Quest for Riches

*Four teenagers discover the keys
to wealth and prosperity*

by **Liliane Grace**
In collaboration with Camilla Mendoza
and Money Mastery for Teens

Published by Grace Productions
Romsey, Victoria, Australia

https://lilianegrace.com

Copyright © Liliane Grace 2018

Second edition 2019

All rights reserved. No part of this book may be reproduced or transmitted by any person or entity (including internet search engines or retailers such as Google, Amazon or similar organisations), in any form or by any means, electronic or mechanical, including photocopying (except under the statutory exceptions provisions of the Australian Copyright Act 1968), recording, scanning or by any information storage and retrieval system, without prior permission in writing from the publisher.

A catalogue record for this book is available from the National Library of Australia
Also available in Kindle and Apple iBooks formats.

Front cover illustration by Jacob Harnwell
jacobhdesign@gmail.com

Book layout by Derek Rawson

Typeset in 10.5pt Minion Pro Condensed

Produced in Australia by Ingram Spark

For all those who are prepared to learn and understand the principles governing wealth and prosperity, and prepared to deliberately create good money habits and a good money mindset.

ACKNOWLEDGEMENTS

Liliane Grace wishes to thank the following people who kindly assisted her with information about India during her research phase: Surya Coape-Smith, Mela Pam Joy of Spirit of India Tours, Himanshi Munshaw-Luhar of Beacon Travel, Rose Witherow, Carmel and Mario Scaringi, and Shyam Burman.

Please note that any errors of fact, especially regarding India, are mine and that, in places, artistic license may have been taken in service of the story.

Foreword #1

If you are aged between 12 and 22, you have in your hands not only a compelling story but also some key principles that I believe will help you better manage your relationship with money.

It's now over to you. Enjoy, learn, and create a more prosperous life!

Camilla Mendoza, creator of Money Mastery For Teens

Foreword #2 for parents and teachers

Since time immemorial, stories have been used to help educate the next generations. It's now time to tell a compelling new story that passes on some learnings I believe are essential for today's youth.

I have spent years coaching people in both life and business. My knowledge and skills have been constantly developing whilst working with people who have different personality types and come from different walks of life and experiences.

Over time I have become passionate about helping women and the younger generation gain an understanding of the concept of money. I have developed a series of workshops for women and youth about mastering money, in which I bring to life the principles required for creating a financially successful future. Having your financial life sorted allows you to live a fulfilling life in all other aspects as well.

Our rapidly changing world has become focused on the here and now, on instant gratification, and much less focus is being placed on preparation for tomorrow. The ability to plan and save up for what we want appears to be a thing of the past. This attitude needs to change and we adults must do all we can to encourage young people to start planning for their financial future. We need to teach them to have more patience and to save their money rather than spending it.

The way we earn money is changing too. More people on the planet means more people looking for jobs. Corporate structures are crumbling under their own weight. It's time to encourage the next generations to become more flexible and self-sufficient, whether that means going where the work is or creating their own businesses and managing their income.

With these goals in mind I came up with the idea of a story that would complement the financial education programs I run for young people around the globe.

As an award-winning author in the Young Adult, 'teaching through story' format, Liliane Grace has taken many longstanding principles and a number of my insights and life experiences to develop a book that is not only a great story but plants the seeds to a sound understanding of one's own relationship with money.

Each one of us has a different relationship with money relative not only to our personality type but also to the influences we received during our formative years. Understanding the factors that determine wealth or poverty is a necessary starting point to managing this crucial relationship with money. Many of those factors are woven throughout these pages.

Camilla Mendoza, Business and Life Coach and
Creator of Money Mastery For Teens
http://moneymasteryforteens.com

Contents

PART I: Setting the Goal

Chapter 1 – The Heroes…

Chapter 2 – February: The Opportunity

Chapter 3 – Deciding To Go

Chapter 4 – Money Plans #1

Chapter 5 – Money Plans #2

Chapter 6 – April: Deposit Due

Chapter 7 – Commitment and Complications

Chapter 8 – Tricky Business

Chapter 9 – July: Balance Due

Chapter 10 – What Do You Pack?

PART II: Achieving the Goal

Chapter 11 – Day 1: The Thrill of the Escape

Chapter 12 – Day 2: Delhi!

Chapter 13 – Day 3: Saving Street Kids

Chapter 14 – Days 4 & 5: Monuments to Love, Death and War

Chapter 15 – Days 6 & 7: Birds and Tigers and Elephants… and a Proposal

Chapter 16 – Days 8 & 9: A Hairy Idea For The God of Wisdom

Chapter 17 – Days 9-11: Living with Peasants and Royalty, Army Colonels and Hindu Matriarchs

CONTENTS

Chapter 18 – Day 12: Digesting India

Chapter 19 – Days 13-16: From Village to Ashram to Seaside City via Overnight Train

Chapter 20 – Days 16-19: Mumbai to Finish

PART III: MASTERING MONEY

Chapter 21 – Strife At Home

Chapter 22 – Struggling

Chapter 23 – Stepping Up

Chapter 24 – Creating a Gap

Chapter 25 – A Balance of Risk and Caution

Chapter 26 – Correcting…

Chapter 27 – Food For Thought

Chapter 28 – Looking for The Way Forward

Chapter 29 – Money Talks

Chapter 30 – The Next Goal

GLOSSARY

THE FOUR MONEY PERSONALITIES

ABOUT THE AUTHOR

PART I
Setting the Goal

CHAPTER 1

The Heroes…

Toni

'And Toni, could you put that news on Tweeter as well?' Mrs S called. 'I never remember how to do those hashtag thingoes.'

'Sure.' Toni checked the time on her phone. Crap. If she was going to make it home in time, she should be leaving right now.

Mrs S poked her greying blonde head back around the door. 'And can you possibly do it before you go? I should have been onto it ages ago. Where has the time gone today!'

She withdrew and Toni heard her doing battle with her kids over after-school snacks and TV rights. Signing into Twitter with Mrs S's username and password – her kids' names, of course – Toni began tapping furiously. #kidsparties, #healthyfun, #clowns, #facepainting…

She definitely wasn't going to make it home on time. Picking up her phone, she texted a quick message to both parents. Still working. Meet you at school. Her mother texted straight back: Getting paid this time?

Hope so!!!!! she replied. But seriously, if Mrs S didn't offer anything for today's two-plus hours of computer support, she'd have to quit. It had seemed like a great opportunity to pick up a few tips about running a business from a friend of her parents, whose innocent little kids' parties biz was going ballistic, but seriously, child labour was OUT.

Toni parked her phone and frowned at the screen again.

`#easybirthdaypartyplanning, #affordableparties, #popular...`

Eric

Eric's father switched on the ignition then paused and looked into the rear vision mirror. 'Seat belt on?' He had been asking that question ever since Eric had first strapped himself into his booster seat at the age of five.

'Yes, Dad,' Eric replied mechanically. He was in a sticky spot. His online chess partner had just made a very good move. Eric contemplated the state of play thoughtfully as his father reversed out of the driveway and the car moved smoothly up the street.

It was already dusk and the streetlights were alight. They drove in stop-start fashion through the traffic to school for a meeting that his parents did not particularly want to attend. Eric's father was talking about it again now, in a low voice into the mic of his earphones to Eric's mother, who was probably working late at the clinic again.

'We'll need to pull funds from his university savings account to do this,' his father was saying. 'Is it really going to be worth it? Expensive fun, I think.'

Eric could imagine her reply: anything that took an opposite position to his father's. His childhood had been a battleground of parental verbal conflict until they finally separated. Ah! Smiling, Eric made his move and waited for the response from his chess partner.

Jackson

Jackson shoved the last bite of sausage into his mouth and swore when a big drop of tomato sauce landed on his shirt. Shit! Did sauce stain? Chewing fast, he took his plate to the sink and turned on the tap, leaning in toward the jet of water to direct some at the red trail next to his button.

'Jackson! Come on!' his mother called from the front door. 'We're running late!'

He swore again, rubbing furiously. They were *always* running late. If his mother hadn't been running late with dinner, he wouldn't have eaten so fast and spilt the sauce. He could feel his dinner going down in lumps. He'd probably end up with a stomach ache tonight.

'I don't know why we're bothering to go!' he shouted back. 'If you've already decided I can't do it!'

His mother appeared in the doorway. 'We haven't 'already decided'. We just don't think it's likely. What are you doing?'

He didn't answer. Some of the redness had faded but it was still clearly there.

'Oh Jackson!' his mother exclaimed as he straightened up and turned around. 'Sauce, right?'

He nodded. 'And I suppose you've been rubbing at the front?'

'What else are you supposed to do?'

'Take the shirt off and run water from the back. You've probably forced the stain more deeply into the fabric now.'

'Oh.'

She sighed. 'Never mind. That shirt was on its last legs anyway. Have you got a clean one to change into?'

'We haven't got time.'

'We're already so late, what's another minute or two?'

Brooke

Brooke peered into the rear vision mirror to check her make-up. She'd smudged her mascara but it kind of looked good like that. Cocking her head, she considered the effect. Sort of made her eyes look bigger... She wondered if any of the boys would notice... Especially Ben. She wanted him to notice. A bit of gloss on her lips would help the effect. She dug the gloss out of her little zip bag, trying not to see the tube of Seashell Pink lippie, lying there innocently among the other stuff. She hadn't been able to use it once since she'd accidentally taken it from the supermarket...

Memory flash: the cashier who'd been processing her stuff being called away; the new cashier popping the lippie into the plastic bag without realising it hadn't been scanned yet; Brooke's confused moment, a mixture of not realising then delayed reaction-realisation, then not saying anything, then the impossibility of saying anything since she hadn't said anything and more stuff was piling on top of the lippie... The guilt ate at her every time she looked at the innocent little silver tube, but she couldn't take it back now – could she?

Suddenly realising the time, Brooke leaned on the horn and a moment later her mother squeezed her bulk into the car. 'I've told you a thousand times not to honk. It's rude.'

'It's also rude to be late,' Brooke said. 'And I want to get a seat with my friends, which I definitely won't be able to do at this rate.'

'Which one of us was cleaning up after dinner?' her mother demanded. 'I didn't see you helping.'

'We can do that when we get back!' Brooke exclaimed. 'So is Dad coming?'

Her mother shrugged and tutted as the car engine turned over without starting. 'I told him about it. I'd be surprised. You know what he's like.'

Yeah. Brooke gazed out of the window as the engine finally fired and they headed off. Yeah, I know what he's like.

CHAPTER 2

February: The Opportunity

The auditorium was still quite empty when **ERIC** and his father arrived. The tech staff were doing sound checks and flicking through the guest speaker's slide show, and a few students were filing along the rows dropping pamphlets onto seats. Eric trailed behind his father, plugging his next chess move into his phone.

'Nice play,' a voice said in his ear, and he looked up to see his friend Chris hovering, phone in hand. Then Chris added, 'But I think I've got you cornered now,' and stood still to key in his reply. Both skinny, slightly hunched and bespectacled, they were called 'the brainy twins' by teachers and students alike, even though they weren't related at all – in fact, they had completely different genetic backgrounds. But they were both Asian, and to a Westerner, that dumped them into one category.

'Where are you sitting?' Chris asked, looking up again.

Eric shrugged, indicating his father, who had paused to speak to a teacher. The teacher was smiling and nodding and glancing at Eric, his prize student. That was another reason they were called 'the twins': both Eric and Chris were top students: they wanted good marks and they went after them.

'You going on this India trip?' Chris asked.

Again, Eric shrugged. 'Dad thinks it's a waste of money. You?'

'I think so.'

Eric gave a little nod and then focused back on his phone. 'Cornered, you reckon?' he murmured.

Smiling, Chris crossed his arms and waited for the master's next move...

TONI stepped into the auditorium and did a quick scan for her folks. Nope. Not here yet. She'd beaten them, after all.

There were knots of people standing around the hall, students in uniform and parents and teachers talking in clusters, but few people had chosen seats yet. She caught up with various friends and their parents, but restlessly, glancing around. Mr Baxter, the school principal, was on stage speaking with the guest speaker, a heavy-set Indian woman with long, straight, black hair wearing one of those traditional Indian outfits, a little top and a matching sari or – whatever they were called – draped around her waist and over one shoulder. There was no way Toni would show her midriff if she wasn't model-thin! But then, belly dancers were often plump. Maybe they thought that was beautiful over there...

She slipped into the second row and picked up the pamphlet lying on a seat. 'India Cultural Tour – Discover the riches of India in a three-week feast of stimulating experiences!'

Toni scanned the text then pulled out a pen and began to fill in her details...

The auditorium was full and buzzing when **JACKSON** arrived with his parents. They parted ways inside the door; his folks to take seats at the back, and Jackson to join his mates up the front. He was bumping fists with his buddies as he edged along the row to the seat they'd saved for him when the loudspeaker crackled into action and the principal began to speak.

'... trip to India several years ago that made a profound impression... global community... important to connect cultures... build understanding... blah blah blah... Delighted to be welcoming Seema Paravati from Eastern Discovery Tours...'

The Indian woman took the microphone and began to speak in that melodic way Indians had. She thanked the principal and welcomed the students and families, and explained that she would give a short overview of the planned tour and then open the floor to questions.

The trip would be three weeks long, including travel time, and scheduled in September, the off-season, in order to keep costs down and enable the students to experience Indian school life. They'd need a few days to acclimatise and then the program would be packed full with excursions, home stays, and other unique experiences that would take them right into the heart of life in India. They'd be travelling the Golden Triangle from Delhi to Agra, where they'd see the Taj Mahal, and on to Mumbai, and they would do one leg of the journey on Indian public transport, which was an experience in itself…

The slideshow clicked past the 'India Tour' intro slide to a map of India with the route outlined in red, then to an image of the Taj, then to one of a village with cows walking down a muddy road, then colourful Bollywood dancers, then a spread of spicy Indian dishes…

'Damn,' **BROOKE** muttered, as she and her mother entered the auditorium. 'They've started.'

The hall was dark and quiet; all eyes were on the slide of an Indian holy man sitting on the side of the road with his begging bowl. The speaker's voice said, 'Every fifty kilometres you travel, the food, language, backdrop and people change, so you can have many different experiences in the same day.'

'Can you see any spare seats?' Brooke's mother hissed.

'One there,' Brooke whispered, pointing. 'You take that one. I'll stay here…' Until she found her friends – surely they would have saved her a seat…?

'Okay,' Brooke's mother headed off and Brooke peered around the dark auditorium, searching for her friends' heads. A slide of teenage girls painting an elephant in bold colours and patterns caught her eye and she focused back on what the speaker was saying.

'The most widely worshipped Hindu god deity is Lord Ganesha: The Elephant God, who is one of five prime Hindu deities. He represents perfect wisdom and is highly loved and worshipped by his devotees. Ganesh is considered to be the remover of obstacles and a bestower of prosperity. Followers of Ganesh always pray to him before beginning any new venture in order to remove any obstacles that would block their way. His image can be found at the entryway of temples and in places of business. As students you'll be interested to know that Ganesha is also the patron of literature,' she added cleverly, with a glance at the principal. 'Actually, in modern day India festivals honouring the elephant-god are celebrated yearly, and an elephant encounter is planned for you on this trip!'

A low murmur of voices rippled through the audience. The Indian speaker went on to talk about the home stays, explaining that they would vary from a pretty basic rural village to living at the local minister's home – it would be luck of the draw. There was a slight titter from the audience again in response to this.

Students would join the host family in all of their normal life activities, she said, whether they included working in the fields or making handicrafts or serving in a shop or going to a traditional dance class. They might be asked to help care for children or to prepare meals. All of these experiences would deliver thought-provoking insights into the lives of everyday people in India. But they would also visit royalty; aside from palace tours, they would meet an actual prince or princess.

'Cool,' Brooke thought. Ah! There they were! She darted towards the brief flash she had seen of a girlfriend's face...

Temples and forts and one of India's most beautiful national parks were all on the agenda, the woman enthused. Their experiences would be as varied as a tiger safari and community service at an orphanage. This was just a taste of some of the wonders of enchanting India awaiting those who signed up for the trip! Smiling broadly, she added that she would be available to answer questions in a moment; meanwhile the Principal had some information to give.

Mr Baxter took the mic and raved on again about his trip to India several years ago that had made such an impression on him. The tour needed a minimum of twelve students to be viable. One male and one female teacher would accompany the students, most probably Miss Harris (Sports, very capable, trim and somewhat grim) and Mr Plowright (History/Geography/Social Sciences, overweight, fun-loving).

And now, were there any questions?

The cost came up immediately, and when **JACKSON** heard the amount, he subsided into self-protective disinterest. He'd been fascinated and engaged by the slides, even spellbound, some part of him eager to go, but he knew what his parents were going to say without even having to ask them: *'Too expensive'*.

Hearing the amount needed for day-to-day expenses, **BROOKE** sparked up. She could afford that! Wow – only twenty dollars a day to cover drinks, snacks *and* souvenir or gift purchases!

When **ERIC**'s mother enquired about health issues, he looked around in surprise; he hadn't realised she'd be there. 'If your child has a weak constitution, by all means bring your own medications,' Seema replied, 'but most will be easily available over the counter. The main thing is to eat only hot, cooked food while you're in India, and drink only bottled water, and then you will be all fine.'

'Three thousand,' **TONI** thought, eyes narrowed as she calculated. She had just over a grand in her account at the moment, and her birthday was coming up so there'd be the usual few hundred from her grandparents, and surely her parents would kick in? She'd really have to screw Mrs S down for an answer about the work she was doing over there now; if she was going to take this trip she couldn't afford to do any more freebies.

When she caught up with her parents at the end of the meeting they immediately agreed that it would be a superb experience and she should go – they'd meet her half-way on costs.

'I was thinking of starting a social club at school,' she told them as they signed the bottom of the form. 'I reckon I could make some money out of that!'

ERIC's parents came together awkwardly for a few moments. It was uncomfortable watching them – their separation was still fresh and they hadn't yet figured out how to relate to each other. Eric stood between them, turning from one to the other. 'You won't need to use the uni money,' he said. 'I'll pay for it.'

'I'm concerned that all the extra activity will interfere with your schoolwork,' his father murmured.

'He can discipline himself to manage both things.' Eric's mother glanced at her watch; she was due back at the hospital in half an hour. 'Marks aren't everything; they've got to show social skills and initiative and self-management as well. Raising the funds to go will be an excellent goal – it's the sort of thing that looks very good on a CV.' She turned to Eric. 'We'll want to see a plan, Eric, for how you're going to raise the funds *and* keep your schoolwork on track.'

'All right,' Eric said. He was thinking about the couple of tutoring jobs he'd had over the last year. Maybe he could ramp that up and take on a few more students… There were about six weeks before the deposit was due; he'd have some sort of idea by then.

'It really does sound lovely,' **JACKSON**'s mother said as they drove home. 'It's the sort of trip I would have loved to take at your age…'

'You'd love to take it *now*,' her husband interjected, turning onto the main road.

'Well that's out of the question and beside the point,' she said firmly. 'But even for Jackson… We'd love to say yes, Jackie, you know that! But what with school fees and Katie's dance classes and your sports costs and the hike in interest rates and the extra loan we're paying off…'

'Yeah, yeah,' Jackson mumbled, watching houses and streets blur past.

'And you've had so many of those tummy upsets lately. I'd be worried that your constitution isn't strong enough for all those foreign foods and germs… And isn't Pakistan experiencing political unrest at the moment?'

'That's a whole other country, Mum.'

'Yes but it's right next door and you just never know…'

'It's things like this that make me think we shouldn't have enrolled you in Brightwood College,' **BROOKE**'s mother said heavily as they pulled out of the school driveway. 'It's a strain to keep competing with people who are at such a different income level to us. I should never have let your father talk me into this school. As if the fees aren't enough without all this extracurricular stuff! It's supposed to be one amount for the year and that's that; not all of this extra this and extra that…'

'But Mum, all my friends will be going! I *really* want to go. It sounds amazing!'

'And I want you to go! I'm just saying I don't think we can afford it right now.'

'Maybe Dad will pay?'

Her mother sniffed. 'Did you even see him in the room tonight?'

Brooke stared outside into the darkness. They drove in silence for a while, until the various images of India that were revolving through her memory pushed her to blurt out, 'You've always said travel broadens the mind!'

'Of course it does, and I don't want you to miss out, Brooke honey.' Her mother sighed. 'Look, we'll see what we can do…'

Brooke smiled. Maybe the Elephant god would help her to overcome these obstacles.

What would you do if you were one of the characters in this book?

Would you want to go on a trip like this?

Would you offer to pay (some of it? all of it?) or would you expect your parents to cough up?

CHAPTER 3

Deciding To Go

Brooke had always liked elephants. They were so majestic and powerful. She'd ridden a horse at a friend's farm once and had loved the height and grandeur she'd felt sitting up there; she could just imagine how great it would feel to be sitting on an elephant's back! She'd been drawing elephants almost obsessively since the India Trip Info Night, and daydreaming about actually being there. The exotic images from the slides had continued to rotate through her mind… the colour, the romance! She could just see herself wearing one of those gorgeous saris with jangling silver bangles all the way down her arm and dark make-up around her eyes…

Downstairs the doorbell rang and she heard her mother moving slowly to answer it, then her father's voice, a low rumble. Leaping off the bed she darted out of her room, eager to hear his decision.

Her parents were both still standing in the entrance when she began galloping down the stairs. 'Hey Dad!' she called, 'Whaddayathink?'

He looked up at her, his frown not quite dissolving even though he was smiling. The lines between his brows were quite deeply etched, she noticed, as she landed in front of him, and he looked greyer than she had remembered. Was it that long since she'd seen him?

'How about a hello first?' he asked, ruffling her hair.

'Hello,' she said. 'So? What do you think?'

He shook his head, laughing. 'If you can find a way to package and sell your enthusiasm you've got it made, honey. But right now, unless we win the lottery, your mother and I can't see it happening. We're both flat broke.'

Brooke pouted. She knew it was childish but her feelings always just poured out of her. She wore her heart on her sleeve, her mother often said. She glanced at her mother, who rolled her eyes, obviously not believing the 'flat broke' statement. But then, much as Brooke's father had an uncanny ability to generate big sums of money, he also had the ability to lose them just as quickly – one of the reasons for her parents' dramatic break-up several years ago.

So it wasn't going to be easy to get either of her parents to pay for this trip. Both her parents were crying poor. She was going to have to control her emotions and get creative…

'Would you like a hot chocolate, Dad?' she asked suddenly. 'I just bought a new cappuccino maker – I can make you the best hot chocolate you've ever had! Honestly, café quality.'

'I'd love to, sweetheart, but I'm in a hurry today. You ready to go?'

'Yeah.' Brooke looked at her mother again. Her face was bland this time. She raised her brows just the tiniest bit and shook her head just the tiniest bit and gave the tiniest of shrugs.

When Brooke came back downstairs with her bag, her parents were arguing about bills her father was supposed to be paying. Her mother was saying flatly, 'No, I can't. We've had the dentist *and* the physio this month, and somehow I got caught by *two* red light cameras and you know me, I *never* shoot a light! So I'm up to here in bills.'

Brooke hated hearing these conversations. She usually did a pretty good job of blocking them out and, for that matter, not worrying about money at all. Somehow things always seemed to work out without her having to worry about it. There'd be food on the table and her mother would pay for the extra clothes and stuff she needed, and she'd go on all the excursions her friends went on despite all the talk of no money – so this India trip would surely work out as well.

'I'm ready,' she said, planting a kiss on her mother's cheek. 'Seeya Sunday, Mum. Have a nice weekend.'

§ § §

She would just say, 'Thanks so much for all the work experience, Mrs S, but I'm saving up for a school trip to India now so I've got to prioritise paying work,' **Toni** thought, as she walked up the street from the bus stop. That should do it. It was completely reasonable! And if Mrs S didn't offer a good enough rate to keep her on, she'd just find something else... but what? Dad had offered her work at his business but that was dead boring. Good money but repetitive, tedious filing and stuff that was boring as shit. Her mother reckoned she should offer to *run* the kids' parties for Mrs S and help her expand, but why take a wage when she could run her own functions and keep the whole profit?

The idea of co-ordinating social events at her school had been growing at the back of Toni's mind. The principal had loved the idea of Toni running an Indian-themed dance to raise money for the India trip, although he'd quickly suggested that this should be a shared venture between all the potential travellers to India. *'Brightwood College Students Show Fundraising Initiative'* – she could just see him visualising the headline of a feature article in the local paper.

Toni's initial lovely vision of running social events by herself and keeping all the profits had faded away, but as she did the maths, it still looked pretty promising. They would have the use of the school hall and be able to put notices in the school newsletter, he had told her, or even give special flyers to each student in Year 9, and that was close to three hundred, so if they just got 200 takers at, say, fifteen bucks each, they'd make three grand! And even taking off hire of the music or DJ or whatever and refreshments and some Indian decorations, such as a few eye-catching posters, surely they'd clear at least a couple of grand for the night?

Toni swapped her bag to the other shoulder, thinking about

everything they'd have to do. Maybe it was just as well he wasn't going to let her keep it to herself; she was definitely going to need some help to put this gig on, so she'd make the twelve (or however many other travellers) earn their share of it! She shrugged, sauntering on. It would work out.

Eric sat at his desk and studied the strategy he had been working on:
Open new savings account – check.
Place ads for new tutoring students – check.
Seek testimonials from the parents of existing students – check.
Break down the total into monthly and weekly amounts – check.
Mark calendar with the due date for the deposit and balance – check.

Now he just needed the students to roll up.

Putting his phone aside, he pulled out his Science text and returned to his homework.

Jackson lay on his bed, replaying the latest soccer match in his mind. If Ben hadn't appeared out of nowhere and elbowed him just then, he'd have had a go at the winning shot. He reckoned he would have got it in, too. Jackson narrowed his eyes, scrolling the almost-win sequence again in his mind. What a glorious moment that might have been...

A ping from his phone caught his attention; he glanced at it and frowned. He really should get out of this group chat. Picking it up, he read the latest comment: '*So excited about India trip. The olds have said yes!!*' Laura had just posted. Another ping and Brooke added, '*Me too! Mine havent confirmed yet but im sure they wont want me to miss out!*'

Jackson scowled and tossed the phone aside. He stared at the ceiling and tried to summon the soccer match again, but it had been replaced with slide images of India. He didn't understand why he was so drawn to go! It was a third world country with beggars and crap on the roads and traffic chaos – surely he'd have a better time on a trip to the States or somewhere like that? Not that that was on offer either, but really, he should just chill and let this one go. There'd be other better opportunities down the track.

He closed his eyes and tried to relax the knot in his stomach.

How do <u>you</u> feel when your parents talk about bills and money issues?

How strategic are you when it comes to stuff or experiences you want to have?

Are you a team-player or do you prefer to be in charge?

How quickly do you give up when it all looks too difficult?

CHAPTER 4

MONEY PLANS #1

What a blast! **Toni** was utterly delighted. Three hundred and seven kids had turned up to the 'India Fundraising Trip Bollywood Dance', which was pretty much everyone from Year 9 plus some blow-ins from a few other year levels and a few friends from off campus. The school had given them the hall at no charge, which was sweet – so long as she 'returned it' in perfect condition, and she was on track for that. So far no damage… Toni peered around the dark auditorium at the throng of bopping heads, but everyone was behaving – dancing, making out, taking selfies and sending Snapchats…

The DJ was playing some decent music. He was the older brother of one of the girls in her class and he'd charged them a rock-bottom fee – hoping for repeat business and some likes on Facebook and Instagram since Toni had said she intended to run another one later in the year. And he was good. He'd found some great Bollywood tracks and video footage that he'd projected onto one wall, injecting a pretty lively vibe into the event. The decorations had been low cost: they'd pinned colourful swathes of fabric around the walls and even overhead, and a couple of the arty kids had painted posters of elephants and Indian style patterns for the doors. It was all so authentic that some other kids were now keen on signing up for the trip, which would make Mr Baxter very happy! And the school canteen had agreed to provide drinks and snacks at cost price

– two of the India-trip students were selling them right now from a little stand in the foyer. All in all, a very successful venture. She was looking forward to counting the cash!

Becoming aware that someone was speaking to her, Toni turned to see **Jackson**, a guy she'd gone through school with since Year 7. So far she'd barely exchanged two words with him over all those years, but looking at him now, Toni wondered why. He was cute. And he was trying to tell her something but she could only catch the odd syllable.

'What?' she shouted, then shrugged when his mouth moved and she could again hear nothing. She pointed toward the door and they wove their way through the crowd and stepped outside.

'What did you say?' she asked, ears ringing.

'Great night,' he grinned. 'Have you done this sort of thing before?'

'Nope. But I think I'll be doing it again!'

'You should. What gave you the idea?'

'Oh, I'm always having ideas for raising money! I was one of those lemonade-stand kids. I had my first lemonade stand when I was about five years old and then my brother got me collecting cans and bottles for refund when I was seven… I'm always doing something! Hey, you going to India?'

'Nah,' he shook his head and looked away. 'Sounds good though.'

'Then go!' Her gaze ran over those broad shoulders and slim physique, the long brown fringe that he kept tossing back, the thoughtful eyes as he turned to look at her that were right now making her blush. *Why hadn't she noticed him before?*

'Can't,' he shrugged. 'My folks aren't keen.'

'Why not?' she asked, curious. 'It'll be a great experience. Honestly, I don't think you should give up so easily! Talk 'em 'round, Jackson. Remind them how educational it will be for you to see how the other half lives… you'll appreciate *them* more. Seriously!' she added, when he looked dubious. 'My brother went to China on exchange and when he got back he kept going on about how he appreciated life here and the whole family way more.'

Jackson laughed. 'Right, I'll tell them about your brother. Should make all the difference.'

'Travel is good for your character,' she added emphatically, unperturbed. 'Make your case!' Suddenly, it was really important to her that he sign up for the India trip.

'So how much you going to make from this gig?' he asked, nodding in the direction of the hall.

'Three grand.' And that was when the penny dropped. 'Is it the money? Because if it is, you should definitely join my India Fundraising Team – Never Be Alone Raising Money Again!'

He laughed, enjoying her spirit, and she smiled back. Toni knew she was pretty. Tall, slim, blonde spiky hair, wide-spaced blue eyes… She didn't like to be vain, but good looks *were* an asset…

She seized his arm with an earnest expression. 'Jackson, have you told your parents you'll chip in? Because that usually makes all the difference.'

Jackson gave her a strange look. Was she for real?

'I'm serious,' Toni said intently. 'Putting on gigs like this isn't that much work. Your parents will be impressed that you're contributing, and we're having a heap of fun in the process!'

Jackson stuck his hands in the pockets of his jeans and looked at her thoughtfully. 'Okay,' he agreed. 'You're on. I'll run it by them again. When's the next event?'

Brooke frowned in exasperation. She'd seen Toni standing right there by the loudspeaker only a few moments ago, and now she'd completely disappeared. Having just spoken to Chloë and Laura about how much spending money they were planning to take to India, Brooke wanted to find out what Toni thought. It would be really embarrassing if she were the only one without enough cash!

A cluster of people near the door moved and she saw Toni entering. It was going to be difficult to talk to her in here since it was so noisy but she really wanted to find out. Especially since she was on the point of asking for more hours at The Burger Place. That lady at the India Trip Info Night had said they'd only need twenty dollars a day but Laura and Chloë were talking about taking thirty or forty! Over three weeks that would really add up... But she did NOT want to be the only one who didn't have enough money to do or get everything she wanted.

Brooke kept her eyes locked on Toni's blonde head and began weaving through the crowd in her direction.

Eric shook hands with Josiah's father and turned to leave. His own father was standing in the doorway waiting to drive him home.

'Thank you again,' Josiah's aproned mother called from the kitchen. 'We appreciate you coming out on a Saturday night,' she added, coming to the doorway with a saucepan she was drying. 'I was surprised you'd be available. I thought all teenagers were out raving or raging or whatever it is you young people do on a Saturday night.'

Eric smiled politely. 'I'm not the raging sort,' he said.

'Well, that's a blessing for us, then.' She smiled. 'Jo's finally getting his head around some of that complicated maths we can't help him with.' Waving the tea towel in farewell, she withdrew into the kitchen.

'I'm proud of you,' Eric's father said briefly as he unlocked the car door.

'Thanks.' As he climbed into his seat, Eric wondered if his father was proud of him for tutoring more students or for raising more money or for not going to the school social. It could have been any and was probably all of them. He wondered, for a brief moment, how the social had gone, then noticed a text from Chris: Parents have changed their minds. Not going to India now :-(

What would you do if you were one of the characters in this book?

How would you raise the money if you were going on a trip like this?

Would you contribute to the whole trip or just cover your spending money?

How would you sell the idea to your parents?

Do you get strategic about realising your important goals?

CHAPTER 5

Money Plans #2

'So what happened?' **Jackson**'s mother asked in a low voice, following her husband through the dining room into the kitchen.

'I don't know. I'm trying to find out,' he replied, as the door closed behind them.

Jackson contemplated the closed door. He was gearing up to ask them about the India trip again. He'd decided to put in a full day on his homework first to make a good impression, and he was actually pretty impressed himself: he'd achieved quite a lot. Amazing how much you could do when you just got down to it. He suspected that much of his dislike of homework was actually caused more by his resistance to getting started than the actual homework itself. Once he'd decided to get it done, he'd managed to knock off quite a few subjects in just a few hours. He looked with satisfaction at the number of assignments he had ticked off in his school diary.

He could hear their voices in the kitchen, his mother's slightly elevated. 'Oh my god! *Ten thousand?* We've lost ten thousand?'

Jackson froze, listening. His father's voice was answering but Jackson couldn't hear what he was saying. Probably telling his mother to be quiet, because when she spoke again, her voice was lowered too.

This put a different colour on the whole thing. If they'd lost money, pretty much three times as much as he was going to need for the trip, they definitely wouldn't be up for it. He felt his whole body sag with disappointment, and the colourful images of India that had been swimming around him ever since that conversation with Toni began to fade. But, as he stared glumly at his school diary, a scribbled note caught his eye: '*Toni fundraising – lunchtime Tues*'. Her bright, optimistic face appeared before him, and Jackson felt a renewal of desire and determination. He began to pack up his books, thinking hard.

Moments later the door to the kitchen opened and his father emerged, saying, '… much more. We should count ourselves lucky.'

'It was just a stupid, risky thing to do,' Jackson's mother said, following him out. 'We should have known better.'

'He's a friend. We trusted him. And it seemed to be working.'

'Uh, Dad,' Jackson interrupted. 'This is probably a bad time but I wanted to talk to you and Mum about something.'

'Sure,' his father said distractedly. 'Need help with some schoolwork?'

'No. It's all good. Got heaps done,' he added. (Hint, hint.) 'I've just been thinking again about that school trip to India.' His mother began to frown and he hurried on. 'I know you don't think we can afford it but I've realised I was expecting you guys to pay for the whole thing, which isn't fair. So I was wondering how you'd feel about it if I pay some too.'

'With what?' Jackson's father asked. 'Your savings from your paper run? You don't have much put aside, that I'm aware of.'

'I'll think of something,' Jackson said. For some reason, he didn't want to mention the social club idea yet. 'I just can't seem to get that trip out of my mind. Uncle Dave had such a great time in Cambodia he's gone back there to start an orphanage. You never know, maybe I'll find some great life mission for myself if I go.' He was surprised to hear himself say this, but it wasn't that far wide of the truth. Jackson had always been inspired by stories of people helping others to overcome serious odds. He and his parents often forwarded YouTube clips and stories to each other about that sort of thing. If the trip to India wasn't just about him but about something bigger than him, maybe they'd be more keen on it.

Jackson's father ran a hand through his greying hair. 'Well, let's have a look at it. Just not now; I've got to get back to someone about something that's urgent.'

His mother was still frowning; she was wearing that worried, tense look Jackson hated as she watched her husband leave the room. But turning back to Jackson she did her best to smile and touched him lightly on the arm. 'It sounds like a lovely idea, Jack. Maybe we've all been thinking too small.'

Eric checked the time again. His student was now running twelve minutes late. This was very irritating because the next student would be here in forty-eight minutes and he didn't want to make her wait. And meanwhile *he* was stuck waiting, wasting time... There was no point getting into his own studies if they were going to turn up any second; he'd barely get started when he'd have to stop, and he hated that. The extra tutoring work hadn't affected his own schoolwork – yet – but he was beginning to feel concerned as his study time shrank. He did *not* want to lose his lead position in the classroom hierarchy, not even to Chris.

He sighed heavily and decided to check his bank balance in the meantime. That was something he could do very quickly, and it was a gratifying experience because the balance was growing steadily; he was on track for making the India trip deposit, he noticed with satisfaction.

'First fund-raising event takings: $4,555.00. Not bad, eh?' **Toni** grinned.

Jackson whistled. 'That is wicked!'

'Only problem is,' she continued, her expression darkening, 'sharing the profits with *all* the kids going to India.' She plugged a number into her phone calculator. 'Which means, after expenses, we've each paid just over three hundred bucks toward the trip expenses – assuming that twelve people are going – which is peanuts.'

Jackson made a face. For a few golden moments it had looked like the India trip was in the bag...

'The school's happy enough to help promote us all in the newsletter and local paper – you know, how resourceful we all are, fundraising for educational travel abroad, blah-di-blah,' Toni said, offering him some orange-coloured chips, 'but we're going to have to be full-time fundraisers at this rate.'

'What are these?' he asked, crunching. 'They taste sweet...? Savoury-sweet...'

'Sweet potato chips. My fave.'

'Cool. So... great promo for the school but not much in it for us.'

'Exactly. I'll have to come up with more ideas.' She propped her chin on her knees and wrapped her arms around her legs.

'*Everyone* on the India Fundraising Team will have to come up with more ideas,' he corrected. 'Anyone who wants to benefit will have to put in.'

She didn't seem to hear him. She was munching dolefully on sweet potato chips and gazing out into the distance. Toni didn't look confident that other people would be useful, Jackson reflected. Maybe she was so used to doing things her own way that other people just cramped her style. Was bringing him in cramping her style? He felt stuck between a rock and a hard place, as his parents often said: help her raise money and make only a tiny fraction of it or strike out on his own, which he wasn't that confident of doing anyway...

'We've only got four and a half months to the deadline for the final payment,' Toni said through a mouthful. 'We'll either need a really packed events calendar or make a shitload of profit.' She swallowed, grinning, and turned her blue eyes on him. 'What if I suggest to Baxter that each student should be responsible for raising their own funds? It can be a competition!' There was a wicked sparkle in her eyes.

'So you think they'll toss their plans for student co-operation in favour of your plans for student competition?' he asked mildly, burying his own twinge of panic at the thought of having to generate all of the money on his own.

'Damn. Put like that, it doesn't sound good, does it?'

Their hands collided in the opening of the packet as they both reached in for more chips.

Brooke stood next to her manager as he frowned over the roster. 'How many more hours?' he asked.

'At least four,' she said. 'Or maybe eight? I'm saving for a school trip to India.'

'Can you do Sundays?' he asked, pencil poised.

Brooke thought quickly. She didn't want to block out time that might cause her to miss out on any socialising with friends but there was unlikely to be much of that on a Sunday morning. On the other hand, if she were late home on Saturday nights, the Sunday morning shift would be a killer.

'From ten?' she suggested.

'Nine,' he replied. 'We open at ten so you need to be here before that to help set up.'

'Okay...' she said. Working was clearly the way to make money but the problem was that it really interfered with your life! How were you supposed to enjoy life if you were always putting in hours at some boring job? It was no wonder that her mother was so tired and fed up all the time...

The thought flickered across her mind that she must check in with her parents about the trip. They hadn't said anything else about it but surely they weren't going to let her miss out?

There are four basic 'money personality styles'.

Before we share what they are, what are you noticing about yours?

Here are a few clues:

Some save diligently

Some are very entrepreneurial/creative and resourceful with money

Some are quite risk-averse and cautious

Some like to 'keep up with the Joneses'

Some are 'easy come, easy go' where money is concerned

Some want to share their wealth with others...

How do <u>you</u> behave with money?

CHAPTER 6

April: Deposit Due

Eric had reimbursed his parents for the India trip deposit they had paid some time ago, but this tutoring gig was starting to irritate him. The rate of pay was okay but you had to put in a lot of hours to make any decent money, and that took him away from his own study – and online chess. He was even beginning to get his anxiety rash back. Eric lifted his shirt and examined the small but itchy, red pimples that were peppered across his stomach. They were both ugly and uncomfortable. They would have to go, and he had a plan.

Last night he'd initiated a new strategy for making money: babysitting. Babysitting was not something he had ever considered before, and he'd only agreed to it reluctantly to help out some friends of his parents who were stuck with a last minute sick sitter. It had taken quite a lot of persuading by his parents before he had finally surrendered and said he would help out, just this once. But arriving at their elegant home at 6.45 pm he had found all three children already in pyjamas, watching him with clean faces and wide eyes from behind their mother. All children had listened meekly to their father's instructions about the evening rules (one story each and then lights out for all but the eldest, who could read for half an hour in her room before putting her light out).

Eric already knew that Asian children were generally more obedient than Western kids – he'd often been quietly shocked by the behaviour of school friends toward their parents – but he'd been very pleasantly surprised by how easily the evening had unfolded. The two youngest had each presented him with a picture book to read and then sat on either side of him on the sofa, following the story with minimal commentary, just pointing to pictures occasionally. One of them had tried for a second book but before Eric could remind the little boy of his father's rule, the older sister had intervened and the child had acquiesced. Wow. This eldest child had also requested a story, though she was old enough to read her own, and hers had been quite a long chapter out of *The Hobbit*, but he figured he had to do something to earn the money…

In fact, Eric had enjoyed reading the stories more than he had expected, but the best part of the evening was what happened next: the elder sister made the two youngest children politely wish Eric goodnight, then she took them by the hand and led them out of the lounge room. Eric heard them speaking to each other as they climbed the stairs, and then all went quiet. Was this it? Was there really nothing else for him to do? He sat on the edge of the big leather lounge suite, listening, head cocked to one side, a slight frown puckering his forehead. Ten minutes later the big sister was back at the doorway saying goodnight to him. He replied, and was about to ask if everything was all right when she closed the door and pattered away. Eric was free.

He stood there for a moment, wondering what to do next. A great grin broke out on his face as he realised the nerve-wracking part of the job was over and the next three hours would be money straight into his pocket while he did his homework. Paid to do his homework! Beaming, he carried his school bag to the dining table. There was a dish of sweet Chinese dumplings on the table for him. Tasting one, he approved and ate the other two as well, then wiped his sticky fingers on the napkin that had been folded in a neat triangle beside the plate, and unloaded his books onto the black teak table. For the next two hours he worked solidly, and then logged onto his favourite game. When the children's parents returned, grateful and generous, he spontaneously offered his services again 'any time' – and if they knew of other families who needed babysitting, they could pass on his number.

Toni stood in the school's administrative office with an envelope containing the $1297.00 deposit for the India Trip. She felt very wealthy and very satisfied. It felt excellent to be paying for something you wanted to do with money you had earned, even if it meant you had pillaged your savings.

When skinny, hook-nosed Mrs Lambeth finally slid aside the glass screen, Toni announced why she was there and enjoyed a moment of congratulations before the administrative officer began to remember how many people she knew who had been to India and come back with a belly problem. Or was that Bali? Mrs Lambeth wondered aloud. Was it Bali belly or Delhi belly? Never mind; you had to be careful, wherever you went.

Toni's smile had frozen by the time she escaped. Walking across the oval she spied **Jackson** and gave him a wave. The India Trip Fundraising Team was working on three upcoming events at once: a trip to the beach before the warm weather completely faded, a trivia night, and then a trip to the snow! Thirty kids had already signed up for the beach trip.

'All done!' she declared, arriving in front of him. 'You?'

'What?' he asked, beginning to dribble the soccer ball in a ring around her.

'Paid the deposit. It's due tomorrow, you know,' she replied, rotating to face him.

'Oh, that.' He concentrated on flicking the ball up with his toes and balancing it on his foot. 'Yeah. All under control.' It wasn't really, but she didn't need to know that. 'Book the bus?' he asked, hoping she wouldn't pick this up as a change of subject.

'Yep,' she said, taking the bait. 'The Fund is cleaned out now, so we'd better get more sign-ups asap.'

'Yeah,' he agreed. 'Or we'll be doing cake stalls.'

'You bake?' she asked, with interest, and he gave her a look. A manly, brows raised, 'Me? As if!' look.

She laughed. 'I make a mean hedgehog!'

'Happy to taste it and test,' he offered, and when she snatched at the ball, he kicked it out of her reach and darted after it; Toni was soon hot on his heels.

But he was thinking as he ran. Last night his mother had come to him privately for 'a word'. He was brushing his teeth at the time, and she had closed the bathroom door and said, 'I've got some money saved, Jackie. It's all mine and it's for special things. I can see that this trip to India is important to you, so I'm going to pay that deposit and if you manage to pay it back that's lovely but I don't want you to feel you owe me anything. No, no!' she hushed, when he tried to speak through the toothpaste foam. '*We're* the parents and it's our job to provide you with these experiences. When you're earning it will be different. Then *you'll* be responsible, but for now it's up to us, and that's as it should be. We've got some funds coming to us that we should be able to use for the balance but we'll deal with that then. Meanwhile, you just save up to cover your own spending money and that will be fine.'

He had spat the bubbles out of his mouth and objected strenuously, but she wasn't hearing him. So now he was left feeling guilty and inadequate next to Toni who'd just paid the whole deposit herself. And troubled: he felt absolutely blank as to how he could raise the kind of money he was going to need. But he was becoming determined.

Toni had caught up with him and was heading for the ball. Lining up the goal posts, he gave it a good, hard kick and it sailed into the back of the net.

Brooke was digging around in her schoolbag for the snack bar she remembered stashing in there when her fingers encountered crumpled paper, and immediately she was struck by the realisation that they hadn't yet paid the deposit and it had been due yesterday. She yanked the school newsletter out of her bag and hurried with it to the laundry where her mother was pulling wet and strangled clothes out of the machine.

'Mum! The deposit's overdue!'

'What deposit?' her mother huffed, bending and pulling.

'For the *India* trip, remember?' Brooke insisted. 'It was due yesterday.'

'Oh.' Her mother stood up and brushed a strand of hair from her red face. 'I'm sorry, honey. It doesn't look like you're going to be able to go.'

'What?' Brooke stared at her mother in horror as bright images of India crumbled around her. 'Why not?'

'Well Dad hasn't fronted up with the money, has he?' her mother replied in a matter-of-fact tone, 'and you know how things are for me.'

'But Mum!' Tears were filling her eyes and she wasn't even trying, so this must *really* matter to her. '*Everyone's* going,' she wailed. 'Laura and Chloë and Toni… I'll be the only one who doesn't go! And they'll all have this amazing *educational* experience and I'll be here working at The Burger Place and going to school all by myself while they ride elephants and see the Taj Mahal and meet princes!' Put like that, it sounded like an awful fate – the worst. She *mustn't* miss out.

Brooke's mother frowned. She picked up the washing basket and gave the flywire door a sharp kick. It burst open and she stepped out promptly, basket in her arms. Brooke caught the rebounding door and followed.

'You know I want you to go,' her mother said, pegging the first item on the line. 'It's not that we don't want you to go. It's just the realities of life. We're broke, honey. There's only just enough coming in to pay the bills, never mind a trip to India!'

Brooke watched her mother hang her school uniform, the hated symbol of school-imprisonment while friends went *Overseas*. She felt desperate. She cast around for something, anything, some argument that would finally convince her mother that this was critically important, that all stops should be pulled out so that she, Brooke Hamley, could join the India tour.

'You going to give me a hand or just stand rooted there like a tree?' her mother asked drily.

Of course! 'Of course!' she babbled, grabbing some socks and pegging them wildly. 'I'll do the rest! I'll do anything, Mum! I'll do all the house cleaning between now and the trip if that will help!'

Her mother raised a brow and shook a towel out. 'That'll be the day.'

'Honestly, Mum! Seriously! Put me to the test!'

Her mother pegged for a moment in silence and then asked, 'I suppose it's a non-refundable deposit?'

Brooke squealed and wrapped both arms around her mother in delight.

'Eech! That's wet,' her mother exclaimed, peeling a damp t-shirt off her arm. 'You got me with that promise – I'd like to see you doing the housekeeping. That'd make the stress worthwhile for me. All right. I'll go out on a limb and stick it on the credit card. I know what it means to you. But you'd better keep your word, missy. That's sweeping, vacuuming, mopping, washing on the line *and* folded, table set every night, and the dishes washed...'

Shit. God, when would she think before she spoke? But still, it was only for a few months... 'Okay,' Brooke said, working to keep the wobble out of her voice. 'Thank you so much! I'll put the form on the kitchen bench.' And she scooted off inside.

How far would <u>you</u> go for something you wanted to do?

Do you think parents should be solely responsible for providing special experiences, or should the child contribute?

CHAPTER 7

COMMITMENT AND COMPLICATIONS

India had a population of 1.2 billion, **Jackson** read. Wow! That was, he discovered, more than a sixth of the world's population – insane! He'd seen pictures of crowded Indian streets and marketplaces, of course, but here at home you could always escape the crowd and find some peace and quiet somewhere; in India, he suspected, that would be next to impossible. Though surely most of those people were in the cities? Surely the countryside wasn't crowded…?

Reading on, he was intrigued to find that people ate with their fingers and meals were often served on banana leaves. Cool… he was looking forward to eating off banana leaves! And no need to do the dishes! Awesome. Eighty-four per cent of Indians were Hindus and most of them were vegetarian; the few who weren't wouldn't eat beef because the cow was sacred to them, whereas Muslims wouldn't eat pork because they considered pig to be unclean meat. These cultural differences were so interesting. The Jewish kid in his class wouldn't eat pig or shellfish. Funny how the whole world had different beliefs and customs and everyone thought theirs were right.

Jackson was beginning to feel pretty damn excited about the upcoming trip. Now that his parents had agreed he was going, and his deposit was paid, he seemed to be bumping into information about India wherever he went. There'd been a program on TV last night about Indian culture, his mother kept forwarding him short video clips about Indian history and monuments and lifestyle, and there seemed to be way more Indians around his neighbourhood than he had ever seen before. Plus, the Asian grocer he passed every day on his way to the bus stop had Bollywood posters tacked to its windows – faded too, which suggested they'd been there for a while. He'd never even noticed them before!

The cost of the trip still gnawed at him though. His parents didn't talk about it much but Jackson felt as if his whole family was constantly wading through a heavy undercurrent of anxiety about money. He watched his father leave for work early and return home late, frowning and preoccupied and often irritable. He'd eat dinner and then disappear into his study where he'd remain until after Jackson had gone to bed.

Jackson was determined that his father's long work hours, fatigue and constant worry would not be his fate. Was the answer simply to study hard and get good grades? Sitting at his desk when he should have been writing an essay, he began to watch clips about young entrepreneurs who had made a mint developing an app or some other great product that was selling squillions. Twenty-one and already a millionaire! *Cool.* That would be the way to go! But even if he didn't come up with something brilliant like that, his generation wasn't knuckling down to years of employment in one company like his father's had; instead they seemed to dance about from one interest or occupation to another.

Jackson knew that his father wanted him to join the family air conditioning business when he left school, and the job security in that was comforting, but the idea of all those hours in the factory made his stomach tighten. He didn't think he was the type to chuck a backpack over his shoulder and head off into the unknown, travelling and bumming around, but he definitely wasn't the sort to spend years doing the same old thing over and over, day in and day out…

His computer pinged and he glanced up to see a message from his Uncle:

'Hello from Cambodia'.

'Hi there,' he typed back. 'How goes it?'

Well... if you can cope with tropical weather, flash flooding, beautiful people who delight in the simplest things, stunning scenery, incessant hawkers, deep-fried tarantulas, the odd bout of the runs, constant red tape hassles, and great WiFi but no hot water – you'd love it!

Deep-fried spiders???

Don't get me started. I hear you're going to India soon.

'Yeah.'

That should be great. Keep me in the loop.

Will do. How's the orphanage going?

Constant red tape hassles but gorgeous kids. We truck on.

Good luck.

Thanks, mate.

His uncle had walked away from a well-paid, high-flying corporate job to start this orphanage. He'd spent ten days in Cambodia on holiday, come home and quit his job. There must be something pretty special about these third-world countries, Jackson mused. At any rate, this trip had better be worth the stress he was putting his family through...

Eric would never gamble but his mathematical brain was drawn to the challenge of unravelling the probability of winning a lottery. He'd been researching the appropriate algorithms on the net and had spent the last couple of hours checking the maths for himself. There didn't seem to be a way of rigging the system. You had to purchase a ridiculous number of tickets to have any hope of winning. He found himself agreeing with one of the commentators that your best strategy for profits was to buy zero tickets...

On the other hand, he discovered, entering contests was like gambling in a casino where the house *wanted* you to win. Those prizes were publicity for the company rather than a loss. The smaller the contest and the more specific the eligibility requirements, the bigger your chance of winning. A contest for an iPad had caught his attention a few weeks ago. Now *that* was something he'd be interested in winning, but how big was the pool? What would his chances be? There was no point entering if the odds weren't good. And much as he'd like some of those prizes, the contests rarely offered money, which was the reward he was really after at the moment.

Tearing himself away from the screen he went to brush his teeth. He wanted to be up early enough to have a last read of his history essay before printing it to submit.

Brooke burst into her room and tipped the contents of the shopping bag onto her bed. It had looked so pretty in the change room but would it look as good here, in front of her mirror? That was the real test. She tore her t-shirt over her head, yanked her jeans off, and slipped the dress on. It was so light and silky-smooth... beautiful. And the colours! A melting sky-blue with unexpected splashes of orange, like a sunset. The shape of it was complimentary too, she thought, turning from side to side in front of her mirror and admiring the sweetheart neckline and waist-hugging lines. She felt a rush of delight. Yep, it worked in her bedroom!

'Brooke!' her mother's irritated voice rang out from downstairs. 'Where are you? Get your arse down here! You haven't done anything you promised!'

'Coming,' she called back. She lifted the dress a little to check if shorter would look better, and turned from side to side again.

Her mother's voice and footsteps were growing louder as she approached. 'The washing's been rained on repeatedly for the last three days and there's stuff out there I need to wear; the table hasn't been set for dinner; and you ran out so late this morning that you didn't clear up after breakfast.'

She gave the customary tap on Brooke's bedroom door and opened it; then stood there, framed by the doorway, tired, angry, and now, brow furrowing in despair. 'What's this?'

'What's what?' Brooke asked, feigning innocence but caught like a rabbit in headlights.

Her mother nodded at the dress.

'It was on special,' Brooke said, pulling it off quickly. 'A really good deal – half price, Mum!'

'Half of what?' her mother asked tightly, still standing there in the doorway.

'Remember, I made more this week because I've got another shift now!'

'Half of what?'

'One hundred and twenty.'

'So you spent *sixty dollars* on a dress when you're saving for a trip to India where clothes are going to cost next to nothing?'

Brooke flushed. Grabbing at her t-shirt she turned away to change and so that she wouldn't see her mother's furious expression.

'Well, *half-price!*' she exclaimed from inside the t-shirt.

'That doesn't make it cheap, Brooke. Honestly, love, when are you going to *think*?'

'The other girls are getting a new dress for the next social and...' her voice trailed off. She picked her jeans up off the floor and poked one foot in, pulling at the fabric that always got stuck around her ankle and hopping to balance herself. These jeans were always so tight to put on.

'The other girls...' her mother echoed, sitting on the edge of the bed. She sighed. 'Brooke, honey, you don't seem to understand. We. Can't. *Afford*. The same stuff as 'The Other Girls'. You don't seem to understand how tight our finances are. Maybe I need to go over all of our expenses with you so you get the picture. I'm a nurse trying to pay off a mortgage by myself, not a… a… whatever those other mothers do. I wish it was different but it's not.'

Brooke zipped up her jeans, swept the dress off her bed and stuffed it back into the bag. '*Okay*. I'll return it. If I can.'

Her mother sighed again. For a while, neither spoke, then Brooke burst out with 'It's not fair!' just as her mother said 'I hope you –'. Both stopped and her mother continued in the gap: 'No, life isn't fair. But complaining won't help; helping will.' She heaved herself off the bed and walked to the door. 'Now put that damn dress away and come help get dinner ready.'

Brooke watched her go, arms folded across her chest. She felt angry and sulky and disappointed all at the same time. She'd had one lousy minute of feeling like a princess and now she was right back to Cinderella. With her own Ugly Stepmother to boot… Okay, that was mean; her mother did her best. But why did some people have to work their butts off and get nowhere while other people did stuff-all and made a fortune! It just wasn't fair.

She stood in the middle of her room, frowning. Glancing up, she saw her pouty reflection in the mirror, and in the same moment realised that she and her mother were angry with each other for the exact same thing: poor money management. Her mother was pissed off with her for spending money she should be saving for the India trip, and she was pissed off with her mother for not earning more, for not being able to easily provide her with all of the things she wanted to have.

Brooke's arms dropped to her sides and her expression in the mirror changed from angry to unhappy. *She* was the one not being fair. She had pressured her mother into letting her go to India and it was just causing way too much stress. She should just let it go. Suck it up and let it go…

Toni faced the other India-travellers on her Fundraising Committee with a grim expression. The excursion to the beach had not been as well booked as she'd expected and the Trivia Night for Parents had gone well but not nearly as well as the Social so profits had been much lower. It seemed that only the India-Trip-parents were up for supporting the fundraising, and they were the ones already dipping into their pockets, so the outcome had been disappointing. At this rate, they'd have to run an event every week if they were going to cover everyone's trip costs! Not that they had to, of course; the Committee was just there to help. Students – or their families – were basically responsible for their own fees, but it seemed like quite a lot of them were counting on the fundraising activities a fair bit. Meanwhile there were some kids who weren't participating at all, saying they had the cost of the trip covered already, like that Asian boy – Andrew? Eric? Then there were the few who had dropped out, like Brooke, although she'd already been replaced by that new kid, Robbie. (Brooke was still hanging around and offering to help – maybe hedging her bets?) Jackson was valiantly supporting the Fundraising Committee but even he looked divided, as if he wasn't all there...

Toni turned back to the white board and wrote 'Enquire: Bus Hire' and 'Ski Equip't'. At their last meeting she had suggested a snow trip during winter. They were only planning a day trip to keep costs down so surely there wouldn't be much else to cover? Everyone could bring their own lunches... A few of the kids were already on their phones searching for prices, and they had to make a final decision about where they'd go – somewhere close enough for a day trip but far enough to promise a good snowfall, not that you could ever count on the weather to co-operate.

'I reckon we should do some easy things like sausage sizzles and selling chocolate,' a kid at the back called. 'This snow trip is going to be a lot of work and a lot of risk.'

'Yeah,' someone else said. 'Sausage sizzles are the go. My Scout group holds them every year – you can make a few hundred bucks easy, and you only have to put in an hour or so each. It's a breeze.'

Jackson looked up. 'Good idea,' he approved.

Toni felt betrayed. 'We've already announced the Snow Trip,' she objected.

'Do we have any sign-ups yet?' the sausage-sizzle-suggester asked.

'No, but that's because we haven't given prices yet. We've just said it's coming.'

'I think we should do some easier stuff first and save that for later.'

'Okay,' Toni agreed lightly. She held out the marker pen. 'Want to take over?' If they weren't going to let her be the boss of this venture, she wasn't going to do all the work!

'What for?' the kid asked, not moving.

'Like, who's going to order the meat, the sauce, the bread? Who's going to get permission? Who's going to hire the barbeque? Is anyone going to make salads?'

'No!' someone yelled. 'Meat, bread, sauce. Done.'

'Okay,' she went on. 'Who's going to advertise it or make signs or whatever? Who's going to sort out the roster so everyone takes a turn? Who's going to organise the money side of it?'

'Sell sausages, make money.'

She gave the person a hard stare. 'We'll need petty cash and to hire a barbeque. You got a spare one?'

Jackson was looking at her, impressed. (Good. She'd won back some authority.) 'I'll suss out hiring the barbeque,' he said, holding out his hand for the marker.

Are you a social entrepreneur?

The traditional business bottom line was profit or loss: business success used to be measured in monetary terms only.

Today's business leaders and consumers are so much more aware of the world around them, of the origin of products, and of the effects of their demands on others and on the Earth, that they are now demanding ethical products, sustainable development and socially responsible business practice. A whole new set of criteria are emerging as the 'quadruple bottom line' of 'full cost accounting':

i) Social: This means looking after one's workers and suppliers, eg. by providing suitable working conditions (and barring sweatshops), by employing disabled people or others who have been deemed 'unemployable', and by giving a percentage of the profit to the community to stimulate the local economy. 'Fair trade' is a new standard ensuring fair prices between companies in developed nations and producers in developing countries. Campaigns like B1G1 ('Buy One, Give One') enable members (consumers and businesses) to make a real impact on the world.

ii) Environmental (ecological): Sustainable business cares for the environment, does not pollute or degrade, and applies the 3 Rs of Reusing, Recycling and Reducing waste.

iii) Financial: A monetary profit is essential – without it, the business will collapse.

iv) The future: A long-term perspective where business today must benefit future generations, or at least do no harm.

People, Planet and Profit – the common good

The bottom lines of sustainable business, or 'social capitalism', are now considered to be the economics of the survival of our human species.

In this model the needs of citizens, communities, and the Earth carry the same weight as the demands of shareholders.

More and more business leaders and individuals are prioritising the whole over self, and discovering the emotional and practical and even financial benefits of giving and of solving social problems in the course of doing business.

The new responsible social enterprise wants to have made the world a better place.

This is the new bottom line.

CHAPTER 8

TRICKY BUSINESS

It was excruciatingly painful watching her friends bubble with excitement and plans for their upcoming India trip. **Brooke** kept a bright smile pasted on her face and squeezed her misery into a tight little ball deep inside her. No one was going to know how shattered she was. She had told them her mother was sick (small fib to save face), and now they asked her sympathetically, every time they saw her, 'How's your mum, Brooks?' Which actually made things even more uncomfortable. She'd wobble her head a bit and say, 'Okay' or 'A bit better', and quickly change the subject, though it would wander back to India pretty soon – to what they were packing and how excited they were and some snippet someone had heard about that exotic land, and how sorry they were that Brooke wasn't going...

It was just as well that someone else had just decided to go and been able to take her place. It would have been the pits if she hadn't been able to go *and* her mother had lost her deposit.

Brooke had hung onto her extra shift at The Burger Place because clearly she had to earn more, and that part was good. She liked the larger number on her pay slip and if she was honest, it wasn't, like, the most horrible job in the world – she did enjoy chatting to people as they made their orders. If she could just get graded at school on her gift of the gab she'd be their top student! But how would she ever make enough money to pay for something big like an overseas trip on this sort of wage? Brooke had heard that some of the other kids, like Toni and Eric, were paying the whole thing themselves, and that had given her a major shock. How could kids have that kind of money? She'd assumed their parents were rich and just gave it to them but then she'd heard they were paying with money *they'd earned*. Holy crap…

She had kept the pretty blue dress as compensation for not going to India, but she hadn't been able to bring herself to wear it at the party last weekend. The others had worn the new clothes they'd been talking about: Laura turned up in a really short yellow shift and Chloë in an almost matching really short pink shift, and Brooke had thought about the floaty blue dress hanging quietly in her wardrobe and kicked herself for not wearing it. It was a bugger when your friends had more money than you did. It sucked. It was *horrible*. But at least she didn't have to take on that whole load of housework any more, although not doing it made her feel guilty now, knowing how much there was and how much her mother already did. You couldn't bloody win.

The babysitting gig had deteriorated somewhat. By **Eric**'s third visit to that first family, the children had become confident, noisy, resistant monsters. It turned out that their compliance the first time was only due to their shyness; once they got to know him, they were bouncing all over the place like they'd eaten jumping beans for dinner, and even the big sister couldn't manage them. And then, after they'd finally gone to bed, there was someone at the lounge door every fifteen minutes needing a glass of water or reporting that someone else had fallen out of bed – yeah, right! – or *something* that kept him from his homework.

Eric had struggled on gamely but the whole thing was beginning to be more trouble than it was worth. It wasn't as if he had ever *wanted* to be a babysitter – man! But the word was out and each week some Asian parent rang to make a booking. The only comfort he could take from this bizarre situation was his swelling bank account. Between the tutoring and babysitting, his balance was growing steadily larger and he wasn't far away from the day he'd be able to walk into the office at school and pay out the rest of what he owed for the trip.

The savings he had already accumulated had been very helpful, of course. They'd given his cause a significant head start. He was glad his parents had been so insistent on him developing the habit of saving from a young age. What had he been – four? – when they'd opened an account for him? His first bank account had been a drawer in his father's desk with an official child's pay-in book and a special cash tin that was all his. Every month they would unlock it and add up the coins he had saved, and he'd touch the clinking pile with pleasure.

Once the tin was chock-full and heavy, they'd taken it to the bank and opened a real account. He remembered standing beside his father in front of the teller, barely able to see who was serving them because the counter was so high. The teller had had to stand up and lean forward to see him, her specs on the edge of her nose, and she'd congratulated him on saving so much money. She'd asked how he'd done it and he'd looked at her blankly, not knowing what she meant since it was surely obvious. His father had explained that he had special jobs over and above basic responsibilities like helping to set and clear the dinner table. The earning jobs were ones he was expected to perform every Saturday morning, like crawling all the way around the house with a damp rag wiping the skirting boards. This had been his special job because he was the shortest; as he grew taller, he'd graduated to dusting tables and ledges and windowsills, and then to ornaments and other delicate things.

He'd never resented these jobs because they were so mindless that he could think his own thoughts while his hands worked – apart from the time he had accidentally bumped an ancient Chinese vase that was a family heirloom. He could still remember the 'oh no!' feeling as a pit opened up in his stomach and adrenaline raced through his body, and he reached for the vase in filmic slow motion. It had literally seemed as if time had slowed down during those long moments as it wobbled and tipped over... He had been jerked out of his daydream and had caught the thing, hands trembling, body trembling, and set it back on the polished wood, breaking out in a sweat as he remembered how priceless and special and unique this vase was, and how his grandparents had brought it carefully from China, wrapped in many layers inside a solid box, because it had been in the family for generations and couldn't be left behind. It was still on that side table and now he wondered how much it would actually be worth. He'd watched *Antique Roadshow* once and had been amazed by how much some things were worth, things that looked quite ordinary, while other things the owners thought were treasures turned out to be fakes and not worth much at all.

It was probably not a bad idea to become a collector of valuable items. If you could choose the right things and patiently hang onto them for years, they would appreciate in value and you could spend your life doing whatever you wanted while your possessions paid for your lifestyle... He wondered if he would ever be interested enough in artwork to collect enough of it to make that strategy work for him. His father had quite a few valuable pieces; most of his wealth came from property but he had inherited the old family interest in beautiful, classic works of art, and every few years he would acquire a new investment. Basically they were pretty well off because Eric's father been very smart with his money, saving his salary conscientiously from the very first week, and then beginning to invest in property and eventually the odd artwork. And of course they'd had his mother's excellent salary as a doctor as well. Even though his parents were separating now, both of them would remain comfortable.

Eric felt confident that he, too, would find a vocation that would allow him to become reasonably wealthy. For a long time he had assumed he would pursue a career in medicine, like his mother, or perhaps in engineering, like his father; the sciences came so easily to him that it would probably be one of those two. But he was also drawn to IT and had begun to dabble in designing software for apps, and wouldn't that be a cool way of earning money that he could get into straight away –

much better than babysitting and much quicker than a four-plus-year uni course! Well, maybe not apps since they were already mostly free or cheap, but by the time he was out of school there'd be some other tech marvel taking off that he could be part of. Surely.

Meanwhile he was grateful for the financial education his parents had given him over the years – in particular the injunction to always repay his savings account whenever he withdrew a large amount. He could have paid for the whole India trip at once but he hadn't wanted to decimate his account without immediately being able to replenish it. He was on track with that.

§ § §

The house was gi-normous. **Toni**'s family had several wealthy friends but this was ridiculous! You could get lost in here. Everything was marble and polished and great big empty spaces, like the entrance hall that was big enough to play a ball game! The windows were huge and looked out onto beautiful gardens and rolling green hills, and pictures as large as what you'd find in the national art gallery hung on the walls. There was a theatre room downstairs apparently, and a library, and a study, and about five bedrooms and three bathrooms and three different living areas, and now Toni and her family were being led from the beautiful living room to a dining room that had a long table set with candles and serviettes and shining silver cutlery, just like in the movies!

She gazed around in amazement, wondering what the owner did to be able to afford this stuff, and wondering how much it all cost. Like, that little square painting above the sideboard that was just an abstract mess of lines like something she could have done in kindergarten – what was that worth, for instance? Before she could stop herself, Toni had asked. Her mother rolled her eyes and gave a slight shake of her head, and Toni felt a small flush of embarrassment – oops, private, shouldn't have asked that… But their host, a tall man with a huge voice and laugh, didn't blink an eye.

'Seventeen thousand,' he said. 'That's a Tony Tuckson.'

$17,000?!!! Toni was staggered. Maybe she'd take up art... Could Toni Walshe become as famous as Tony Tuckson? Her skill level was about the same as that crazy abstract, she reckoned...

Most of the dinner conversation rolled over her head. She was engrossed in the delicate flavours of a delicious goat's cheese soufflé, followed by lightly baked fish with asparagus and green beans in some kind of really tasty sauce, and a green salad with cherry tomatoes and shreds of raw beetroot and carrot and macadamia nuts. But her ears pricked up when their host said he'd done pretty well during the recent economic downturn because 'any time is a good time to make money'.

'But how do you make money if people aren't spending?' she asked.

'True wealth comes about through patience,' their host said. 'Everything goes in cycles: if you buy when people are selling because the price is dropping, and then you have the patience to hold, eventually the prices rise again and you're ahead.' He took a sip of his wine and leaned back in his seat. 'Warren Buffet for instance; he amassed his fortune by buying investments and businesses when everyone else wanted out.'

'Who's he?'

'One of the richest men in the world,' her father said. 'Warren Buffet is an American billionaire who made his first investment when he was eleven years old.'

'Seriously?'

Her father nodded. 'He's had his share of losses too –'

'And *millions* at a time,' Toni's mother put in, smiling her thanks as their host poured her another glass of wine. 'Imagine losing *millions*. "Oops, there's another twenty-five million down the gurgler! But never mind, we're still fifty billion ahead."'

'The guy might be rolling in it but he's no miser,' Toni's father said. 'He's signed a commitment to give at least half of his income away – that right, Arnold?'

'At least,' their host said. 'I think it's way more than that.'

'How does someone earn that much?' Toni demanded.

'Not doing time-for-money, that's for sure,' Arnold said drily.

Time for money? Toni asked her father with her eyes.

'A job,' he said. 'Getting paid for hours worked. If you want to be wealthy, you want to set yourself up so that you're earning passive income, which is money that comes in whether you're working or playing or sleeping. Usually from investments, or royalties from books or music, or employees who run your business for you. To be wealthy you have to have money working for *you*, rather than you working for *it*.'

'So if you're not likely to write a bestselling book or song or whatever,' Toni said, 'you've got to own a business or invest.'

'That's it,' Arnold agreed. 'But not any old investment. Too many people follow any financial advisor who comes along – usually the one making the biggest claims – and end up with property that won't appreciate in value or stocks that are on their way down. You have to buy wisely, which means studying the company and the market and the trends. There are x-factors of successful investment, like knowing what to buy and when to buy, and having the patience to hold. Buffet is in it for the long haul. He doesn't look for immediate profit; he looks for longevity.'

'So does anyone get rich quick?'

'Sure. It happens. When the Soviet Union was dissolved in the nineties, for instance, a lot of business was privatised and the ones who got into that game early made a squillion.'

'You mean communism going out and capitalism coming in?' Toni asked. 'Private businesses instead of the government running everything?'

'More or less. But the "get rich quick" market is a dangerous game. It's not for folks who want to build a sustainable fortune. If you want to make serious money, you've got to actually study the subject, just like you're doing with Maths and English at school. You can't use an eeny, meeny, miny, mo kind of strategy. That's why lottery winners rarely keep their windfall: they don't have a wealthy person's mindset – they haven't educated themselves about money and they don't have a strong saving habit; they've got a poor person's mindset, so they just spend the lot and within five years they're back where they were – or sometimes even worse off.'

'Even if they've won, like, fifty million?' Toni demanded.

'Even if. I think the stats are that most lottery winners are broke, even bankrupt, within five years, and have broken relationships to boot.'

'Why broken relationships?'

'Going from rags to riches sets off all sorts of jealousy and difficult situations,' he said, and a small muscle twitched in his jaw. 'Friends and family start hitting on the winner for money to pay *their* bills and fund *their* dreams, and pretty soon the winner's in hot water because he or she is trying to spread the jackpot between twenty relatives and a bunch of charities and new cars and houses and boats and travel, and the poor sucker's never learned how to manage money in the first place.'

'Tricky!' she murmured.

'That's just the beginning of the slippery slope. There are many traps for the unwary… If the winner tries to hang onto it all for themselves, friends and family get resentful and jealous, and if they're married, the couple themselves might not agree on how to spend or manage the money, so divorce is common. Even if they're smart enough to recognise that they need help, they often fall prey to financial planners who take advantage of their ignorance… All sorts of things can go wrong.'

'This is why Dad and I have attempted to drum the importance of saving into you,' Toni's mother said. 'And getting out there earning money so you start learning how it all works. So many parents will talk to their kids about drugs and alcohol but not about money, and then they wonder why their kids haven't got the first clue.'

'I am eternally grateful,' Toni said grandly.

'Cheeky bugger,' her mother snorted.

'I really am,' Toni said more sincerely. 'Most of the kids at school go on about how hard it is to get money out of their folks and don't twig that they could be finding their own way of making some.'

A door banged somewhere in the house followed by the sound of loud voices and running footsteps. Toni glanced at their host's face, wondering who had arrived, and saw that he was looking in the direction of the noise with a grim expression.

'My son,' he said, noticing her watching him. 'Brought up in the lap of luxury and doesn't appreciate any of it. If you're paying attention to your parents, good for you, Toni. There's so much I could be passing on to Lucas but he won't listen. My mistake was giving him too much. I didn't realise until too late.'

He stood up and began to collect their dishes. The place might be palatial and the meal restaurant quality, but he had served it all himself and had apparently prepared it all himself too – no maids or cooks. Toni was very impressed.

'Was your family rich when you were growing up?' she asked.

'My parents were immigrants who arrived in this country with nothing and then worked like the blazes. Dad's a property developer now but he began as a labourer.' Arnold paused in the doorway to the kitchen with his load of dirty plates. 'Our family is enacting a typical pattern: the first generation has nothing so it values wealth and works hard to achieve it; the second generation consolidates; but the third has no memory of lack and so they don't appreciate the wealth and begin to dissipate it. That's what I've got to look forward to – unless I can prevent it.' He grimaced and disappeared into the kitchen.

'Where's his wife?' Toni whispered. 'Is he married?'

'They're divorced,' her mother replied in a low voice.

'And she didn't get half of it? Or did he already have so much that you'd barely notice?'

'They had a prenup – so she couldn't touch a lot of his family wealth.'

'A what?'

'Prenuptial agreement. Lots of wealthy people set them up before the marriage so that if they split up the partner can't clean them out. So his wife couldn't touch a lot of his money. That's one of the reasons he doesn't get on with his son. Everybody's pissed off with each other.'

So wealth didn't buy happiness, Toni reflected. Comfort, beauty, new experiences... but not happiness. The house was magnificent but he had large-scale personal problems to match. How did you manage your life so you had it all?

The door from the kitchen opened again and their host appeared with a dish bearing their dessert: chocolate truffles and candied orange rind. Very posh.

The pile of junk gathering in **Jackson**'s family driveway was classic. Were they really going to find people who would want to buy this stuff? Broken lawn mowers, axe heads with no handle, chipped dishes, old toys, puzzles and models that had missing pieces… surely not. But he kept his mouth closed and followed his mother's instructions, stacking piles of stuff on the wobbly trestle tables.

The first people were already pulling up in front of their home even though the ad in the local paper had said their garage sale began at 8 a.m. and it was only 7.30. His mother smiled cheerily at these potential customers, who were now climbing out of their car and wandering to the fence to peer at their stuff.

Surely eBay would be a better way to make money than this! Although you couldn't sell crap on eBay… Oh well, he supposed the garage sale was worth a try. Jackson had parked all of his old stuff on one table and any revenue from it would go straight to the India trip. If it didn't sell here, he'd try it on eBay – and not selling here was a very likely development: the heavy grey skies promised rain. Jackson could just imagine the chaos when the heavens opened and they tried to get everything back under cover…

His mother called out to him to help her with a heavy item, and he stared in surprise. 'Your old sewing machine, Mum? I thought you said you would never sell that, not ever, not even if we were starving!'

She smiled and flushed. 'Oh well, you know, I was joking. But the thing is, it's been broken for years and it's beyond repair, so what's the point of hanging onto it? Just for nostalgia doesn't seem like a good enough reason when it's gathering dust in some corner of the garage where we don't even get to see it. If we had a bigger place I'd display it, at least, or if we had the funds I'd have it professionally cleaned and confirm that it's beyond repair, but none of that is a priority right now, and sometimes these old machines can bring in a few hundred so it's worth a try. Come on, you grab the heavy end. I think we should put it over there where it's a little under cover in case it rains.'

Jackson hoisted his end of the machine and they inched it over to the spot his mother had chosen. He knew what this sewing machine meant to his mother. He knew how many childhood memories were woven around it. He felt the edge of anger that here they were, good, hard-working people who always did their best, and yet they were constantly struggling and unable to get ahead, having to scrimp and save and steal from this account to pay that one, and do without, and chase bargains, and decide things by prices rather than just doing the damn thing they wanted to do.

Standing with arms folded, he watched a steady trickle of customers wander in through their front gate and fossick around amongst their old, worn stuff, and the anger brewed and simmered inside him. He was going to find a way to make money, heaps of money, and he was going to start *now*. This India trip would be the first goal and then he'd set more goals until he had earned so frigging much that he could retire his parents and buy his mother as many antique sewing machines as she wanted. He wasn't going to get stuck in the factory like his father. He was going to find something else that he loved doing that paid a mint, but in the meantime he would use whatever skills or strength he had to earn as much as he could. Right. There was an idea!

Marching inside, he found a piece of cardboard and a thick marker pen, and wrote a sign that he took back outside and propped up on his table:

NEED ODD JOBS DONE?

NEED SOME GARDENING?

NEED HELP MOVING HOUSE?

CALL JACKSON ON....

A JOB and running your own business, is where you trade time for money:
someone pays you to carry out certain tasks.

Many entrepreneurs launch their own businesses
because they want to be independent and autonomous, only to find they've just created themselves another 'job' where they are overwhelmed by an abundance of tasks they haven't been trained for, and they no longer have time to do the one thing they love to do and are good at.

This pattern is described in The E-Myth by Michael Gerber:
A pie-maker (who loves making pies) opens her own shop and then finds she has to employ others to bake the pies because she is so busy running the business... and not enjoying herself anymore.

Both of these options can feel like treadmills. It's worthwhile taking the time to ask yourself how you can be richly paid for doing what you most love.

Imagine earning so much that you can give half your income away!

If you have money to give, where can you give it?

Even if you don't have much spare cash, how can you be of service?

How do you feel about your current finances?

How do you feel about the state of your family's finances?

To what degree do you or your family plan and strategise for financial success,
and to what degree are you just 'doing the days' as they come and hoping that one day you'll break through to wealth?

Do your parents give you everything you want?

Should they?

Do they provide for your basic needs but make you buy the stuff you want over and above that?

Do you save?

Do you save regularly?

Do you get paid for working around the house?

Which jobs should you be paid for, and which should simply be your contribution since you're a member of the household using all the goods and services?

CHAPTER 9

July: Balance Due

At last! **Eric** handed over the balance for the India trip and relished the moment when he would advise his babysitting clientele that he was No Longer Available. He would send *that* email tonight.

Receipt in hand, he walked out of the school admin building and headed toward the library where he was meeting Chris to brainstorm their plan to build an app. As he walked, he pondered the great domain name that had popped into his head during breakfast that morning. Before they started on the website he would jump online and see if it was already taken. If not, he reckoned he would buy that name and then sell it later for a profit. He smiled at the thought of how easy this could be.

'I screwed up,' **Toni** announced to her parents, who were sitting at the breakfast table with coffees and newspapers and toast.

They both looked up, her mother with raised brows and her father with his head cocked to one side. 'How so?' he asked.

'The balance,' she said, landing heavily in the seat opposite them. 'It's due this Friday and I haven't got enough. That beach trip was a fizzer and so was the Trivia Night – we just didn't raise enough.'

'How much are you short?' her mother asked.

'About twelve hundred,' Toni grimaced.

'Oh well, bad luck,' her father said gravely. 'Valiant effort. Next time.'

'Da-ad!'

He grinned. 'Hey, it *was* a valiant effort. We're proud of you, hon. No problem. Put the form on my desk and I'll fix.'

'Thanks, Dad,' she beamed, wrapping her arms around him. 'I'll pay you back. I had just wanted to get it handled by the deadline *myself*.'

'We know,' he said, his voice muffled. 'And we're proud of you for that. But you gotta roll with the punches: being in business brings all sorts of ups and downs.'

'She's gotta get back on the horse,' her mother corrected. 'What's your next venture? Fall down five times, get up six.'

'I will,' Toni said cheerily. 'We're going to keep running events after the deadline's over because quite a few kids are still paying parents back. So yeah, we've got sausage sizzles and stuff planned. I know – boring! But the others went along with my ideas so I guess I've got to help them with theirs.'

'Well, keep inspiring them to greater things,' her father said, and then his phone rang and her mother's phone buzzed with a message as he was answering and they were both swept away into their own business worlds again. Toni watched for a few moments, feeling a little deflated, then set about making her breakfast.

s s

So the garage sale takings weren't amazing but he'd scored two jobs from his ad. The old guy across the road wanted **Jackson** to mow his lawns, and watching their family cleaning out their garage had reminded him that his needed doing too, so perhaps Jackson could help him with that, too, being 'such a strong, young man'... Hopefully the pay would be reasonable – Jackson had no idea what people charged for mowing and labouring. He guessed he'd better find out.

Meanwhile he had the unpleasant task of facing his parents to ask for the balance for the India trip, which was due tomorrow. Jackson sat staring at the TV without taking in what he was watching. He knew things were still tight, money-wise. He knew this trip was a big pain in the bum for them. But he was so keen to go that he couldn't give up on it now.

Sighing, he seized his courage and went to his father's study. He hesitated for a moment outside the door… then knocked.

'Yo?' his father called back.

Jackson opened the door and looked in. 'Sorry, Dad, I know it's a pest but that India trip has to be paid out tomorrow.'

'Shit,' his father said, grimacing, and the awful feeling in Jackson's stomach tightened and curdled.

'All right, son,' he added, frowning, still not looking at him. 'Leave me the paperwork and I'll get onto it.'

'I'll pay you back,' Jackson said, hovering. 'It just might take me a while. You know, at one-lawn-mowing-job-at-a-time rate.'

'Sure,' his father said, kind of dismissively.

'Bill!' Jackson's mother called from outside in the hallway. She came into the room, still speaking: 'Do you know where –?' then stopped, seeing Jackson and the look on his face and her husband's dark expression. 'What's up?'

Neither spoke at first. 'Just talking about the deadline for the balance,' Jackson said finally, feeling the pain all over again.

'Oh,' she said.

'I'll sort it,' Jackson's father said irritably. 'Now, if you'll just let me…'

'I'm trying to find the power board that used to be in the kitchen,' his mother interrupted.

'It's in the garage on the bench,' Jackson's father said, returning to his work pointedly.

'Okay. Thanks.' She looked from him to Jackson, and hooked her arm through her son's as they both left. Closing the study door behind them, she hung onto his arm and walked with him to the lounge room. 'Don't worry, Jackson. This too shall pass, as they say. We're just going through a rough patch.'

'So you keep saying,' Jackson said, and then wished he hadn't.

His mother frowned and wiped the hair out of her eyes tiredly. 'Some rough patches last a while. Dad had to dip into your college fund to pay the mortgage, which he hates doing. Sorry. I shouldn't have told you that. We'll repay it. It's just that things are very, very tight at the moment.'

'You must really wish I wasn't going,' he said sourly.

'No, we're really *glad* you're going,' she contradicted, pulling on his arm and making him face her. 'We *want* you to have these experiences, Jack. We had a long chat about it with Uncle Dave the other night. It's just that we're a bit up against it at the moment. Anyway, don't you worry. We do have some money put aside for a rainy day that we'd promised ourselves we wouldn't touch unless it was an absolute emergency, so that's there as our safety net if we really need it.'

'I *will* pay you back,' he said, a fierce edge to his voice.

Her eyes softened and she reached up and planted a kiss on his cheek. 'I know you will, love. You don't need to but if that makes you feel better, you can pay us back. No rush.'

'I will,' he said again, and he gave her a tight hug.

Brooke had finally opted out of the chats about India. She couldn't stand it any more. She lay on her bed, her silenced phone beside her, feet pointing up at the ceiling, flexing her toes. The ceiling was such a vast, blank canvas. She wondered what she'd paint up there if she could. 'Brooke Michelangelo'... It sure wouldn't be angels and Biblical characters! Maybe she'd paint a beautiful sky – a sunset scene? Or a night sky with millions of luminous stars... Or a great big elephant. No! No thoughts of India. She dragged her attention away. An abstract pattern, perhaps? Or the story of her life? Boring... Or maybe she could paint a vision of the life she wanted to have! A life in which she was famous (at something) and surrounded by adoring friends and fans and stunningly beautiful and slim and maybe even a bit taller, and she'd paint herself with heaps of money poking out of her pockets to show how wealthy she had become! Brooke grinned, scissoring her legs and visualising the magnificent, prophetic picture on her ceiling.

Her mother knocked at the door and opened it. She looked in. 'Bit more of that Monopoly game we started while you're waiting?'

Brooke dropped her legs to the bed and they bounced. It was rare, these days, for her mother to propose a game, but she often suddenly wanted more time with her daughter when Brooke was about to head off with her dad. 'Okay.' Brooke swung her legs off the bed and followed her mother downstairs.

They were not very far into the game when it became apparent that her mother had an agenda. 'I've been thinking,' she said, sorting through her pile of notes. 'I've been thinking that it might be helpful for you if I explained to you exactly how much I make and how much the bills are so you can get a sense of how finances work in the adult world.'

Brooke screwed up her face a little and waited. She wasn't sure that she wanted to hear this…

'Pause the game for a moment while I show you?' her mother asked.
'Okaaay…'

'All right then.' Her mother counted out a bunch of yellow and blue and green notes and placed them on the table. 'This is how much money I make – my wage. I earn $52,000 per year.'

Wow. That was heaps. They were rich! Why did her mother complain so much?

'That works out at about $4,333 per month. Now, this is what we pay each month on the mortgage.' She removed $1,680 from the pile and set it aside.

Shit! Nearly half of it was already gone!

'And this is what I pay on food.' $900 was subtracted from the pile – it was looking a lot less rich now.

'And then we have bills – power, gas, phone, internet…' Another $1,040 was withdrawn from the pile of income.

'And then there's petrol and car maintenance costs. Let's estimate three hundred dollars.'

'And then there's stuff like doctor, dentist, physio, clothes, shoes, gifts…'

'There's nothing left,' Brooke said.

'That's right,' her mother said. They both looked at the empty space where the money had been.

'In fact,' Brooke's mother said, 'we are mostly living beyond our means. Which means we're spending money we don't have.'

'Shit.'

'Precisely.'

'How can we spend money we don't have?'

'Credit card. Borrowing against the mortgage.'

'So this is why we don't go on holidays very often.'

'’Fraid so.'

'So you really never could afford India.'

Her mother shook her head sadly.

'Then how were you going to do it?'

'Oh, I don't know! Borrow again. Work harder – get more shifts. Hope your Dad kicked in.'

Brooke leaned across the table and hugged her mother. 'I'm sorry,' she said.

'You weren't to know,' her mother replied. 'We didn't educate you. Silly of us – we just didn't think to.'

'So… what are we going to do?'

Her mother shrugged. 'It's a bit of a vicious cycle. You just work as hard as you can and hope you get ahead. This is why your education is so important, Brooke. The better your job, the more you earn…'

No more goofing around in class, Brooke thought, sitting up a little. She really did need to get her act together. If this was the reality waiting for her in the adult world, it was going to be a horrible future if she didn't earn much. Then again, some people dropped out of school early and still made heaps, so that *couldn't* be the x-factor. But, whatever. You had to be smart. You couldn't just drift and dream along as she'd been doing…

'So when you go shopping for clothes, Brooke,' her mother said gently, 'if you can avoid the big name brands and just get the plain ones, we'll be spending half as much.'

That really hurt. Brooke visualised herself walking along the street with Laura and Chloë, the two of them wearing snazzy Gucci or Burberry, and her in a no-name... Maybe she could just wait for the sales?

'In fact, is there something else you can do for entertainment other than go to the mall? Just looking – window shopping – that pretty soon leads to actual shopping.'

'Yeah.' Brooke sighed. 'This sucks.'

'You could learn how to make your own clothes, you know. Your aunt Sara is a brilliant dressmaker – she'd teach you. And then you could create your own style instead of looking like everyone else. Lead the field...'

Brooke shuffled her fake money. She wished it was real. She wished the real world wasn't. 'I hate sewing,' she said.

'But you're very creative,' her mother pointed out. 'You might find that you like it if you're working on something special instead of just hems and buttons. What if you could create something pretty, like that blue dress you bought?'

Brooke thought about it – the measuring and cutting and pinning. Could she be bothered?

'It might turn into a career,' her mother added craftily. "Brooke Hamley, Fashion Designer".'

Brooke waved a hand dismissively.

'You used to love helping me organise the costumes for your dance concerts when you were little,' her mother continued, gaining in enthusiasm. 'That's a potential career: Wardrobe Manager for a theatre company. You're going to want a stimulating career, Brooke, and that would be fascinating. It's worth thinking about it.'

'I've got to like sewing though,' Brooke said. 'You're getting carried away, Mum.'

'Maybe. But it's worth exploring.'

'I like photography too. And drawing.'

'I know. You're very creative. You could be a photographer – in fact, you could probably take photos and sell them online. There's a huge demand for stock photos.'

'Most people want free ones.'

'There must be some that are paid for. Or you could draw pictures at kids' parties – or do face painting.'

'All right! I've got the idea. You want me to bring in some money.'

'I want you to have a better sense of the real world,' her mother corrected. 'And I want you to start valuing your skills and doing something with them. I can promise to meet all of your *needs*: food, shelter, love… but I can't promise to provide all your *wants*. You've got to start taking some responsibility for those.'

'Okay. Fair enough.' Brooke wished she could be more gracious about all of this but it felt like her world was falling apart and tumbling in pieces around her. She'd been living in a lovely dream world where everything was provided for her and now she was being asked to wake up and grow up. It hurt.

'And, you know, don't get focused on what we don't have. I do that way too much, too,' her mother said. 'We have so much, Brooke. We have each other, a home, our health…'

'Except that you're at the physio every second week.'

Her mother made a face. 'I'm still able-bodied enough to go to work and you're in perfect health. Come on, tell me three things you're grateful for.'

'I dunno.'

'Surely you can think of something!'

'Well, *you*.'

'When you sound so grudging, it doesn't feel like you appreciate me at all,' her mother said in a hurt tone.

'Sorry.' Brooke covered her mother's hand with her own. 'I do appreciate you.'

'Thank you. What else?'

'Yeah, our home. Being healthy.'

'You have to come up with three new ones, not the ones I said!'

'Okay. One: food, especially pizza and chocolate. Two… sunny days.'

The doorbell rang and Brooke leapt to answer it. It was her father, and he entered with a mysterious smile and an envelope that he flashed around in front of her face.

'What's this, Dad?' she asked, taking the proffered envelope.

'The balance for your trip.'

'What?!' Brooke shrieked, ripping it open. $100 notes fluttered out and fell to the floor.

'Brooke – careful!' her mother exclaimed, standing up.

'Don't lose it,' her father laughed. 'There's two grand in there!'

'Wow! Dad, you're amazing!' Brooke threw herself at her father in a wild hug. 'I thought I couldn't go! This is wicked! This is awesome!'

'How–?' began Brooke's mother in slightly tense voice.

Her ex shrugged. 'Tell you later. Don't worry – it's all above board.'

Brooke looked at her mother with shining eyes. 'Three: Dad, and this trip to India!'

CHAPTER 10

WHAT DO YOU PACK?

Brooke's bed was covered in clothes. She had been buzzing around happily between her wardrobe and her chest of drawers, singing to herself and tossing items over her shoulder onto the bed, and now her cupboard was empty and her bed piled high. A little frown puckered her forehead as her gaze flitted between the open suitcase on the floor and the mountain of garments on her bed. They were not going to fit. She picked up a top decisively, folded it, and placed it in the case. That one was definitely going. She picked up another, considered, folded it, placed it next to the first. And she always wore those jeans with that top, so...

'I know it looks awkward,' **Jackson**'s mother said, tying the moneybag around his waist, 'but you really do need to be careful. These countries are full of starving, desperate people who are all terribly jealous of our wealth and they'll be looking for opportunities to steal. Just one moment of inattention, and...'

"Our wealth'!' Jackson echoed, laughing. 'As if!'

'Compared to them, we're very rich,' she said, beginning to poke Indian rupees and American dollars into the pocket. 'You know that. It's just that their standard of living is so much lower and everything's so much cheaper there. If we *did* live in India, we'd be considered quite wealthy.'

'They won't *all* be thieves. Uncle Dave reckons he doesn't even lock the door, and that's a similar sort of –'

'Uncle Dave has been living in his community for a while now. He's almost a local. You're a tourist. You'll stick out a like a sore thumb, especially travelling in a group with other Western tourists.'

Jackson's mother unzipped the money belt again and pushed the money out of the way to make room for his passport.

'Ugh!' Jackson protested. 'All this crap around my waist is what's going to make me stick out like a sore thumb! Can't I just be careful?'

'Not safe enough,' she replied smartly, zipping the pocket up again and pulling his t-shirt down over it. 'I've heard that they come along and slice your backpack open with a razor blade and then grab your wallet and run.'

'Really?' he said, impressed. 'Honestly, Mum, I'm pretty fast. I'd catch 'em.'

'You don't know your way around there,' she said, patting and pulling at the t-shirt in an attempt to conceal the bulk around his waist. 'They'd only have to duck into a side alley –'

Jackson mouthed a swear word. He dropped his head on an angle and lowered until he was level with his mother, and looked at her sideways, brows raised. 'Mum, if the teachers and tour guides say we have to use them, I will, but if no one else is, you can be sure *I won't*. I am *not* going to be the only joker wearing a money belt.'

His mother sighed and straightened up. 'All right,' she said, hands in the air, stepping back. 'I give up. But don't say I didn't warn you. Don't expect to write home for more money every time you get pick-pocketed.'

'Every time! Man, you must really think there are some bad dudes over there.'

'Not bad; just... needy...'

Jackson put a hand on each of her shoulders and looked at her squarely. 'I will be careful. Okay? No one is going to rob me.'

For a moment he thought she was going to cry. Then she sniffed and straightened up and pulled him into a tight hug. 'We're so proud of you. We're going to miss you, Jackie.'

Almost all of the clothes were now in the suitcase and just a few stragglers had been returned to the cupboards and drawers. Feeling successful, **Brooke** sat on the case to close it and reached for the zip. She tugged but it only moved a few centimetres. She pulled again. Was something in the way? No. Kneeling next to the case she leaned on it heavily with her upper arm and elbow, and tugged at the zip again. Not a hope. Okay. Maybe she had packed too many clothes. She'd take some of the warm ones out; she probably wouldn't need those.

'All packed?' **Toni**'s mother asked. 'Did any of the tips I gave you help?'

'Perfect. The school list of what to take was pretty good but sticking socks inside shoes for more space was a great idea – and rolling my clothes – that was all handy. And putting bright stickers on the case so it's easy to recognise.'

'You travel often enough, you figure out what works best.' Toni's mother glanced at her phone. 'So! You're ready?'

'Yep.'

'Remind me what time we leave in the morning.'

'All students to meet at school at eight-thirty,' Toni recited. 'Bus to airport. Stand in queues for two hours. Go through customs, etc. Flights depart one-o-five p.m. Loooong flight."

'And no duty shopping this end,' her mother instructed, texting a message to someone as she spoke. 'Or you'll be stuck carrying stuff the whole way. Get it on your return trip.'

Toni nodded. 'Good advice. So where's Dad?'

'He's going to be back late tonight – working on a surprise,' her mother smiled, and then when Toni was about to ask. 'Just wait. You'll see…'

Shit. There was no way all of this stuff was going to fit! **Brooke** flipped the lid open again and began to pick a few items out. But she *really* wanted to take all the other things she'd packed… She frowned, gave the case a brief, frustrated kick, and then scooped armfuls of clothes out and dumped them back on the bed.

Hang on! There was a list, wasn't there? The school had given them a packing list… Maybe that would help. Now, where had she put it?

Eric's suitcase and carry-on luggage were neatly packed and standing by the front door, ready for departure day tomorrow. He was getting a last hit of computer time before he had to shut down and leave all of that behind for three whole weeks. They were allowed to bring their phones but that was all, and the internet was so dodgy over there he knew he couldn't count on being able to do any digital stuff while he was away. That was an unsettling prospect. Three weeks with nothing but dodgy internet. Geez.

He had several browser pages open at once. He'd been checking out political trouble zones in the region just in case – he couldn't imagine either of their two teacher companions thinking to do that. And he'd been researching moves on his favourite online chess site and reading a blog by this young guy who was so good with numbers that he was the youngest ever Professor of Maths at Oxford Uni, or something like that, and now worked for a mega successful company that assessed betting risks for football and the races.

Ah! The domain name he'd come up with! He'd checked its availability with Chris a few weeks ago and had meant to buy it but then the bell for class had rung and he'd forgotten all about it. He'd better do that now before they headed overseas. It was pretty cheap, he remembered…

He opened a new window and typed in the URL for the domain registration company and then the URL he wanted to buy… and then stared in disbelief at the message that it was no longer available. How could that be! It had been his unique idea – how could it be taken all of a sudden?

Sitting back with arms folded and jaw set, Eric thought it through. He'd heard that there were people who made their living buying and selling web addresses… they probably had a robotic worm sussing out whenever someone came up with a new site name, and if you didn't claim it straight away, they would grab it because once they knew someone out there valued it, no doubt others would too and they could hike the price up. Damn. It had been a bloody good name, too. He should have bought it as soon as he'd thought of it.

Oh well, he knew now. He'd never make that mistake again.

Brooke smiled tiredly. The case zipped up and everything she needed was in there, plus just a little bit extra. It was late though, and she was feeling exhausted. Her plan to have an early night so she'd be up fresh for the big travelling day had gone to the dogs. Her mother had popped in at nine-thirty to say goodnight, been alarmed that she was still not ready and stayed for an hour helping, but after she'd headed to bed Brooke had just swapped a few more things around and now suddenly it was already after eleven!

There was one more thing she should do before she hit the sack. She'd take the case with her to the bathroom and stick it on the scales. It would be awful to arrive at the airport and have to unpack stuff in front of everyone, to say nothing of having to leave things behind. Especially as they were going on the school bus so she wouldn't have her mum at the airport to give her excess stuff to.

Brooke seized the suitcase handle and lifted. Holy crap! Were there bricks in there or what? Suppressing a flicker of concern, she hefted it up and carried it in little bursts to the bathroom, treading as quietly as she could past her mother's room.

The case dwarfed the scales and she couldn't see the numbers. Dragging it onto its side, she prodded it around until it was reasonably well balanced and then peeked at the reading. One and a half kilos over the baggage allowance… that should be okay!

'I wish we could go to the airport with you,' **Jackson**'s mother said. 'But at least we get to pick you up from there when you get back. Now, have you got your passport?'

'Yep,' said Jackson.

'Visa?'

'Check.'

'Wallet? Money belt?'

'Yes – curses.'

'Plane ticket! Oh my God, lucky I remembered to ask you that!'

He patted his travel wallet. 'It's all in here, Mum. Stop worrying.'

Jackson's father poked his head around the door. 'Didn't you hear me beeping? We've got to go.'

'Sorry, darling; just doing all the last minute checks.'

'Yet again,' he said, rolling his eyes. 'Come on, son.'

Jackson hoisted his backpack and reached for the handle of his case but his father got there first.

'I'll take it. You'll be dragging that around for the next three weeks.'

'Thanks, Dad.'

His father nodded, a little curtly, and Jackson felt a rush of affection for him. It wouldn't be easy, sending your son off on an international holiday while you had to stay at home and slave away to pay for it. He followed his father out to the car and watched as he opened the boot and laid the case on the old blanket.

'Thanks, Dad,' Jackson said again. He wanted the thank you to convey more than just case-carrying thanks; he wanted it to mean everything that he felt: the gratitude and indebtedness and hope and fear and… but he just didn't have that sort of relationship with his father. It was easy to talk to Mum but he could never seem to get the words out with his father.

Jackson's father looked back at the house and shook his head in amazement. 'Where is that woman? Whatever is she doing now?' The next moment, the front door opened and his mother appeared. She slammed it behind her and hurried towards them, buttoning her coat.

Brushing her teeth, **Brooke** was struck by the realisation that she might not have left room in her case for her toiletries bag. Her reflection in the mirror was instantly wildly alarmed. Ten minutes to leaving the house and she still had packing issues to sort out! Shit!

'So what's the surprise, Mum?' **Toni** asked, glancing at her watch. 'We've got to go, like now, and Dad isn't back yet.'

Her mother read a text on her phone and smiled. 'I think you'll find that he is, honey, *with* the surprise.'

Baffled, Toni followed her mother to the front door with her luggage and as it opened she saw her father out by the front kerb, opening the door to a strange, shining, new Toyota Landcruiser.

'What the –?'

'We splashed out. Something for us to play with while you're having adventures overseas,' her mother grinned. 'Business is going okay, so… Dad wanted to at least give you a quick run in it before you left so he pushed the purchase through to pick it up this morning. Come on!'

'You packed the first aid kit I gave you?' **Eric**'s mother asked. 'It's got the Immodium for diarrhoea, and Panadol, antibiotics, antiseptic cream, etcetera. Make sure you take whatever you need at the very first sign so that you nip it in the bud. Once those bacterial infections get a hold of you they can be really nasty.'

'Yes, I've got it,' Eric confirmed.

'And you're clear on the exchange rate? Remember that they expect you to barter so don't pay the first price they tell you. Work them down.'

'Okay.' He did feel just the slightest twinge of anxiety at the thought of bartering. It was so much easier to just walk into a shop and pay the price that was displayed. Oh well. He wasn't such a big spender anyway, so hopefully he wouldn't need to buy very much…

Brooke's father had actually turned up to say goodbye at the school. He lifted her case out of the car and carried it over to the bus for her. (Her case looked old and battered standing next to some of the others, she noticed with discomfort.)

'Have the best time, Treasure,' he said, and wrapped his arms around her in a farewell hug.

'Thanks, Dad. And thanks so much for this,' she added in a low voice. Her mother was standing nearby and still cranky with her ex about the whole thing. It was almost as if she would have preferred to lose their deposit rather than miraculously come up with the rest of the money and let her go. Luckily they'd been able to hold Brooke's spot, even with the new kid joining the trip as well, but it was still a touchy subject with Mum.

'You're welcome,' he replied. 'Money well spent – it will be a great experience.'

'Yep!' she beamed. She was actually going! Three whole weeks of no school, no work, no family stress – just fun and adventure!

'Now remember, stay with the group,' **Jackson**'s mother reminded as they milled around the bus. All cases had been squeezed into the baggage compartment under the bus and they were minutes away from the 'climb on board' instruction. 'It'll be easy to get lost so be careful...'

'I will,' he promised, distracted by friends and the whirling excitement in his stomach. 'Don't worry.'

'Impossible,' his father said. 'You know your mother.' He gave Jackson's shoulder a squeeze. 'Have a great time, son.'

'I will, Dad. Thanks for everything.'

His father nodded, and the instruction came to board the buses. The first few students leapt up the steps while others hugged parents yet again.

They were going to India!

PART II – Achieving the Goal

CHAPTER 11

Day 1: The Thrill of the Escape

Everyone's high spirits on the bus were dampened a little once they joined the queues at the airport and found themselves inching towards the check-in counter at a snail's pace. But perhaps it was just as well that the process took so long – someone had forgotten to pack their passport and ticket, and an urgent message had been sent from the bus to their parents to meet them at the airport with the missing items.

Toni contemplated the teachers who were accompanying them as the queue took one more step forward and everyone prodded their luggage or dragged it that tiny distance. Miss Harris, the Sports and Outdoor Education teacher, was a small, compact, older woman with short, iron-grey hair who seemed to be always frowning and disapproving of someone or something. She'd be a helluva lot of fun on a trip like this – *not*. Toni couldn't understand why she'd been chosen, or volunteered, whichever the case may be. Perhaps to balance out good-natured Mr Plowright, the well-padded History/Geography/Social Sciences teacher, who was constantly laughing and joking with his students, and was one of the school favourites. He already had a little knot of students hovering around him, while Miss Harris stood on her own at the end of the line, her eyes raking the terminal for a sign of the summoned parent.

Brooke had been caught big-time by her now two kilos of overweight luggage. If it wasn't for a few of the other girls letting her squeeze some of her stuff in their cases, she'd have been hit with something like a hundred dollars in extra fees – before she even left the country! It was either that or put some of her belongings in the bin, which was *not* an option. So much fuss over two itty-bitty kilos! She'd have expressed her disgust if she weren't feeling so embarrassed and stupid and a big nuisance as she watched her friends unzip their bags to squeeze her stuff in…

But what was she going to do coming back, especially if she wanted to buy things in India? Worrying about that took the shine off the walk from the check-in counter to the security area, although her concern dissipated once she arrived there. Having never travelled overseas before, the experience of going through Security was a thrill. Standing in the queue and peering ahead, she hoped desperately that someone would be arrested for carrying drugs or something – not anyone in their group, of course, just someone else, so she could see what would happen…

Surly security officials barked at them to move their gear onto the conveyor belt, and then they each walked through the body scanners. They'd already been told to remove jewellery and belts, so when a buzzer sounded as *she* walked through, Brooke experienced a pleasurable stab of panic and had to go back, wide-eyed, until the officer pointed out that the aluminium wrap on the lollies in her pocket had triggered the scanner; minus the roll of jubes she was able to walk through without incident.

Once they were through security, bright shops with 'Duty Free!' signs beckoned, and Brooke begged for permission to have a look.

'Five minutes,' Miss Harris allowed, checking her watch, and Brooke scampered to the shelves. Her mother's sad/annoyed expression had travelled with her all the way on the bus, leaving a slightly guilty taste in her mouth. She'd buy her mum a bottle of her favourite perfume! Perfume was supposed to be cheaper in duty-free, wasn't it? She knew exactly which scent her mother loved, so this would be easy – although there was that moisturiser her mum liked too! Maybe one of each? Wow, they had the best labels in here! Louis Vuitton bags and everything! Two of her favourite brands of sunglasses… Brooke's dad had slipped her some extra money as he hugged her goodbye so she could spend up without affecting her India supply!

'I wouldn't buy anything now if I were you,' Toni murmured, brushing past. 'You'll have to carry it all around India. Get it on the way back.'

'Oh. Thanks. Good thinking,' Brooke said, and she began, reluctantly, to unburden her arms.

'No probs. My mother travels heaps. She had lots of tips.'

Seeing Eric examining iPads, Brooke approached him to pass on this advice.

'I know,' he said briefly, 'just researching for later. Some of these prices aren't really much better than you can get in a usual store anyway, or online.'

Really? Brooke looked back at the shelf of perfumes. But she thought duty-free meant a good saving…? Maybe she should check for herself before buying.

Jackson was doing his best to repress his excitement and maintain his cool, but boarding the plane and discovering the on-board entertainment system had triggered off a truly childlike delight. He and his mates had settled on the same action film, which he'd started watching as soon as they'd taken off, but he was restless, distracted by what the crew were doing and the view from the window and the many Indian and Asian passengers and the trolley that came up the aisle with drinks and snacks and lunch in specially packed trays…

Even some hours into the flight, when others were nodding off, he was on high alert, noticing everything. He'd made a trip to the loo and had pushed every button and opened every door in that tiny compartment, flushing the toilet twice and remembering the scenes in airplane hijack movies where incriminating stuff was dumped down the toilet. Walking back to his seat along the narrow aisle he half-hoped something dramatic would happen… and imagined himself tripping up the hijackers (they wouldn't expect to be threatened by a teenager), and seizing their weapons while the plane nose-dived toward the ground and passengers screamed, and he dashed to the cockpit to save the day…

Eric had been to China twice with his family, so when they landed in Singapore for their connecting flight, he was the only one who knew his way around – aside from their teachers. It was a great relief to stretch his legs after some eight hours in cramped quarters! He'd watched a couple of documentaries and the action film all the guys were watching, had read a bit of the ebook on his phone, and had tried for some shut-eye, but sleeping was never easy on a plane.

He and Brooke bumped into each other again in the Duty Free shops, and then Toni appeared and informed them that it was risky buying stuff overseas because of warranties – hard to take back if you had a problem. *He* knew that; he was just doing research, but Brooke obviously didn't. Anyway, Miss Harris wouldn't allow them long in there – she wanted everyone walking as much as possible during the one-hour stop-over to get their blood moving before they were strapped in again. It was probably a good idea but if she was going to be this bossy the whole trip…

At last they were on board again and the final leg of their flight to India began.

CHAPTER 12

Day 2: Delhi!

The first thing that hit them when they stepped off the plane was the intense heat. Heat and humidity. It was already early evening, but it was *so* hot. The airport looked like any airport, as they walked through it to collect their luggage, except that there were so many Indians everywhere! As soon as they arrived at the exit, eager for their first glimpse of India, they were besieged by a number of men, intent upon helping them to find transport and literally taking the cases out of their hands in their eagerness. Mr Plowright thanked them in his good-natured way, retrieved their luggage, and shepherded the group away from them and towards the mini-bus that was already waiting. They climbed aboard and slowly joined the stream of traffic exiting the airport.

They had known India was going to be crowded and noisy but this was unbelievable! **Brooke**'s mouth hung open as she stared through the window. There were people and vehicles *everywhere,* and it seemed as if every single driver was beeping his horn! You'd have thought peak hour traffic would be over by now, since it was eight p.m., but the streets were so congested with cars and buses and trucks and cyclists and motorbikes and cycle rickshaws and auto-rickshaws and people crossing everywhere that at times their bus was hardly moving. None of the drivers seemed to be following the lanes, and none of the pedestrians were using the crossings – people just went weaving through the traffic holding up their hands to stop cars, which stopped! Unbelievable. You'd never get that at home, but here they were, stopping in the middle of the road to let pedestrians past. It was just utter chaos wherever she looked, but, somehow, 'organised chaos'!

At one point, when they were waiting at a traffic light, Brooke let out a squawk of fright when someone rapped on the window of the bus and a tall, skinny Indian man with terrible teeth stared in at her. When she looked back at him in horror, he broke into a big friendly smile and held up a brightly-coloured teddy bear.

'What's he doing?' she asked in alarm. Mr Plowright turned around in his seat and laughed.

'Trying to sell his goods. Want to buy a bear, Brooke?'

'Not right now,' she said, shaking her head at the man, who looked crestfallen. A moment later he brightened up and waved a feather duster. Laughing now, she shook her head again, and he shrugged and moved along to tap on someone else's window, but just then the light changed and the bus lurched forward. He melted away into the crowd.

As they trundled alongside the pavement of the main road, Brooke gazed at the activity happening there. Every square centimetre of space seemed to be packed full. People were selling their wares, their goods often spread out on blankets. Grubby children hung around or played with sticks and stones; some waved cheerily while others just stared at the passing bus with the barest of interest. Beggars sat here and there, impassive and still, wrapped in dirty cloths.

The bus lumbered around a corner and she saw a stretch of unpaved, sandy ground with broken bricks and garbage dumped on it and the next minute she was staring at a stunning building that looked like it had to be thousands of years old, and *it* stood next to shacks…

'Far out,' she breathed.

Eric liked to be comfortable, and that meant comfortable in the same old way that he was used to. He'd nursed a private worry for the whole flight, plus some weeks before leaving home, that India would be too much for him and his bed would be awful and he wouldn't sleep well and the food would make him sick… Of all of the students who were on this trip, he was the most prepared for the chaos and noise and intensity, having been to China twice, but while he might have Asian roots, he'd been born in the west and he liked his space and quiet; he found the crazy busyness and constant blare of horns disturbing. So when they arrived at their accommodation and were led to their rooms, he was relieved to find that the room was okay – and so was the bed, he discovered, when he parked his case next to it and gingerly sat down.

They had half an hour to settle in before meeting in the dining room for supper and a brief orientation talk. Excited voices rang out in the hallways as students poured backwards and forwards, checking out each other's rooms and commenting on everything. The first person to visit the loo burst out of it with reports of the squirty tap next to the toilet, a self-cleaning alternative to paper that had to be seen to be believed. Did some Indians really not use toilet paper at all!

When they were summoned to the dining room, they found snacks waiting for them: 'aloo paratha', or fried Indian roti bread with mashed potato inside and a smear of lemon pickle on top, and 'idli sambar', dumplings made of fermented rice and lentil batter that you dipped in chutney, along with glasses of 'lassi', a sweet yoghurt beverage, and spicy chai teas. The Indian proprietor welcomed them formally, with much head-wagging, and Miss Harris immediately trained her most severe expression on some of the boys at the back who were prone to mimicry… Then she and Mr Plowright reviewed the itinerary and the warnings:

- Dress modestly
- If you see shoes outside a shop or a home, remove yours before entering
- Only eat hot, cooked food – don't eat salads or have anything with ice in it, and only eat fruit you can peel
- Use bottled water to brush your teeth, especially if you have a weak

constitution, and your anti-bacterial drops or wipes before eating

• Let us know immediately if you feel sick, and that means any loss of appetite, headache, nausea, vomiting, diarrhoea. However if you feel sick it's not necessarily a tummy bug – it might just be that your stomach is dealing with the different spicier diet

• You can use travel cards and debit cards and there are plenty of ATMs but it's mostly a cash society, especially in the markets and bazaars, so make sure you've got enough on you

• But don't carry too much – as tourists you will stand out and pickpockets are always lurking in large cities

• And don't keep cash in your backpack because zips can be undone in a crowd easily – put it in a money belt or bumbag, and don't sling your backpack over one shoulder because it can be grabbed in an instant by motorcyclists as they pass you

• Stay with the group! But if you get lost, stop walking and phone one of the teachers or go to the designated meeting spot (a new one would be established when they arrived at each new site)

• Don't eat or shake hands with your left hand (the toilet reason circulated among the students in a whisper), and always give and receive money with the right hand

• And, above all, keep a sense of humour. You're in a different culture and many things may seem odd or uncomfortable, so relax your expectations and go with the flow…

They were released with reminders that they had an early start in the morning and so to do their best to sleep even though they were all feeling wired.

Eric had ensured that he had a recording of the relaxing baroque music he studied to on his phone. Back in his room he undressed, drew the curtains, plugged his earphones in to drone out the chatter and thuds around him as his co-travellers got sorted, and lay in bed with every intention of going straight to sleep. He was still lying there, stiff, tired, and wide awake, four hours later.

Sanjit, their beaming tour guide, collected them after a breakfast of Indian scrambled eggs, which came with tomato, onion, chilli and spices, and once again they joined the slow-moving throngs on the roads in another mini-bus. The seething mass of people and the unrelenting clamour were even worse this morning, as the locals hurried to work and whatever else they were doing. It was *so* noisy. Horns beeping constantly, brakes squealing, the engines of hundreds of vehicles puttering, people talking…

'India is huge for temples,' Sanjit said into the crackling mic. 'India is known as the most religious country in the world. You will see temples and shrines and small roadside places of worship everywhere around. Today we begin your tour of beautiful Delhi with a visit to a temple to make an offering for a good, safe trip.'

As soon as they had piled out of the bus, **Jackson** felt noticed; Indians nearby turned to stare at them. Some smiled, many just stared; it was as if they were a strange new kind of beast. A few children who had been hanging around the pavement sidled close and beseeched him with their big, dark eyes. He smiled back awkwardly, and then realised they were after money. They were all skinny and bare-footed. He glanced around him, unsure what to do, but his school group was moving toward the gates into the temple. Impulsively, Jackson dipped into his pocket and pulled out a few rupees, which he extended to the nearest boy, who smiled and snatched and ducked away. Immediately three other children pressed close, one of the buggers even reaching into his pocket!

'Oy!' Jackson exclaimed, extracting the skinny hand. The boy smiled winningly at him, but Jackson shook his head, frowning at them. He'd teach them! Besides, where was his group? He fought off a slight panic at finding himself alone and hurried towards the Temple, but soon found the others milling around the gates where they were being sold fruit and flowers to take in as offerings. Jackson joined the tail end of the group in time to hear Chloë say, 'Look!' in a low voice. He followed her gaze to where some ten or more beggars were lining the street. Many sat on the ground with cups or metal bowls in front of them, some raising their hands and faces imploringly to passers-by and others just sitting there passively, as if they had neither the energy nor the desire to do anything about their condition.

'Oh God,' Brooke murmured, and Jackson realised that Chloë was pointing to a specific beggar, a woman with a huge growth on her neck.

'Gross!' someone behind them said, and Chloë snapped, 'Don't! Poor thing... She needs a doctor...'

Jackson heard Brooke whispering to Mr Plowright, and then him saying, 'I know. But sometimes the family deliberately puts them out on the street like that to beg, figuring they'll arouse sympathy... or guilt. I suspect they're here, outside the temple, on purpose. You can't consider yourself a good person if you haven't given to the needy...'

'I'm going to give her something,' Chloë said, and the rest of them watched as she strode to the woman with the tumour and handed her some rupees.

'Me too,' said Brooke, and she followed.

Immediately both girls were approached by more beggars. Mr Plowright went to rescue them, ushering them back to their classmates, who were beginning to walk through manicured gardens towards the Lotus Temple, a beautiful white marble structure in the shape of a lotus flower that was surrounded by nine pools.

There were already lots of people ahead of them on the long path that led to the Temple. They moved forward slowly until they reached the shoe-depositing area. Removing his trainers, Jackson worried that he'd never find them again in the abundance of footwear being abandoned. He joined the queue advancing towards a priest who was blessing their plates of fruit and flowers, but kept glancing back to memorise the position of his shoes in the pile.

Eventually they were inside, where it was cool and quiet and kind of humbling. The Lotus Temple was a Bahá'í place of worship that was open to all, regardless of religion. No musical instruments could be played inside and no rituals or ceremonies could be conducted inside the Temple; it was a gathering place where 'everyone was free to worship God in their own way', the brochure said.

Jackson's school group wandered around in clusters of twos and threes. A class of uniformed Indian school students was being addressed in a corner; the Eastern and Western students observed each other silently. A number of Indians were sitting in pews with closed eyes. He wondered what they were praying for – his prayer was that he'd find his shoes again… Which he did: as soon as they emerged, there they were, just where he'd left them.

From the Temple they toured through New Delhi, which was designed and developed by an English architect. They drove past Rashtrapati Bhawan, the official residence of the President of India, and stopped for a picnic lunch on the grounds outside the India Gate, a 42-metre high stone memorial arch commemorating the 70,000 Indian soldiers who lost their lives fighting for the British Army during World War I, and bearing the names of 13,516 Indian and British soldiers killed in the Afghan War of 1919. **Toni**'s eyes would usually glaze over when she heard stats like this but somehow it was different being here.

After lunch they drove to Qutub Minar, a 73-metre high tower built in the 12th century by the first Muslim rulers in Delhi. When they descended from the bus to have a closer look, Toni read an inscription declaring that the tower had been built with material obtained from demolishing 27 Hindu temples. Wow…

There was a seven-metre high iron pillar in the courtyard; apparently if you could encircle it with your hands while standing with your back to it, your wish would be fulfilled. 'A likely story!' Jackson exclaimed, trying and failing.

They visited an extraordinary Persian-like structure called

Humayun's Tomb that was set in eerily peaceful gardens that seemed to take them back in time. It was more like a palace than a Mausoleum. Toni wondered what it would feel like to have a 47 by 91-metre tomb built for you – not that you'd know, of course; you'd be dead. Which was how they were all feeling by the time they got back to their hotel. She was amazed at how tiring touring was, even when you were being driven everywhere and walking slowly in queues.

Dinner was predictably curry-ish and very tasty, and then they were free to relax for the evening, after writing a compulsory entry in their travel journals.

The following day they headed off on a guided tour of Old Delhi, first to the world-famous Red Fort, a stunning construction in red sandstone with fourteen gates where Mughal emperors had lived for almost two hundred years, and then to Jama Masjid, the largest mosque in India that was built by the same emperor who had built the Red Fort. The girls had to wear burkas to be allowed to enter! The boys teased them as they covered up from head to foot and tripped over the trailing fabric. There was lots of giggling at first, but it soon died away as they became caught up in the majesty around them.

It was quite something to walk through all of these old monuments with their high arches and intricate carvings and tapestries and vast stretches of cool, smooth marble. Toni gazed up at the ceilings and around at her statuesque surroundings in awe. Imagine being rich and powerful enough to order the construction of buildings like these – buildings that would still be standing hundreds of years later... That was some legacy to leave the world. What a land of contrasts this was! The beggars outside who had nothing and would leave nothing, and these incredible monuments to power and wealth that would stand for centuries.

Going from impressive landmarks to a crazy, heart-stopping cycle rickshaw ride in the busy, narrow lanes of the Chandni Chowk, the main street of Old Delhi, provided a refreshing change of pace. This was India to the max! Animals roamed free everywhere – including monkeys! When they finally piled out of their rickshaws to walk through the bazaar, the chaos they had driven through was all the more in their faces. Old Delhi was loud, lively, busy, messy, smelly... Cows stood around eating from piles of garbage that the vegetable sellers had cast aside. Toni caught Brooke walking with her hand discreetly in front of her face in an attempt to shield her nose from the smell of... what? Strewn garbage, rotting food, animals and their dung, spices, diesel, sewage, beggars...? She didn't know what but it certainly took some getting used to.

There were, it seemed, millions of people milling around among the rickshaws, taxis, garland-decorated trucks, and bullock carts – honest to god, bullock carts! People selling all sorts of stuff from shops and stalls: food, clothes, gadgets, souvenirs, spices, fabrics, shoes, flowers, all sorts of shiny glittery items, and live animals in cages... So many women wearing colourful saris! And then if you looked upward, you were gobsmacked by the wiring. Exposed power lines snaked overhead, masses of them, all interweaving in what was surely a dangerous arrangement. If someone had a power issue, how on earth would they know which one of those bundled wires related to which building? When she asked, their guide told them that somehow it all worked. Amazing.

They spent the rest of the day wandering through the Old Delhi Market and gazing at the wares on offer. Each street offered only one kind of product – either food or textiles or even steel. Toni had a crack at bargaining with a vendor for some jewellery. She aimed for a rock-bottom price, trying the old, 'Nah, too much'-and-walk-away act, but when he turned his attention to someone else rather than coming after her she drifted back and ended up buying the bangles anyway.

Jackson was clutching a strange bulge in the region of his stomach and saying there was nothing he wanted to buy. He hovered around when she and a few other brave souls tried the street food, saying he wasn't game to risk it, but when she gave him a taste of hers and he bit into the flaky pastry samosa and the flavor of spicy potatoes and peas exploded in his mouth... he bought his own, and followed it up with some fried Indian bread that you could dip into curries and condiments.

They caught up with the others, and followed Mr Plowright, who was raving about 'mango kulfi', down a narrow concrete alley, the sort of place you'd expect to be kidnapped or mugged, to a tiny shop where they bought slices of frozen mango that were stuffed with some creamy filling. They were already feeling full when their guide insisted that they try the 'jalebi', a curl of dough deep-fried in bubbling oil and then soaked in sugary syrup. He led them to a special location that was quite famous among the locals for cooking jalebi and samosas in ghee rather than oil. 'Ghee' was a type of clarified butter, he explained, that was healthy – Indians considered it to be the nectar of the gods, especially those Indians who followed a health system called 'Ayurveda'; the legendary 'Delhi-belly' was often caused by cooking in oil that was rancid. The jalebi (and samosas) were delicious.

No one was very hungry for dinner that night.

What new experiences do you want to have?

Do you want to travel?

Where? How – in luxury accommodation or living with the locals?

Do you want to backpack on your own or travel with tour groups?

Did you know that your brain develops with every new experience you have?

New experiences literally create new connections in your brain.

You make yourself smarter when you do new things, and travelling is one of the very best ways to do that.

If you ever think your way is the right way, go visit a country on the other side of the world and see how they do it. Surround yourself with people whose beliefs are directly opposite to yours, and your thinking will burst wide open...

How the Monetary System Evolved...

In the beginning people exchanged or bartered goods like chickens and eggs and cows and grains and fruits, and services like blacksmithing and harvesting.

From there, to allow for exchange between people who may not have possessed goods the other party wanted, coins and precious metals were introduced as an intermediate medium.

Paper money and cheques evolved after that.

Plastic 'money' (credit and debit cards) heralded electronic payments, which has now been enhanced by 'photonics' (fibre optics) – online banking at close to the speed of light.

New developments indicate that the next wave of money exchange may be via 'blockchain' technology. A digital ledger records cryptocurrency transactions chronologically and publicly, using encryption, which makes them safe from corruption and eliminates middlemen.

CHAPTER 13

Day 3: Saving Street Kids

Eric was in some kind of fish bowl. He was pushing his way through what seemed like hundreds of sardines and looking for something or someone, he wasn't sure what, but not finding anything he recognised. A panicky feeling was beginning to tighten his stomach. When he stopped one sardine to ask for directions, it turned into a turbaned octopus, which nodded and smiled and pointed in eight directions at once.

Eric's eyes snapped open and he sat up in bed, heart racing. A dream – thank god! But all too close to the horrible experience he'd had yesterday when he thought he was lost in that crazy, crowded Old Delhi market. He'd lost sight of his group and had urgently asked three Indians for directions to the Town Hall, his group's designated meeting spot. The first one had smiled and nodded and pointed, but just in time Eric had realised that the old man spoke no English and had no frigging idea what Eric was asking! The second Indian had smiled and nodded and wobbled his head 'yes' when Eric asked if the Town Hall was that way, but when he'd double-checked by asking a third Indian, she had smiled and nodded and wobbled her head 'yes' also, even though Eric, in his anxiety, was pointing in the opposite direction! If he hadn't spied Mr Plowright's bald head bobbing above the crowd in the distance, he could have been lost forever in that seething mass of humanity! He could have been snatched by kidnappers and absorbed into the illegal sex trade!

Eric reached for his specs and checked that his phone was charged. The night before he'd plugged it in and assumed it would be fully charged in the morning, only to find it as a dead as a tack and of no use to him at all when he got lost. Last night he'd made sure he wiggled the lead until it made a proper connection and was definitely charging, but he'd only slept lightly all night, worrying that the plug might have lost contact in the socket again. Today it was charged. He felt enormously relieved.

Outside, the interminable hooting and honking of horns was already in full swing. The sun was slanting in through the dusty window; they were headed for yet another hot and humid day. He sighed.

Suddenly two legs dropped over the edge of the bunk above him, almost whacking him in the face, and Jackson jumped to the floor and ran desperately for the bathroom. He'd barely closed the door before Eric heard the sounds of illness…

Oh god. Not that too. Eric stood up and dragged his case out from under the bed. Flipping the lid back, he saw the first aid kit his mother had packed, neatly tucked among his underwear. He pulled it out and unzipped the contents onto his bed. There were cures and preventions and all sorts of things in here… When Jackson emerged, pale-faced and shaky, Eric held out two containers of tablets and a sealed bottle of water.

'My mother's a doctor,' he said.

'I've got some, somewhere,' Jackson murmured, a hand on his stomach.

'Just use this for now. Save you looking. I've got heaps.'

'Thanks.'

'Did you notice the open sewage yesterday when we were on the bus?' Eric tutted, watching as Jackson unscrewed the bottle. 'Seventeen million people approx., and half of them live in slums with no basic services like water, sanitation, electricity *or* sewage systems. It's not surprising there are so many germs around here.'

Jackson swallowed the tablets and handed the pack back with thanks. 'It's a different world, isn't it?'

'No health infrastructure,' Eric continued. 'No public health. It's dire.'

It did seem dire. Back on their bus later that morning they were again confronted by crowdedness and clamour, dirt, animals, poverty, smog – and colour. So much colour! **Jackson** sat with his face close to the window, gazing at the activity outside. It seemed as if there were peak hour traffic jams every day, every hour in Delhi. The roads were choked with cars and those auto-rickshaws and motorbikes. Women rode the bikes side-saddle in their colourful saris – there went one with a child on the handlebars! Crazy! You'd never get away with that at home.

Toni nudged Jackson and he looked in the direction she was pointing. A family of five were all crammed onto one motorbike: Dad driving with one child in front of him, Mum hanging on behind him, another child squished between the two parents, and a third child clinging on at the back – and only Dad wearing a helmet. He was marveling at this sight when another motorbike zigzagged past the bus, its driver so loaded with goods that you could only see him from the chin up, plus his hands on the handlebars and feet on the pedals; every other part of him was concealed by parcels that were strapped onto his body or the bike.

What a chaotic place this was! Jackson wondered how similar it was to his Uncle Dave's experience in Cambodia. He still felt unsettled in the guts and overwhelmed by the intensity around him, but it was exhilarating too. The sense of freedom was exhilarating – you weren't as locked into predictable patterns out here as in the west. Kids didn't automatically go to school, and while they probably should, there was something wonderful about a country where you could fall between the cracks and do your own thing…

He had cause to rethink this attitude some hours later when they were being guided through Salaam Balaak, an award-winning school and orphanage dedicated to rehousing street kids. It turned out that many of the children living on the streets wound up begging or in the sex trade simply because they had become separated from their families in

Delhi's congested streets, and were never able to find them again. Others had run away from abusive families or had run to the city in search of opportunities, and discovered life there to be harsher and more difficult than they had expected. Alone and defenseless, they were soon picked up by pimps or absorbed into street gangs.

Jackson's school group was guided through the orphanage by an ex-resident of the house, a young university student wearing a Salaam Balaak t-shirt who spoke enthusiastically about the organisation that had rescued him some eleven years ago. The Trust's charter was never to take a child against his or her will, he told them. Instead, they first offered to help find the child's family, and if that wasn't possible, they educated him or her about the safety, free meals, and schooling available at the Centre… and persuaded the kid to check it out. But it was always, ultimately, the child's own choice to accept shelter or not.

Salaam Balaak owned five residential shelters like this one, and also some thirteen 'Contact Points', or day centres, where kids could come for medical aid and check-ups, for education, play, and just to talk. So many of them had experienced neglect or abuse that many were aggressive or frail or physically disabled, their guide said, as they paused outside the door to the room that doubled as a dormitory and a schoolroom.

And when they entered the Children's Room there were certainly some children who looked sullen or limp, but most of their faces lit up at the sight of their visitors, and some of them immediately came close. Jackson and his group were invited to mingle with the kids and read them stories or listen to them read, and within minutes dark-haired children were crawling into his lap or sitting close on either side of him, holding his hands and staring at him with large eyes and shy smiles. They listened closely when he corrected their faltering English, immediately echoing his words like perfect, obedient students, and calling him 'uncle', which felt weird.

His school group was invited into the kitchen to help prepare lunch for the children: dahl, a spicy lentil stew, and rice, which they ate out of tin plates with their hands. (Jackson and the others made a donation and bought small serves for themselves.) After lunch they played ball games and hopscotch together and then watched the kids demonstrate a traditional folk dance. Some of the girls got up to have a go as well but Jackson resisted... That night, when his school group was back at their accommodation, they watched *Salaam Bombay*, the film about street kids that had inspired the orphanage.

After the film, a conversation sprang up about begging. Everyone was feeling confronted by it. Miss Harris instructed them to firmly extend their arm, palm outward, as beggars approached them in order to give a clear 'stop right there' message. 'Once you start interacting with them they won't let up until you give them something,' she said, 'even if you're polite. If you don't want to be hassled, you have to be very clear. Remember that many of them are earning more begging than they would in a proper job!'

'That's hard to believe,' **Brooke** murmured to the girl next to her. 'They look absolutely destitute! It's so sad...'

But Mr Plowright seemed to be agreeing with Miss Harris. 'It's a very organised industry,' he said. 'They even have their own territories and some people mutilate themselves or get out there with someone else's baby in order to appear more needy. It's almost impossible to know for sure who is genuinely needy and who is putting it on, so if you want to give, you just have to trust your instincts.'

'There are over a million people in Delhi living on the equivalent of eleven U.S. dollars a month – or less,' Eric informed the group.

Shocked exclamations reverberated around the room, and Toni seemed to speak for everyone when she declared, 'It doesn't matter how cheaply you can live here, that's just *wrong*. Why doesn't the government do anything about it?'

'I'm sure they are,' Mr Plowright replied. 'India is dedicated to being a welfare state, by which they mean justice and equal opportunity for all, but most of the programs for feeding people and for empowering women and the lower castes are run by non-government organisations. With such a huge population and extensive corruption, it's not easy to create systemic change. There are spiritual aspects to the issue as well. Many Hindus believe that beggars are suffering for sins committed in past lives, and so it's 'God's will' for them to suffer. That's why they can just walk past beggars without doing anything – they don't want to interfere with the beggars' karma.'

More murmurings and mutterings within the group as they digested this information.

'The people do contribute as well,' Mr Plowright reassured them. 'When they can afford to they'll donate to their temple or mosque, and then those organisations look after the needy, like the Sikh's Golden Temple in Amritsar where they apparently feed some 10,000 people a day. Mr Baxter helped out there when he was in India. He was one of hundreds of volunteers cooking massive pots of rice and dahl and making thousands of chappatis – all of it free. He said it was very moving, even the job of washing truckloads of dishes.'

'Speaking of moving,' Miss Harris intervened, 'it's time you kids moved off to bed. We've got an early start in the morning.'

A group of cheerful Salaam Balaak volunteers met their bus the following morning to take them on a 'City Walk'. Quite a few students had purchased the Trust's t-shirts so they made a very cohesive group as they left the bus at New Delhi railway station to begin their walk, meet some actual street kids, and watch the volunteers in action. As many as 500 street children might sleep in and around the railways station, their guide Chitra told them as they encountered the first few kids, hovering in grubby clothes and bare feet. Some of them hung back suspiciously, but others sidled close and enquired, 'America? Eengland?'

Toni came into step beside Chitra when they set off, and asked what she did when she wasn't being a tour guide.

'I am study journalism,' Chitra replied. 'I have many ambition. I wish to travel to USA and your great country also. I will obtain my degrees but I will always return here to my mother country and help my people.'

'What sort of journalism will you do?' Toni asked. 'Like, TV or newspaper or radio?'

'There is not many radio in Delhi, isn't it?' Chitra said. 'We have much newspaper reading and two earth TV channel and several cable but not yet much satellite. I wish to research and write about India's economic situation. For example, we have much growth potential but this is danger of being held back by lack of welfare provision and insufficient social investment. We receive much little Foreign Aid here in India.'

Having deciphered the broken English, Toni wanted to ask how Chitra had found herself on the street, but she also didn't want to pry. 'Where do you live now?' she asked instead. 'Are you still at Salaam Balaak?'

'Oh no. I am live with other ex-residents very nearby. After the eighteenth birthday we have to leave the shelter; we must live somewhere else with other graduates. Salaam Balaak pays us to be tour guide at the school and to lead city walks, and we study very much. Some of us have other employments as well.'

'Oh,' Toni said. That seemed fair. She was itching to ask 'the' question, but they were turning off the main dusty road into a dark alleyway and Chitra began to share her story with the group by pointing to a doorstep that had once been her bed… It turned out that she had become lost at the age of eleven when her family made a rare trip into the city; she hadn't been in a hurry to find her parents because she was often beaten, but she hadn't expected to never find them again either. Nor had she expected life on the streets to be so hard. She had spent many of the months that followed in hiding, afraid of the older boys in the street gangs who might have forced her to have sex, and afraid of the police who often did the same… She was relieved when she was eventually rescued by a Salaam Balaak volunteer – although she had been very suspicious at first; he'd had to work hard to win her confidence.

Their male guide, Vikram, said that he had enjoyed his freedom on the streets at first: no one to tell him what to do, mastering the art of pickpocketing and rummaging through garbage for food, sampling illegal drugs... But then the dream soured. The boys constantly fought each other to be gang leader and he was often hungry. His hopes for the future were dying and he was becoming dependent on drugs. He was rescued just in time.

Toni reflected on the number of times she'd been told as a child to think of the starving in India when she didn't want to finish her dinner. She'd usually retort that her mother could send her leftovers over there. Now, speaking to people who had actually eaten out of rubbish bins, she felt a pang of guilt and regret, and was glad they hadn't witnessed her sarcasm.

There was lots happening at the Contact Point they visited. A line of kids trailed toward a table where a few Salaam Balaak staff were doing medical check-ups while others engaged children in games or in writing and drawing on the walls of buildings – their version of school!

'Legit graffiti!' Jackson grinned.

The Brightwood College students spent the rest of the day, their last in the city, with the children. Tomorrow they would be heading to Agra and the Taj Mahal!

Have you ever gone hungry?

How do you feel when you observe people living on the streets?

Do you give them money or ignore them? Why?

How far would you go to help yourself if you were stuck on the streets?

Would you steal, cheat, sell your body for money?

CHAPTER 14

Days 4 & 5: Monuments to Love, Death and War

They left Delhi under overcast skies, a light drizzle spotting the windows of the bus. **Toni** was feeling a little weak this morning after a night on the loo. She'd taken tablets instead of breakfast and was sitting quietly, arms resting lightly on her gurgling stomach, and gazing at the now familiar city sights as they left smoggy Delhi behind and passed through industrial areas, and then into a long stretch of agricultural countryside. Around her the others were speaking quietly or sleeping, and she was soon drowsing too... until the urge to go became sufficiently intense for her to signal to Miss Harris and request a toilet stop. There was a service station approaching, fortunately, and as she waited by the door for the bus to pull in and let her off, a queue of students was already piling up behind her. The door creaked open, but before she could disembark, Miss Harris grabbed her sleeve and said, 'Do you have any paper?'

'Paper?' Toni asked blankly.

'*Toilet* paper,' Miss Harris said, but she was reaching into her rucksack as she said this, and pulling out a squashed roll. You will probably need this.'

'Oh. Thanks.'

She burst out and half-ran, half-walked to the building, searching for the universal language symbol for a toilet. There it was! She opened the door cautiously and immediately backed out again, stepping on the toes of someone who was suddenly right behind her.

'Ouch!' Chloë exclaimed.

'It stinks in there.' Taking a big breath of fresh air, Toni stepped forward again into the cramped, dark space and closed the door behind her. No light to be found. She could just make out a wooden bench with a hole in it. No toilet seat. No flushing buttons or chains; just a bucket of water standing on the dirty cement floor with a scoop hanging off its side. Grimacing, she 'sat' over the hole to do her business, trying not to make contact with the bench, trying not to breathe, and trying to be as quick as she could.

Miss Harris met her at the bus with a spray bottle of disinfectant, a box of wipes, and a grim smile. Toni received them gratefully.

'Hanging in there?' Jackson asked as she passed him on the way to her seat.

She made a face. 'How are you going? Still feeling like shit?'

'I wouldn't use that word,' he advised. 'I'm getting better. By tiny, tiny increments.'

Toni sank into her seat and returned to gazing out the window as they continued towards Sikandra, a garden mausoleum built in 1492 by Akbar, a ruler of one of the last dynasties of the Delhi Sultanate. It seemed weird to go halfway across the world in order to visit tombs, but apparently that was what people built in those days, and this one was apparently pretty special.

All eyes were trained on the four-storey, red sandstone building as they approached, parked and piled out of the bus on stiff legs, only to be assailed by pushy hawkers when they joined the queue. Eric stopped to read a plaque detailing the history of the place, but Toni's attention was captured by the large marble inlay on the gate, and the four white, marble, dome-shaped minarets up above.

Once through the gate, they found themselves in a lovely green park where peacocks strutted and black deer could be seen grazing in the distance.

'Wow, this is awesome,' Brooke exclaimed, joining Toni on the tree-lined walkway. 'So beautiful – and look!'

'What?' Toni looked away from the deer to follow Brooke's pointed finger.

'Monkeys!'

There were indeed: monkeys clung to the trees and looped through them, startling flocks of parakeets. This was good for the soul after the noise and smog and intensity of Delhi.

The tomb itself was impressive. The imposing building as they approached was one thing, with its four white marble minarets and intricate patterns on the walls, but the design of the entrance was something else: it forced them to bow their heads as they entered. A cunning architectural decision, Toni reflected. Talk about humbling your visitors! That was some power.

She was even more impressed when their guide directed them to the circumferential gallery around the tomb where the slightest whisper carried across to the other side. 'Whispering walls', they were called. Toni had never considered architecture as a career before, but she was beginning to. It was no small thing to be able to influence a person's feelings and thoughts in this way… Music had a similar mood-changing effect; Toni had often wished she 'had that power', but she'd never mastered an instrument. She remembered visiting her parents' rich friend, Arnold, and experiencing the grandeur of his home. That was nothing by comparison with the magnificence surrounding her now, but what if you were able to design homes that inspired people and lifted their spirits? That would be satisfying. And it would surely pay well…

After lunch they joined the traffic-jammed streets of Agra in order to view the unconquered Agra Fort, built in 1565 by the Mughal (Moslem)

Emperor Akbar – he whose tomb they had just visited. Well, not built *by* him; he ordered the building of it, **Eric** read in his tour guide as they approached. It took eight years to complete and cost three and a half million rupees. Closing his eyes, Eric calculated rapidly: about 70,000 dollars. Peanuts by today's reckoning but that would have seemed like a fortune back then. Property: if you bought it when it was cheap and sold it years later when the price had gone up... well, you could get *very* wealthy.

As usual, there were heaps of locals sitting around outside the imposing construction, only this time a few of them were playing traditional music, which really set the scene. Eric continued to read his tour guide as they inched forward in the queue. Apparently a clever counterweight system had been designed to raise the massive gate. He would love to see that in operation! Lifting his chin, Eric gazed up at the towering ramparts of the Red Fort, as it was known. Only 30% of it was open to the public; the rest was reserved for the Indian Army. That would be pretty cool – having your barracks stationed in an actual fort.

Jackson, who was standing next to him, nudged his shoulder. 'Look at that dude. I reckon he's pickpocketing – or about to.'

Eric watched the slight Indian who was hovering behind a couple of heavy-set Westerners. Just then someone behind them bumped into Jackson, making him lurch into the people in front, and they temporarily lost sight of the potential thief as everyone apologised and regrouped.

'There he goes,' Jackson said, pointing. 'I reckon he did it. And that was probably a mate of his creating a diversion by bumping into us.'

'It was too far away,' Eric said doubtfully. 'And their 'targets' don't look as if they've noticed anything.'

'They'd be pretty sharp around here.'

Someone different stood in front of them now; a fair-haired person wearing a t-shirt that said, *Life begins when you leave your comfort zone*. Eric snorted. He was just as alive when he sat at home in front of his computer researching stuff that interested him!

They had finally reached the gate of the apparently impregnable military structure that had been inhabited by all the famous Mughal emperors who had invaded India over many centuries. And there was no doubt about it. For sheer scale it took the prize – it was grander than anything Eric had ever seen – and the interior was stunning. Akbar's son Jehangir had built rose-red palaces, courts and gardens, and then *his* son Shahjehan embellished the place with marbled mosques, lavish palaces and pavilions of gem-inlaid white marble. It might have been a fort but it had the elegance and majesty of an imperial palace. The whole place was immaculately maintained and utterly impressive.

When they arrived at the rooftop, they were struck by the beauty of the Persian gardens, Yamuna River and surrounding landscape. There, like a jewel in the distance, lay the Taj Mahal, their destiny first thing next morning.

Eric would have liked to return to the Fort that evening for the light and sound show that was scheduled, but instead they were driven to the 'Baby Taj', yet another tomb, this one built for Itmad-Ud-Daulah by his daughter Noorjehan. The family had a rags-to-riches story that was pretty interesting. A poor Persian called Ghiyas Beg (not a pun!) hadn't wanted kids but his wife gave birth to a daughter and – big stroke of luck – when she was older, Emperor Akbar's son fell in love with her and married her. She eventually commissioned this first ever all-marble tomb for her father, and dad's name got changed from 'Beg' to the mouthful 'Itmad-ud-Daulah', which was probably considered impressive in those days.

There were few visitors when they arrived in the cool of the early evening, and the 'Baby Taj' (so named because it had inspired the big one) was quite small so they were able to explore it in leisurely peace. Arched doorways and octagonal towers, pure white marble inlaid with semi-precious stones… It was exquisite.

By the time they got to their new accommodation Eric was beat. A long drive, hot weather, and *three* sites. He fell into bed and was asleep almost instantly.

Brooke was not impressed with the early rising but apparently the best time to see the Taj Mahal was at sunrise or sunset, so they were hauled out of bed at an ungodly hour and piled onto the bus with omelette sandwiches to eat on the way. Through the dark streets they trundled, passing groups of Indians huddled around small fires with cows for company. They were transferred to electric vehicles for the last stretch because there was an injunction against motor vehicles approaching the Taj in order to prevent vehicle pollution damaging the building.

They arrived at the gates as the sky was growing pink. Brooke let out a breath in awe at her first sight of it, framed in the archway of the main gate. An optical illusion had been created by the builders so that the Taj seemed to change size, appearing smaller as you moved closer and larger as you moved away, though you'd expect the opposite to happen.

Once they were through the gate, the magnificent structure looked like it was floating in the distance on a magic carpet. A waterway, flanked by rows of dark cypress trees, led from the main gate to the Taj. Its still waters reflected the morning sky and the Taj itself, which was glowing pink. Their group set out on the paved path toward the monument, and Brooke began to take photos.

They had been told that this mausoleum had been built by Shah Jahan in memory of his wife, Mumtaz Mahal, who had died giving birth to their fourteenth son. *Fourteen!* Brooke had nearly choked when she heard that number. But what a romantic gesture of love! What a tribute! What if she were to marry a man who loved her so much that he built a monument like this in her honour... Still, there was no way she was having fourteen kids. Her man had another think coming!

Eric was reading aloud from his guide to the little knot of students around him, and Brooke caught the words: 'No cost was spared to make it the most beautiful monument the world had ever seen. White marble and red sandstone, silver and gold, carnelian and jasper, moonstone and jade, lapis lazuli and coral were fashioned by 20,000 skilled workers to make the emperor's dream a reality. It took 22 years to complete – a symbol of eternal love where Shah Jahan now lies buried too, reunited at last with his beloved Mumtaz.'

The Taj rose in front of them, serene and perfect, its flawless double dome flanked by four tapering minarets, its pure white marble glowing pink in the sunrise. The symmetry of the structure was breathtaking.

'The artists' hands were cut off so that they could not replicate their artistry anywhere else,' Eric read, and a little explosion of swear words and exclamations burst from the listening students. '... although some historians dispute that claim. This timeless wonder, that has been described as having been designed by giants and finished by jewellers, is still the inspiration of poets and painters, writers and photographers from all over the world. The architecture combines elements of Persian, Turkish, Indian and Islamic styles of architecture. The marble has an uncommon lustre and quality. It is inlaid with semi-precious stones that were crafted by hand. This extravagant gesture of love truly deserves its status as one of the seven wonders of the world.'

They had arrived at the steps and now began to ascend the huge white marble terrace. At the top, Brooke turned around for a view of the walkway and surrounding lush Persian gardens with their reflecting pools. Stunning. She was about to take more photos when a security man approached her sternly and told her to put the camera away or he would have to confiscate it. No filming allowed on the premises. Disappointed, Brooke tucked it away in her backpack.

She donned the white shoe covers they had to wear and joined the others in walking quietly through the richly decorated hallways, admiring the latticework, the paintings, the patterned floors and carved ceilings, the arched windows and doorways... just beautiful. The chamber that held the jewel-inlaid tombs of the Empress and, a little to one side, the Emperor, was a little wiffy – there was only one tiny window and she guessed that many thousands of 'the great unwashed' passed through here every day. But the discomfort was insignificant by comparison with the beauty and grandeur.

On the way out Brooke saw Toni and Jackson laughingly posing on the lovers' bench, and felt a quick pang of envy. An official Taj photographer offered to take a picture of them, and they gestured for the rest of the group to join in. Brooke squeezed in close and beamed.

They were back at their accommodation by mid-morning and had a couple of hours to pack their bags in readiness for the trip to Bharatpur via Dayalbagh and Fatehpur Sikri. One cursed, the other a ghost city…

Dayalbagh was the headquarters of a religious sect founded in 1861 and finally due for completion in 2018. A Sadhu, or wise man, had cursed it at some point, declaring that it would never be ready, and indeed it had been under construction and subject to alterations ever since construction began, **Jackson** learnt. The place was a combination of a temple, church and mosque, reflecting Hindu, Christian, Buddhist and Sikh elements.

This structure had the central dome, exquisitely carved pillars and marble splendor of the other grand sites. Some believed it would rival the Taj when complete, but it didn't strike Jackson that way and anyway, he was over visiting monuments. What he found more interesting were the bits he learnt about the residents of the Dayalbagh community.

They began the day with prayer at 5 a.m. and then worked in the fields for several hours before being free to do their own work. In the evening they came together for a prayer and to prepare a meal in the communal kitchen where unlimited food was provided for the residents at a very low cost – *a fraction of one cen*t. They were prohibited from using TVs, fridges, washing machines or other appliances, and commuted on bicycles or battery-operated autos. Kind of like the Amish communities in Philadelphia, Jackson thought. He couldn't imagine going without phone, computer, internet and all of that. But on the other hand, India was already giving him a taste of life without all the gadgets, and he hadn't yet really missed them. Obviously if you'd never had it, you wouldn't notice it not being there, and maybe if your life was very full of new experiences, like this trip, you'd get to be less attached to it... He could just see his mother celebrating at the thought of him spending less time on electronic devices!

Dayalbagh experienced, they boarded the bus once again for the drive to Fatehpur Sikri. Jackson didn't think he could have taken this much driving at home, but out here it was always fascinating. The streets through Agra were crammed with people and vehicles, all beeping constantly and no one following the lanes. Their driver explained that using your horn was a kind of insurance: if you had an accident you could honestly say you'd honked to warn the other party!

Once they left the township area the roads were not so busy and it was not uncommon to see chooks, ducks, pigs, bullock carts, cattle and tractors, as well as the expected trucks and buses, cars, motorbikes and cyclists. They passed through villages where children played in the dirt, women carried bundles of grass on their heads, and buffaloes were being driven by a herder to graze. Time warp...

As they approached 'the ghost city of Fatehpur Sikri' Miss Harris announced that there were some 46 buildings in this complex and they would not have time for a thorough look; they had two hours at the most.

Automatically resisting the beggars and pedlars hovering around them as they emerged from the bus, Jackson couldn't help noticing the collection of goods one vendor had spread on a blanket on the ground: safety pins, camphor, cotton buds, bangles, beads, little cellophane-wrapped bags of lollies... Seeing him looking, the woman scrambled to her feet, eager to sell him something, so he shook his head firmly and walked away, feigning interest, instead, in the white-garbed musicians who were sitting on rugs playing their music and singing.

The entrance to the city was 54 metres high, a true giant's door. They craned their necks to stare up at it, and then walked through it into a large expanse of paved squares and manicured green gardens that housed an array of red sandstone buildings – mosques, tombs, Turkish baths, halls, hunting towers, women's quarters, stables… This deserted city had been built by Emperor Akbar as his capital in the late 16th century but was only inhabited for fourteen years due to a shortage of water. It seemed to be quite perfectly preserved.

Jackson wished he could visualise the place alive and busy, but he didn't know enough about the period to fill those gaps in his imagination. This would be the perfect way to learn history: instead of reading a dry textbook, take a trip around the world! He would definitely be up for that! In the meantime, he would find Mr Plowright and pick his brains.

By the time they left, the sunset was casting a rosy glow on the buildings and Jackson was beat.

What's your favourite occupation?

Do you have a career in mind?

How much do you think you would earn in one year?

Would you like to have a major impact on the world

or would you prefer to live quietly, doing your own thing?

Are you hoping that luck will transform your circumstances from 'rags to riches'

or are you planning to create that magic yourself?

Do you agree that 'Life begins when you leave your comfort zone'?

Could you live without any devices?

CHAPTER 15

DAYS 6 & 7: BIRDS AND TIGERS AND ELEPHANTS... AND A PROPOSAL!

Once again they were up early, this time for a cycle rickshaw ride through one of the richest bird areas in the world, the Bharatpur Bird Sanctuary, also known as the Keoladeo Ghana National Park. **Eric** and Brooke were paired up for a cycle rickshaw that was pedaled by a smiling, grey-bearded Sikh wearing a sloppy brown jumper and a black turban. 'Narm-ah-stay,' he said, bowing to them as they climbed aboard. 'I am Varen.'

'Narm-ah-stay,' Brooke echoed, 'I'm Brooke and this is Eric. What does that mean?'

'Namaste? This is a beautiful word what mean: "I honour the divine inside you",' Varen explained. 'Ready to go?' He took his seat and began to pedal.

It was still cool this morning, and the Sanctuary was a blend of greens and browns wherever they looked. Birds and fowl perched in trees and on sandy banks, and the waterways reflected the washed-out skies. There were over 300 species of birds living here, Varen told them, and the park attracted bird lovers from all around the world, especially during the hibernating season. But there were also many species of flowers and animals such as antelope, boar, snakes and jackals –

'Jackals!' Brooke scoured the grounds for a skulking wild dog.

'Yes, and lizards and turtles, and much many fish also.'

'Are they dangerous?'

'The fish?' Eric asked, baffled.

'No, dummy – the jackals!'

'We probably won't see any,' Eric said. But when he adjusted his binoculars, he found himself looking through the undergrowth for dog-like shapes rather than focusing on the birdlife.

'This Sanctuary is man-made,' their Sikh guide called over his shoulder. 'It was created when the Maharaj Suraj Mal did constructed a dam, you are understanding, to preventing flooding by the monsoon.'

'And it was a hunting ground for royalty, wasn't it?' Eric asked, reading from his guide.

'Yes. This, too, is being correct.'

'In one shoot in 1938 over 4,000 birds such as mallards and teals were killed by Lord Linlithgow, the Governor-General of India at that time,' Eric read aloud to Brooke.

'Over 4,000 birds killed in one shoot!'

'It was so, yes. But shooting is now prohibited,' Varen reassured them. 'The Park, it was declared protected in 1982, isn't it? This caused great many conflict between the farmers and the government. This was being because they could not any longer graze their cattle here,' he added, shaking his head.

'Will we see any Siberian crane?' Eric asked, lifting the binoculars to his eyes again.

'Maybe yes,' Varen said. 'Usually they are not always here in September, isn't it?'

So did that mean yes or no? Reading further in his guide, Eric discovered that the last Siberian crane was seen in Bharatpur in 2002; they existed in slightly larger numbers elsewhere but now only introduced cranes could be found in the sanctuary.

Suddenly the sky was filled with movement as a whole flock of long-necked water birds rose and flapped away together. They sat and watched for a while, and then Varen pedaled on through grassland and past marshes, skirting dense forest areas and all the while pointing out pelicans and eagles and hawks and larks and geese, with Brooke continually asking, 'Where? Where?' and shooting glances in all directions as she homed in on the bird in question.

Later, when she commented on the beauty of the calm waters, Varen informed them proudly that his name meant 'Lord of water', so this was a fitting employment for him. Brooke was delighted, and asked how long he had been working at the Sanctuary. They were both staggered by his response: 25 years cycling around the same paths... Then again, the park was 29 square kilometres in area and would look different in all seasons, so perhaps it wouldn't feel so repetitive after all. It would certainly keep you fit.

They wound up at the canteen, where an antelope had wandered in among the tables and was now gently butting into a visitor. Brooke squeaked in delight and hurried in its direction for a closer look. Eric bought a bottle of juice and sipped, watching from a distance.

'Pity we didn't get to see any of those big, painted storks,' Jackson said, coming to stand beside him. 'They're a sight, apparently, but wrong time of year. Where'd you get the drink?'

Eric pointed and Jackson headed away. When he returned, he indicated a group of Westerners in their 50s and 60s sitting at one of the tables. 'See that crowd? Apparently they've been up since 3.30 this morning bird watching. You'd have to be mad.'

'They have lists,' Eric said. 'There's this kind of international competition to get the most sightings, especially of rare birds. They're probably trying to up their numbers. Most of the big listers have over 5000 sightings.'

'Yeah? How d'you know that?'

Eric shrugged. 'Read it somewhere.'

'Do you have one of those photographic memories?

'Kind of,' Eric admitted. 'Not exactly, but I remember most things I read.'

'Lucky you!' Jackson said, a touch of envy in his voice. 'Well, I tell you what. I don't think I'd want to be a birder. Up *before* the crack of dawn, camping in all weather, sleeping on the ground, washing out of a bucket, sitting around for ages waiting to see a bird, getting cramp... Doesn't sound like much fun to me.'

'Me neither,' Eric agreed. 'I thought you'd like camping.'

'Yeah, if it's part of a rock climbing trip, or white water rafting, or something *fun*. Not just sitting around waiting.'

Fun, Eric thought. Rock climbing and white water rafting were not his idea of fun. It was just as well it took all sorts of people to make a world.

They had a couple of hours to do their own thing and then drove to the Ranthambore Tiger Sanctuary, arriving in the afternoon for a safari. Another of the hunting grounds of the Maharajas, it was today a major tourist wildlife attraction and had been declared a World Heritage site.

This time their mode of transport was a jeep. No walking was allowed through the reserve, and to see the tigers in the centre, one approached on elephant. All of the students (well, almost all) wanted the elephant option but they were firmly shepherded toward the jeeps, and began their bumpy journey, eyes peeled for signs of the magnificent Royal Bengal tiger whose number had multiplied in this favourable environment.

'It is a very priceless life experience for seeing the tiger busy at his activities of hunting and caring for his young,' their guide, Aman, remarked, as he drove his small tribe of students along a dry and dusty track. 'You will see also some very nice ruins and much other species of animal, such as deer, crocodile, mongoose, and many chirpy birds.'

Toni grinned at Jackson. 'Chirpy birds' – cute. But they'd seen birds; now she wanted tigers!

Aman kept up a steady patter of information for the next couple of hours as they drove through a range of landscapes, from verdant greenery to rivers and lake areas to rocky outcrops and jungle scrub, but not one tiger could be seen. They sighted elephants and deer and birds and ruins, but only distant shapes that might have been tigers and were gone by the time they drew near. Toni was keen to see Michali, the legendary queen of the tiger dynasty who had conquered crocodiles, and her daughter Satara, who had fought with her mother and taken over her lake territory.

'I'd be happy to take over my stepmother's territory,' Chlöe murmured.

'Would you fight her for it?' Toni asked with interest.

'With tooth and nail?' Chlöe queried, but before she could answer the jeep began to slow down and Aman called their attention to the road ahead. Not one, not two, but *three* tigers lay in their path, enjoying the late afternoon sunshine.

'Whoah!' Toni breathed, switching her phone from camera to video. Not that the tigers were moving. They lay there, still and majestic, the largest of them looking straight at the jeep while the other two paid no attention whatsoever. A tail switched lazily from side to side.

'Now what?' Chlöe wondered aloud. 'Do they move or do we?'

No one was inclined to move, beyond taking photos, and they stayed put for a good twenty minutes, gazing at the handsome beasts in front of them. Two other jeeps rolled up and parked alongside, one containing the other group of students, and more cameras were immediately trained on the tigers.

'I suppose we're like the paparazzi to them,' Toni whispered, and she and Chlöe giggled, but perhaps that thought had conveyed itself to the tigers as suddenly they'd had enough of being ogled at. The one that had been staring at the jeeps now rose and stood motionless, while the other two stretched and rose and walked slowly away into the scrub. The remaining tiger opened its mouth in a tremendous roar that sent a shiver through Toni and brought her skin out in goose bumps. There was dead silence in the aftermath of his roar, and for several minutes afterwards.

'That made my day,' Jackson said in a low voice.

'That made my *trip*,' Toni replied.

The sky was beginning to show sunset colours, and around them the bush slowly came back to life now that the potential source of danger had moved away. Their jeeps rumbled back to the gates through growing darkness, and the students emerged, full of moments that would live within them forever.

The following morning they enjoyed another early safari before heading to Jaipur, the 'Pink City', described so because the whole city was either constructed in a pinkish-coloured stone or painted that colour. In fact, the residents were now compelled by law to maintain the pink colour.

'That's rich!' **Brooke** thought, but then remembered that her aunt lived in an area where residents were bound by all sorts of building and garden restrictions in order to preserve a particular heritage 'look', so perhaps it wasn't so strange after all...

Jaipur was also the first city to be planned and constructed geometrically, in a grid pattern. And right at the centre was the City Palace, which was where they had just arrived.

'Not another museum,' a boy behind her grumbled as they descended from the bus.

'This is a *palace*!' Brooke called over her shoulder.

He scoffed in reply.

Brooke was immediately fascinated by the two gateways, one richly decorated for the royal family *that still lived there!* – she so hoped to catch a glimpse of someone royal! – and another more ordinary gate for the 'commoners' and visitors.

They shuffled through into the part of the residence that was open to tourists and discovered, from their guide, that the structure was composed of a series of enclosures of increasing impenetrability from the public outer circles to the protected inner sanctums of the king and queens. *King singular and queens plural*, she noted. So did that mean it was okay to have lots of wives back then?

There were not only seven gates at ground level but also seven storeys, however the architecture didn't grab her attention nearly as much as the opulent decoration: stained glass windows of peacocks, frescoes on the ceilings, vast chambers painted in red and gold and pink, chandeliers and columns… stunning. The two huge, marble elephants standing on either side of the entrance to the King's Hall, with its gold throne, reminded Brooke that the following morning they'd be seeing, and hopefully riding, elephants!

But it was the people who fascinated Brooke the most: the real-life guards who stood on duty in their long buttoned jackets, matching pants and red turbans, and also the royal family on display in photos where they were posing formally. She had a good long stare at a boy who had been crowned (or turbaned) at the age of thirteen (only two years younger than her!), and also at the glamorous queens and princesses in their brocaded saris and rich jewellry.

As ever, there were more buildings than they had time to see – temples and museums full of weapons and carriages and palanquins, which were boxes on poles carried by bearers, just like in the movies. But they made sure that they checked out the display of the largest silver objects in the world, including the man-sized silver jug. You probably needed a jug that size if you were Sawai Madho Singh I, who measured 1.2 metres wide and weighed 250 kg… Crazy! You could have fit six normal-sized people inside that fellow's pants! And apparently he had 108 wives – seriously? How could one man have that many wives?

'Don't go to the toilet,' Toni breathed in passing. 'They're foul.'

They meandered through the museum shop on their way out, and Brooke admired the array of pashmina shawls, silk saris, textiles, carpets, miniature paintings and block prints, but Miss Harris had warned them all that they'd find the same goods cheaper in the market, so she resisted. She hadn't yet spent much money at all, other than on souvenirs that were generally of a fairly crappy quality, leaving her feeling regretful, but she was determined to buy herself a beautiful sari, and something special for each of her parents. Later she was glad she had waited because she did pick up a beautiful block print sample at an artisan's shop-gallery in Amber.

The following morning a spirited discussion erupted in their group when they arrived at the Amber Fort and observed other tourists clambering aboard elephants for the trek up to the top of the hill while they were being ushered towards a set of *steps!!!* Brooke had been busting for her ride on one of these majestic beasts, and she felt cheated at the thought of trudging all the way up to the palace complex on her own two feet rather than riding up there in style.

But just then: 'You can't really want to ride them,' Toni said loudly to someone; 'it's elephant abuse.' Brooke was about to protest – she felt nothing but caring and fondness for the elephants, and she wouldn't be urging them to walk any faster than they could, but Toni insisted that the pressure on their backs and feet was damaging to them and their own drivers pushed them too hard – and, she added emphatically, riding the elephants was demeaning for them in the same way that circuses were; they'd hardly do it if they had a choice.

Eric read aloud from his guide that new government regulations had limited passengers to two, and the hours the elephants worked to three round trips maximum, so things weren't as bad as they used to be when the elephants worked all day in the hot sun, trudging up the hill with four passengers on board, some eight elephants having to give rides to 900 or so tourists. But they were still clearly treated as objects for use, Toni rejoined, and not respected for the dignified and magnificent creatures they were. It was just not right! Besides, some of the elephants were trafficked or forced to work when sick or injured, even having their tusks and ears mutilated. These were wild animals whose spirits were literally broken in order to accommodate human pleasures and be a source of the tourist dollar!

That was enough for Brooke. When sprightly Miss Harris cast the deciding vote by insisting they get some exercise and take the stairs, she surrendered the elephant ride she'd been hoping for and instead held out for an opportunity to paint an elephant when they reached the top. By the time they arrived at their destination, she had realised that painting them was simply another form of animal exploitation.

All the same, at the very least she would go up close and stroke an elephant, Brooke decided, and let it know how much she admired it through her touch. And this she did. While one of the drivers was helping passengers descend from his steed, she approached the elephant and cautiously put a hand to its leathery grey skin. She was surprised by how hot it felt, and how hard and rough. Looking up at its wrinkled face, past the pink and green and yellow painted trunk, she gazed at the small, sad eye of the elephant and was glad they had decided to neither ride nor paint…

'We're going in,' Toni said, tapping her on the shoulder. Reaching past Brooke, she touched its trunk. 'Aren't they awesome?'

'Yes,' Brooke murmured, giving the elephant one last pat before reluctantly moving away.

Their group walked through the gate with its paintings of the elephant god Ganesh, and into a vast, sunbaked courtyard where monkeys squatted and loped around, and scores of pigeons covered the dome roofs. As ever the Mughal/Hindu architecture boasted all sorts of artistic splendour, though when they entered, Brooke was shocked by gaps on the walls where decorative jewels had been prised out and stolen by tourists. She was particularly captivated by the Hall of Mirrors: thousands of pieces of pure glass had been embedded in white marble so that the Queen could 'watch the stars', since she was not permitted to sleep outside in the open air; the light from two candles burning in this hall had been converted into thousands of glittering star-images by the many mirrors. Disgusted that the King had had 300 concubines – *300!* – Brooke was nonetheless intrigued by the lattice screens that enabled the women to watch the men outside without being seen themselves. She and Toni marveled over the 'Hall of Winds': a cool climate had been artificially created by winds blowing over a rose-water cascade within the palace – old-style rose-scented air con! All in all, a fascinating place.

They were given another opportunity to visit the Jaipur bazaar that afternoon, and went their own ways through the noisy, jasmine and spice-smelling streets that were packed with sellers and buyers. **Jackson** soon saw Brooke paying for a wooden statue of Ganesh, and Toni bargaining intently over some traditional white cotton Indian outfits. He wandered around looking at gems and bangles and blue pottery and shawls and silver jewellery and embroidery and decorated shoes and puppets and table runners and table mats and tablecloths and stone carvings and leatherwork and metalwork and woodwork, wondering what to buy his parents. His mother would be easy to delight but his father... What would his father like?

'Watch your back,' Eric said quietly. 'A boy's been following you for quite a while. He's watching you now.'

'Yeah?' Jackson glanced over his shoulder and caught sight of a tall, thin, bespectacled Indian of about his age who was staring at him quite openly from the other side of a stall. 'Okay, thanks.'

'The crime rate in Jaipur is pretty high,' Eric added conversationally, before moving on.

Jackson went back to examining the bangles in front of him. There were approx fifty rupees to a dollar, so if this set of bangles cost thirty rupees that was only about sixty cents – he could buy a whole armful of them for a few bucks...

'The seller over there has a better quality,' a low voice said.

Jackson looked up to see the bespectacled youth standing beside him. 'Thanks,' he replied, automatically holding onto his backpack more tightly.

'That one has genuine silver,' the boy continued. 'This one... it is cheap. It will damage.'

'Okay, thanks,' Jackson repeated, turning away. 'I'll have a look in a minute.'

'I will introduce you,' the boy said. (They were 'sticky', these Indians. They couldn't take a hint.) 'My name is Ahmed.' He held out a hand, ready to shake.

Jackson took his hand tentatively, and Ahmed broke into a smile. 'Come,' he beamed. 'Over here is the shop of my uncle.'

The guy didn't seem to be about to rob him, Jackson thought, and maybe he'd get rid of him faster if he just went and looked at the uncle's wares. 'We're leaving soon,' he said, by way of insurance, 'so I don't have much time.' In fact, he could see Mr Plowright waving in the distance and then holding up a hand with five fingers outspread. Right. Five minutes left.

'Yes,' Ahmed smiled, walking backwards towards his uncle's shop in order to not lose sight of Jackson.

'Watch out!' Jackson exclaimed as the boy nearly tripped over a goat. Ahmed rebalanced, half-embarrassed, half-laughing, as the goat skittered away, and then they were at his uncle's shop, where a great range of jewellery lay spread out on cloths and stands. His uncle appeared almost immediately and more introductions were made.

'Jaipur jewellery is famous,' the grey-haired, portly uncle informed Jackson. 'Your Hollywood stars wear our jewellery. Rihanna. Jennifer Lopez. Angeline Jolie.' Their names sounded strange on his tongue. He beamed and pointed to a silver necklace with delicate leaves in some kind of green stone, maybe jade or emerald, Jackson wasn't sure. 'For your mother?'

The number of rupees was quite a bit more than he had been planning to spend.

'No thanks,' Jackson said, glancing toward where Mr Plowright had been. 'I have to go.'

'You will come back,' Ahmed said with certainty.

Jackson frowned. 'Maybe. I don't know. I can't remember what we're doing next.'

'I would like to speak with you...' Ahmed continued, staying close to Jackson as he edged away. 'For a proposition. A deal. A business deal.'

'A business deal?' Jackson wrinkled his forehead. 'I'm not here on business. I'm on a school trip.'

'Yes,' Ahmed nodded, 'school trip. I also am in school. But you go back to Western country. I think – partnership is good, yes?'

'Partnership? Sorry, I've got to go.'

'You could take some kohl from India and sell in your country,' Ahmed said urgently. 'I will be your Indian supplier. We will make good partnership.'

'I don't think so!' Jackson said, both amused and distracted. 'I'm not in business. I'm a school kid.'

'Yes,' Ahmed agreed again. 'I also. But we can make a business together. Import, export. Perhaps kohl? I can supply for you very cheap.'

'Coal?' Jackson echoed, brow furrowed. 'No, forget it, Ahmed. I'm not interested. And I've got to go. 'Bye. See you. Have a nice life.' He turned determinedly and walked away, and amazingly, the boy didn't follow him.

But the following morning as they queued up to enter the Jantar Mantar Observatory, he saw Ahmed again. The teenager stood at a short distance watching as Jackson and his group lined up.

'There's that boy again,' Eric said.

'I know. He wants me to go into business with him.'

'Really? How bizarre.'

'To do what?' Brooke asked, turning around.

'Sell coal, of all weird ideas.'

'Coal?'

'That's what it sounded like.'

'He probably said *kohl*,' Brooke said. 'It's eyeliner. You know how these Indian women have really thick eyeliner?'

'Do they?' Jackson asked. He hadn't noticed.

Brooke rolled her eyes. 'Yes. It's not a bad idea. Light and easy for you to take in bulk and not hard to sell, I reckon.'

'But he's a complete stranger. And I didn't come here to start a business.'

'What's that about starting a business?' Toni demanded, also turning around.

'The Indian over there wants Jackson to export kohl to Australia,' Brooke explained.

'Really? Cool!'

'I'm not going to!' Jackson exclaimed, surprised that they were taking it so seriously.

'Why not? Buy cheap, sell for more, share the profit with your Indian partner. Why not, Jackson? If you don't, I will!'

'Are you nuts?'

'No,' she replied, gazing at him evenly; 'just being an opportunist, like all good entrepreneurs.'

Shaking his head in amazement, Jackson walked away from them to enter the Observatory. Eric hurried after him. This place was right up Eric's alley; he could see that at once. It was a scientist's paradise: some nineteen gigantic astronomical instruments made hundreds of years ago that were still in working order, although tourists were no longer allowed to climb the steep staircases to the tops of each structure.

'Bummer,' said Jackson, staring up at the world's largest sundial. 'I'd love to get up there.'

Constructed from brick rubble and plaster and bronze, the enormous instruments were designed to view the stars with the naked eye. The whole place had a kind of Stonehenge feel about it, Jackson reflected, gazing around. Not that he had ever been to Stonehenge or knew much about it, but there was something similar about the large, spaced structures... This place had apparently been used for both astronomical and astrological observations. Right now he'd appreciate a bit of foretelling about his future, such as what career he should forge for himself that would encompass travel and adventures like this, and also make him a shitload of money.

Eric seemed to be reading his mind about the foretelling. 'I wonder if we could use these instruments to find out if our homestay is going to be okay,' he pondered. 'I'm not looking forward to it very much.'

'Yeah? Should be all right,' Jackson reassured. He'd noticed that this guy seemed to be quite prone to anxiety. Then again, his own stomach aches were more of a nervous thing than a physical thing, he suspected, although that Delhi sickness had definitely been the food. Geez! He'd come good after taking the medication but now he began to worry that the food they'd be served on homestay would be too rich and spicy for him or not cooked properly and he'd get sick again... Agh! Put it out of your mind, he told himself. Instead, he found himself wondering about that Ahmed boy and his 'business proposal'. How bizarre!

People in developing nations often believe that all Western tourists are very wealthy and some will look for opportunities among these visitors.

> If the sort of proposal Ahmed made to Jackson was made to you, would you consider it?

Do you have a vision to make a difference in the world?

> - perhaps by caring for animals, or by shaking up a whole industry and making it more conscious and responsible?

Today's rapidly changing world means that now people rarely spend twenty-five years in one job.

> How long have your parents and grandparents worked for one company?
>
> What do you feel your career pathway will be like?
>
> Young people used to automatically go into their family's business or industry but today, at least in the west, it's all about free choice, and some people spend a whole life experiencing a varied range of positions rather than building a particular career path.
>
> What are you envisaging for yourself?

'It takes all sorts to make a world,' Eric reflects.

We often want other people to think like us, but we'd lose so much diversity if that were the case.

What do you think?

CHAPTER 16

Days 8 & 9: A Hairy Idea for the God of Wisdom

The following day had been scheduled 'at leisure', and **Toni** was keen to return to the Jaipur market and pick up more of the white punjabi outfit she had bought so that she could give them away as gifts. She talked some of the other girls into returning with her, this time as an independent expedition on the local bus. Mr Plowright was wary of them going on their own but the girls insisted that they'd be careful and stay safe and look out for each other. So, with sketched maps and phones in hand, they headed out to the bus stop and joined a motley crew in the dusty road.

The waiting Indians all stared at the Westerners. Brooke widened her eyes at Toni in a 'What's their problem?' expression. Toni grinned and shrugged in reply, but she was less tolerant when they boarded the bus and someone roughly grabbed her arm and pointed her away from the seat she was about to take to a seat on what turned out to be the 'female' side of the bus. Segregation! Then, since the bus was already quite crowded, they had to squeeze into separate seats between locals. Toni didn't want to be judgemental but it wasn't the most pleasant-smelling experience… She kept her face pointed to the front to avoid the garlic aroma of the toothless old woman on her left and the unwashed odour of the large woman on her right, who held a bare-bottomed baby on her lap. What if the baby…?

The bus driver was yelling and gesticulating at the last few passengers to hurry up and board, and moments later they swung away from the bus stop with a sickening lurch and headed off at speed on what soon proved to be uncomfortable seats and a terrible road.

The woman with the baby poked Toni in the side with her elbow. 'First time India?'

'Yes.'

'Sisters?' pointing to the other girls.

'No. We're students.'

The baby was also gazing at Toni, and now it reached out a plump and dirty hand that held a squashed, sloppy mandarin segment. Toni smiled and shook her head, saying 'No, thank you', but the mother began to insist, 'Yes! Please!' She brought a fresh mandarin out of a cloth bag and broke it in half, offering Toni half and popping a piece into her own mouth.

'No, thank you,' Toni repeated, smiling woodenly, but the woman nodded intently, opened the fingers of Toni's hand and deposited the other half of the mandarin in her palm with a broad smile and the instruction, 'Eat!'

Now what? Toni wondered. Would she offend the woman if she didn't? What if she picked up some bug? She broke the mandarin into pieces and put one of them into her mouth, planning to lose the other pieces as soon as she could, and they smiled at each other as she chewed.

The bus tore along the road, bumping over potholes and swerving to avoid other vehicles and animals. Several times she held her heart in her mouth and her palms grew clammy as the driver overtook another vehicle right in the face of oncoming traffic, and so close that Toni was sure this was to be her last day on Earth. But none of the locals were batting an eyelid; they just sat there stolidly, swaying from side to side with the motion of the bus, everyone sweating in the heat and close proximity of other bodies.

At one point the driver made a sudden stop in the middle of the road and yelled to a guy sitting at the back of the bus who came running up to take a bunch of flowers that the driver was holding out. Then the guy jumped off the bus and ran across the road to a little temple with the flowers while the driver faced the temple and put his hands together in prayer for about five seconds. The guy left the flowers on the altar then raced back to the bus, jumped on board, and they were off again. Toni swiveled around to look at Brooke and Chlöe and Laura, and they all raised their brows and grinned at each other in amazement.

'It's a different world,' Laura said, when they stood outside Jaipur market brushing themselves off after their hair-raising trip, and preparing to enter the chaos in front of them and start haggling for goods.

'You've got to get these punjabis,' Toni declared, leading the way. 'They're gorgeous. And if you see phone chargers, let me know because I keep losing mine. I'm about to buy my third one since leaving home.'

'What are punjabis again?' Brooke asked, frowning 'no' at a vendor who was trying to catch her attention.

'You know, those pants and long-top outfits that Indian women wear. The ones I found have got really pretty lacey sort of stitching on them and they're a great price. I reckon I could get them to give us an even better price since you're buying too. I just have to find the stall...'

Jackson had discovered some local kids playing cricket in the streets outside their accommodation. After watching for a few minutes he was invited to join in; he leapt forward, eager to run and swing a bat and toss a ball after a whole week of touring and travelling.

These kids sure did love their cricket, and they weren't half bad at it. When it was his turn he bowled to an Indian boy who concentrated intently, tapped his bat on the ground three times, then swung out, sending the ball straight back at him like a rocket. Jackson stretched out his arm and enjoyed the satisfying whack as the ball landed in his hand.

The boys cheered good-naturedly, including the one who had been caught out, and despite the lack of a shared language, the next few hours passed so quickly that Jackson was taken aback when the old bus pulled in and he saw Toni and the other girls descending, their arms full of purchases.

He was not so happy to see who followed them off the bus: the tall, skinny, bespectacled Indian – Ah-something.

The fellow came straight to him, beaming. 'Good afternoon, Jackson!' he said. 'I see you are liking the cricket.'

'Yeah,' Jackson replied, hesitating as he tried to recall the guy's name.

'Ahmed has been telling us about his idea for the kohl business,' Brooke said with a meaningful stare. 'In fact, he's had an even better idea.'

'Hair,' Ahmed beamed, nodding. 'Yes, a very good export-import business, isn't it?'

'Hair?' Jackson echoed blankly, tossing the ball back to the waiting Indians since it was clear his game was over for now.

'Oh yes!' Ahmed enthused. 'You have bald peoples, yes? And your womans like long hair?'

'He's talking about extensions,' Brooke said.

'Extensions?' Jackson's mind produced an image of a house being renovated…

'*Hair* extensions. For longer hair.'

'Here in India it is a sacrificial act to cut the hair in the temple,' Ahmed explained eagerly. 'This hair has been put inside mattresses or in the Ganges River but that is not permitted now because it makes the river sick, so there is hair for –' he halted and looked at Brooke.

'For wigs,' Toni interrupted. 'And it's a bloody good idea. Women apparently spend several grand on wigs and hair extensions, and guys who are losing hair spend heaps too. You could rake it in, buddy.'

'What are you *talking* about?' Jackson asked, flummoxed.

'Ahmed wants to start a business with you,' Toni replied. 'With *you*, for some reason. He has his heart set on *you*. He'd provide the Indian goods cheaply and you'd sell them back at home and then send him his cut. It's worth considering.'

Jackson's head was whirling. Him? Run a business? But he was only fifteen and still at school – and this particular idea was sheer insanity!

'My sister's a hairdresser and she's always talking about how much better real hair is for extensions than artificial,' Brooke informed them. 'It holds dye better, for one thing.'

'Whoah!' Jackson protested. 'You guys are getting carried away.'

'You should think about it,' Toni said gravely. 'Really.' She hoisted her bag onto the other shoulder and headed into their accommodation to put away her goods.

Jackson looked at Ahmed, who was smiling at him eagerly.

'What's the matter?' **Eric** asked Toni the following morning. They were about to board a bus for a surprise outing and Toni was hovering at the road's edge, looking in all directions rather than boarding.

'I ordered some more clothes at the market yesterday and the shopkeeper said they'd drop them off here this morning,' she said. 'But I forgot that we'd be out and I don't want to blow my cash!'

'They'll probably just leave them at the front desk,' Eric said. Secretly, he was doubtful, but he didn't want to cause her any upset. 'On the other hand,' he added, 'if this bus operator is anything like the others, we'll be an hour late leaving so they'll probably arrive before we go.'

At that moment Miss Harris poked her head out of the bus and beckoned to them. 'Come on, you two!'

'So much for that idea!' Toni said darkly, with one last glance around. 'I shouldn't have paid up-front,' she muttered, following him. 'That was dumb. I should have just paid a deposit or something. Idiot me!'

This time the bus took them away from Jaipur toward the hills. Eric sat by the window, gazing outside at the people driving bullocks, the roadside stalls with their fruit stands, the motorbikes zipping here and there that were overloaded with passengers and goods... At one point the bus drove over a short stretch of road that was covered with sheaves of rice. They erupted into exclamations when their driver told them these were scattered on the road to be threshed by the passing traffic! It was simultaneously so clever and so strange – wouldn't the food then be too dirty from the tyres and exhaust?

Seeing the locals around them, Eric was reminded that tomorrow each student was to be deposited with a strange family for a two-night 'homestay experience'. He had been avoiding thinking about this for the last few months, and now it was upon him. Tonight they would be allocated their host family, and the experiences were apparently going to be vastly different. Butterflies exploded in his stomach as he wondered where he'd be staying and if it would be all right…

Brooke's face broke into a radiant smile when they reached the end of a long, pitted, dirty road and turned in at 'Dera Amer', and she saw elephants in the distance. Descending from the buses, they were greeted by turbaned attendants offering bottles of water and juice and cold flannels. The owner, Udaijit, welcomed them and they were soon given bananas with which to feed the elephants. Not everyone wanted this experience but Brooke was first in line to hold out the fruit that Laxmi took gently with her trunk and placed in her mouth.

When the elephants had been fed, the students were given paints so they could decorate their dotted trunks. Brooke hesitated. She could hear Toni questioning the teachers and elephant handlers about the appropriateness of riding the elephants, and being reassured that they would be trekking at a slow pace on flat ground through the countryside rather than on a steep hill like at the Amber Fort, and that no hooks were used. In fact, this wilderness retreat was specifically designed to protect elephants and camels, and the tourists who came here to enjoy these beasts were gentle and respectful.

That was good enough for Brooke. Carefully avoiding Toni's eye, Brooke joined the other students in selecting colours and placed herself in front of an elephant's trunk, where she attempted to reproduce some of the traditional Indian patterns she had observed, outlining the leaf-like shapes in white and colouring them blue and pink and green and yellow.

She became aware of Toni standing aside and watching, and Brooke felt uncomfortably like a traitor, especially when each elephant knelt down for two students to climb aboard into the cradle-like, padded platform structure on its back, and Brooke clambered aboard while Toni remained on solid ground. The rest of the group took off at a slow, rocking amble through the dry bush, leaving 'their conscience' standing on the track behind them. Brooke quashed her slight feeling of doubt that she might be doing the wrong thing, and settled in to enjoy the experience. It wasn't very comfortable but it was worth it! For half an hour they trailed along, pointing out monkeys in the nearby trees and passing the odd mud building or villager. At the halfway mark waiters appeared with more drinks for them and to take pictures (for a small fee), and on their return journey they heard peacocks making their loud 'ah, ah, ah' cry, and the nearby 500-year-old monastery sounding its call to prayer. It was exhilarating.

Back at the camp, they were led to a thatched roof, open-air dining room where they could choose locally grown organic dishes from a buffet and eat in comfort at cloth-covered tables. The *naan* bread was freshly made in the tandoori oven in front of their eyes, and the food was delicious. The crowning glory would be to dine here at night, Brooke reflected, noticing the lanterns hanging from the trees, and the candles on the tables. It would be beautiful.

Toni slid back into a seat at her table and declared, 'Toilets are fabulous. Clean. Marble.' Then she placed a small, wooden elephant carving on the table in front of her plate. She'd been browsing the souvenir shop while the rest of the group had been on safari.

'That's gorgeous!' Brooke exclaimed, picking it up for a closer look. 'I'm going to get one too!'

Toni read aloud from the information that came with her purchase: 'Ganesha, the remover of obstacles and the god of beginnings and wisdom,' which reminded Brooke that she had called upon the elephant god to remove any obstacles in the way of her being able to take this trip... and here she was, on her first ever overseas holiday, an adventure that was filling her mind with all sorts of new knowledge and giving her a riot of new experiences!

'You know how men and women sit separately in the bus?' Toni added randomly. 'Apparently that's for sexual protection.'

'Really?'

'Yup.'

After lunch they were invited to scrub the elephants in nearby pools, so by the time they were trundling back along the dusty road later that afternoon, Brooke's cup was full.

Eric, on the other hand, grew more and more unsettled as the hour approached for their homestay experience. He asked Brooke, conversationally, if she was looking forward to it and she said yes, sort of, and that she was hoping to be billeted with the royal family, which would be super cool! Why was he asking? Was he stressed about it? It couldn't be that bad. They were just people, after all, even if their habits were different...

When they reached their accommodation **Toni** hurried straight to the front desk to check if her order of punjabis had arrived. To her relief, it had. Calling to the girls who had shared the order, she took the large package to her room and ripped it open, revealing twelve neatly folded outfits. Toni busily sorted out whose was whose and handed them to the others. But when Laura held one of the outfits up, they found that the stitching was wonky and loose in places, and the final effect much shoddier than the first garment Toni had bought. The others contemplated their purchases a little sourly, and Toni squirmed as she recalled their doubt and her certainty and brusqueness and even, dare she admit it, bossiness about making the order... There was not much they could do about it now: they were leaving first thing in the morning for their homestay experiences.

Have you talked friends into buying things or having experiences that they weren't really up for but 'went along with' because you were strong and clear about it?

Ever regretted any of that?

On the other hand, has someone talked you into doing or buying something that you later regretted?

How did you grow from the experience?

What did you learn? What did you decide for next time?

Would you take the risk of starting a business with a stranger?

What are the pros? What are the cons?

How could you prepare yourself to benefit from the pros without suffering the cons?

Would you head out for an experience among foreign locals or would you stay in the comfort zone of your tour/family/friends?

What are the pros of striking out? What are the cons?

How could you prepare yourself to benefit from the pros without suffering the cons?

CHAPTER 17

DAYS 10-12: LIVING WITH PEASANTS AND ROYALTY, ARMY COLONELS AND HINDU MATRIARCHS

Both **Jackson** and Eric were in Group A, destined for families in Jodphur, the Blue City, second largest in Rajasthan.

'As in, riding pants?' Brooke asked.

'Yes,' Miss Harris replied as they pulled up in the driveway outside a grand hotel. 'The Rajasthani warriors were all excellent horse riders. All right, Jackson. This is your stop.'

'Oh my God!' Brooke gaped. 'It's *gorgeous*.'

Indian royal families were no longer recognised officially by the government; when the country became a republic they had done away with all titles and the royal families no longer held court or dressed up, but they were still recognised as royalty by the people. And Jackson was to be hosted by such a family in their home, a palace that had been converted into a palatial hotel.

The remaining students gazed at the impressive, dark-brick building with its domed rooftops and arched windows that featured peacock designs in the stained glass... and the servant who was emerging from the front door. They called their farewells to Jackson, who saluted his classmates and leapt off the bus with his backpack.

'Khamma ghani,' the servant said, bowing.

What was that? Jackson wondered, bowing slightly and mumbling 'Namaste' in return.

A woman in a red and gold sari appeared and spoke briefly with Mr Plowright while the servant took Jackson's luggage from him. Then his teacher slapped him on the back with a cheery, 'Enjoy!' and climbed back into the bus, and Jackson's comfort zone of familiarity in this world-away-from-home drove away down the long driveway. Jackson was alone with Poonam Singh and her family for the next three days.

He quelled the disturbance in his stomach and followed the woman and her servant inside.

Jodphur was also known as the Sun City because of the bright, sunny weather it enjoyed all year 'round, being on the edge of the Thar Desert, and the village they drove into to drop **Eric** off at his homestay certainly had a desert feel about it. A number of other students had been dropped off en route, but still, the contrast between Jackson's palatial homestay and Eric's thatched roof, small, circular mud house destination was pretty startling.

'These people are very special,' Mr Plowright told Eric by way of encouragement, since Eric appeared to be frozen to his seat. 'We chose them especially for you.'

Slowly, reluctantly, Eric emerged from the bus with his bag over one shoulder. Children stood in the sunbaked street, staring at him. The woman who came to greet him wore a nose ring with a large gold engraved circlet that obliterated half of her mouth. She bowed, murmuring 'Namaste'. Her son would usually be here to welcome the guests, Mr Plowright told Eric, but he was caught up on some business or other and would be back soon. Meanwhile, Amrita would look after him. Taking in the hunched old woman's wrinkled, unsmiling face, for some reason an image from his childhood fairy tale book came to Eric's mind, and he wondered if he were about to be shoved into an oven and eaten for supper...

He waved goodbye to the staring faces in the bus, waiting until it was far away before turning to follow the bent old woman through the gates into her domain.

Brooke had reluctantly let go of the royalty experience and now, after another long drive from Jodphur to Udaipur, they were pulling up outside her homestay billet, a brick home in one of the outer suburbs that had been rendered white but had seen better times. Standing on the steps outside the building, though, were two teenaged girls! Grabbing her bag, she farewelled her classmates and dropped down the steps of the bus.

The girls smiled at her shyly, and one darted inside, returning a moment later with their mother. Miss Harris and the woman spoke for a moment and then Brooke was introduced to her hostess, Shoba, and her daughters, Indira and Fathi. Even as the bus rolled away, the girls were drawing Brooke into the cool interior of their home and asking her how she was finding India and where had they toured so far and where were they going next and where did she live and did she have brothers and sisters and was her school good and –

Relieved as she was to have company of her own age, Brooke was also grateful when the mother sent the girls to their rooms to finish their homework, and led Brooke into the kitchen for a cup of spiced tea and a snack.

It was fortunate that Brooke didn't get to see where **Toni** was dropped off. Udaipur was a city famous in India for its romantic lakeside position – it was called the 'Venice of India', and Toni was billeted to a large guesthouse on a hill with views of a lake and surrounded by farmland and vegetable gardens. This property belonged to a retired army colonel whose wife ran the homestay. There were eight rooms for visiting guests, although half of the guests were away touring at the moment, Srividya informed Toni, after greeting her and leading her past numerous doorways through the carefully maintained house.

The interior was also white, and her bedroom decorated in blue and white with views of the lake. After a week or so of hostels, this felt like serious luxury. Toni parked her bag by the wall, sat on the four-poster bed experimentally, examined the miniature paintings on the walls, and took in the view of the lake and houses and hills. Lovely.

Like Brooke's hosts, this family had two daughters, a sixteen year old who was right now on her way home from school, and an eighteen year old who was chopping vegetables for the evening meal, or so Toni discovered when she entered the kitchen. Their ex-colonel father was apparently out tending the small, ancient temple that was also sited on their property.

Srividya offered Toni a seat at the table and joined her daughter at the bench, and Toni watched and enjoyed the aromas as vegetables sizzled in rich spicy sauces, *naan* was cooked in the pan, rice was steamed, pakoras deep fried, and little chutneys were dished out.

The younger daughter, Naarani, arrived soon and proved to be painfully shy. She greeted Toni and then escaped to her room and chores, not returning until the mealtime. Meanwhile the father, whose name was quite frankly unpronounceable, had entered the house. He treated her to a benevolent smile before speaking to his wife in Hindi at some length while she chattered back to him and the older daughter continued cooking, glancing up now and then.

When it came time to eat, Toni was surprised to find that the father ate first. Srividya served him, her gold bangles sliding up and down her arms as she scooped food onto his plate, and hovered over him as he ate. Toni's stomach was growling but she could only sit helplessly, wondering at this chauvinism, until her own dish was served. It was only a matter of time before she would question this tradition…

Jackson's palatial home, or 'havali', as it was called, had some 18 to 20 rooms, but a family feud had resulted in the two royal brothers literally building a wall smack-bang through the middle of the house, and now each brother lived in one half of the house with his family. Jackson was staying with the brother who was operating the homestay (and his wife and son and a widowed aunt), while on the other side the estranged brother lived with his wife and son, but no one else. Jackson could just imagine the three of them rattling around in their half of the huge building, their closest family on the other side of the wall.

He had been amazed to find that the feud was so deep and old and current that the brothers would literally ignore each other in the driveway if they happened to cross paths. You would think, Jackson thought, watching them pass each other without even a nod, that a princely family would have princely manners and graces, but no, they were so locked into their perspectives that it seemed the issue was at an impasse. He wondered what the feud had been about – or if they even remembered what had caused the original disagreement. He wondered if it was about money. Were arguments in rich families usually about money?

Jackson's parents' quarrels and his own clashes with his father seemed minor compared to this major breakdown in communication, and it gave him pause for thought. He'd always thought that life all-round would be better and easier and that his parents would fight less if his family had more money, and now here he was, sitting in the midst of great wealth (where even the bathrooms were marble), and the people around him were still unhappy and quarrelsome.

His parent hosts were friendly and accommodating, but their son Ghandhiram struck Jackson as lazy, letting the servants do what he could easily have done himself, and behaving as if he were entitled to ease and comforts just because he existed. Ghandhiram seemed to expect that everything he wanted and needed would simply land in his lap with no effort or contribution on his own part, and he showed no particular interest in his Western guest.

Strolling along one of the grand hallways in the hotel, Jackson found himself thinking about Ahmed and his polite persistence, and some respect for the young man's determination to get ahead began to seep through his resistance. What if Ahmed was completely genuine? What if this idea of his was the beginning of actual wealth for both of them? Perhaps, instead of being so determined to not have anything to do with him, he should at least have a proper conversation with the guy and find out more. After all, even if it went belly-up, he shouldn't be too out of pocket, and if it worked out, perhaps he'd even be able to pay his parents back for this trip. It was worth exploring – if he were ever able to find Ahmed again.

Living in the Bishnoi village was like living in a time warp. And for a kid like **Eric**, with his reliance on devices and the internet, the environment he found himself in was extremely uncomfortable. Everything was homemade, including his bed, which was a wooden frame with colourful, woven materials stretched from end to end to form a kind of mattress. The Bishnoi used similar structures as benches; it seemed that someone was always spinning yarn.

The old woman squatted to cook at a fire that was fueled by cow dung and hay cakes, and meals were served on tin plates or banana leaves. The family sat on the ground to eat in the communal kitchen, and each person finished off all the food on his or her plate. Eric was dished a small first portion and when he'd finished it, he was offered more, and then more, but it was clear that he should not ask for more than he could eat so as not to waste a morsel of the precious food.

The old woman was silent and rarely smiled, and the male elders were also very stern-looking. They wore white turbans and *dhotis*, material wrapped around the waist and covering their legs, though not Eric's host, Vinesh, a young, single, and quite cheerful man who wore a white, short-sleeved shirt and long white pants and sandals, and offered an abundance of explanations about his people's lifestyle and history from the moment he arrived home in time for the evening meal.

The Bishnoi were the traditional custodians of the land here, Eric discovered, and they had a bloody history of martyrdom. These people worshipped nature and even prayed to trees and animals, and one of their female ancestors had given her life in order to prevent the chopping down of trees by the Maharajah's men. *Three hundred and sixty-three* other villagers, including children, had joined her in giving their lives to protect the trees before the Maharajah heard what was happening and ordered his men to stop felling the trees – and the people. Needless to say, all meals were vegetarian. Goats wandered freely throughout the gated village, while outside antelope and black bucks could be seen grazing peacefully in the fields. Eric was okay with animals in the distance, though the goats had startled him a few times. As for the camels, he gave them a wide berth.

Water in this sandy, desert village was very scarce and guarded in clay pots, Vinesh said. (Eric was carefully rationing his own supply of bottled water.) Showers were taken in a shared, public room and the water was heated outside on the fire. The toilet room seemed clean enough although it was very humble: plain and tiled with a squat toilet and a water tumbler for cleaning afterwards. (Eric was glad that (a) it was warm and he could shower quickly, and (b) that he had stowed away a squashed roll of toilet paper for 'just in case'...)

He spent his three days watching the local villagers at their work. The clay pot-maker squatted in front of a large wheel that he spun with a stick since there was no electricity, his hands deftly shaping the swirling, moist clay until it formed a simple and elegant pot. Eric was invited to have a turn and politely declined, but they coaxed and urged and finally he surrendered. Soon, however, he felt embarrassed by the stodgy lump he produced that fell apart into fragments. The potter laughed merrily and urged him to have another go. Eric didn't want to but another part of him felt annoyed by his failure and determined to master this thing, so he did, and his next effort at least looked like something and held together, though it was very wonky.

He was invited to have a go at spinning yarn for the rugs they wove from scratch, and firmly declined, but he enjoyed watching two of the craftspeople sitting opposite each other around a frame and weaving a colourful pattern that grew in response to the movements of their busy fingers.

At night, oil lamps lit the mud huts and buildings, but not for long: these people retired soon after dark and rose early, with the dawn. On his second afternoon, as he relaxed on the rugs in the courtyard under the trees and watched tourists examine the Bishnoi wares and make their purchases, Eric realised he was feeling quite contented. By the third morning, he felt as if some knot inside him had been loosened...

Brooke was quizzed over dinner about her life and school. The girls' mother interjected many times into her daughters' questions with remarks about the lack of spiritual and familial duty in the West. Brooke opened her mouth to protest and defend, and had to close it again. When was the last time she had voluntarily helped out with a meal or the house cleaning or attended church? She couldn't remember doing either without being cajoled or outright commanded; she certainly didn't consider it her duty, as these girls appeared to.

'Young people in your country do not look after their parents,' Mrs Bharathi said disapprovingly. 'They do what they like. This disrespect is staining our country also. You see, here we live with my mother-in-law and we all care for each other. The mother finds her daughter a husband. This is how it should be! But now our young people are copying the West and think they should be free to do whatever they want!' Mrs Bharathi tossed her head. 'It is a breakdown of family values and our society will become as sick as yours,' she pronounced to Brooke.

Man! Talk about rude and judgemental, Brooke thought. Indira and Fathi took their guest's side by pointing out that some of this modernisation was important – look at how literacy was improving throughout India! It was natural that with greater empowerment there would be more independence of choice. And in families such as their own, where the mother was a widow, women had to fend for themselves. But yes, on the whole their mother was right. Nuclear families were on the rise and that would become a problem for the elderly and for young mothers who would now be alone at home with their children, and, of course, for widows, unless they had a good support system.

Brooke's teenage hosts returned to their study after the evening meal had been cleared away; their diligence stunned her. She sat with the mother and grandmother and aunt, watching soap operas in Hindi and understanding nothing, and, on her way to bed was disconcerted to find that she was to go with the girls to school the following day. Lying in the strange bed and feeling anxious about this, Brooke figured that surely nothing much would be expected of her given the language issue – she would be the local celebrity, in fact!

And she did stand out. When they arrived at the imposing building the following morning she was the only white-skinned person in the entire school of several thousand brown, uniformed bodies, and it seemed that everyone was looking at her wherever she went. She followed Indira to class, since they were closest in age, and was given an exercise book to write in and an English text to read and answer comprehension questions. This was quite fun since it was so easy for her but as Brooke gazed at the many dark heads bent over their books (apart from when they were snatching glances at her), she was struck by the difference between her school and this one. There was plenty that she didn't understand as everyone around her mostly chattered in Hindi, but what she did grasp was the dedication to study (there was no mucking around) and the emphasis on rote learning: the students were busily memorising facts, and there seemed to be little focus on either creativity or problem-solving. She was surprised, too, to find that in at least a quarter of the classes they were allocated private study because their teacher had not turned up to work. Wow. If only teachers at home had such poor attendance records! Apparently it was rife here.

On their way home after school Indira revealed that she found the pressure to achieve and succeed stressful. But at least she wasn't studying the sciences like Fathi; she was planning to be a nursery school teacher, or perhaps to educate women about family planning and things like that, since fertility rates were greater where women were less educated. Fathi, however, had very academic aspirations. She wanted to study Engineering at the University of Mumbai – which was highly unlikely to eventuate, Indira declared, because their mother would never agree and anyway, only a tiny percentage of girls ever became engineers. It was really not a very girl-like occupation, and there was so much competition in India for any position at all, that Fathi was doomed to failure, especially if she was up against men. And their mother would never allow her to live away from home in Mumbai, that immoral city! And anyway, they couldn't afford to pay for her accommodation over there. Fathi set her jaw and said nothing, and Brooke digested all of this in silence.

She had given her family souvenirs from her country upon arrival, such as miniature stuffed toys of native kangaroos and koalas and little Australian flags, and even a tiny jar of Vegemite, her favourite spread. They had received these gifts politely but without much enthusiasm, so when she learnt that the family had never, in their entire lives, been to a classy restaurant for a meal, Brooke decided to make a real splash and totally impress them. She would treat the whole family to a night out! After all, this was the romantic, lakeside district of Udaipur, and she wanted to experience a lakeside restaurant herself before leaving the next day. So, with Indira's help, she chose a restaurant that looked suitably grand and the whole family (plus the neighbours, who pretty much lived at their place) piled into a taxi for the big night out.

Her hosts were greatly impressed and delighted by the beauty and elegance of the establishment when they arrived, Brooke was pleased to note, and she felt as proud of their position on the balcony, where they had an awesome view of the dark, shining lake, as if she were the owner of the restaurant herself. The food was delicious, in Brooke's opinion, although Mrs Bharathi tut-tutted about the quality of several dishes and claimed that her own or her mother's cooking was better.

But the bill that arrived at the end of a very successful evening gave Brooke quite a shock. Having shared a meal with her classmates for a mere fifteen dollars for all five of them at a restaurant in Jaipur, she had been expecting something similar – just a bit more. But seven people at 1500 rupees each (the mother, the mother-in-law, the two sisters, Brooke, and their neighbor who looked after the girls when their mother was away on a training for work, and the neighbour's young son as well)… holy crap! This one meal was going to cost her almost two hundred dollars!

Toni's family was preparing for the wedding of the eighteen-year-old daughter, a wedding that had been arranged eight months before.

A marriage broker – she could hardly believe there was such a thing! – had taken Priya's astrological details and then looked through her books for a suitable match, which turned out to be a guy called Gokul. Then the two families had a meeting and looked at photos of each other's children, and as they were happy about it, it was arranged that the young couple would meet.

'And then I suppose you started dating,' Toni said. 'To make sure *you* like the guy!'

'Oh no,' Priya replied, narrowing her eyes to concentrate on the fine needlework she was doing. 'I have only met Gokul twice.'

'But you're going to marry him?' Toni exclaimed.

'Oh yes.'

Toni was gob-smacked. 'What about love? What about choosing for yourself?'

Priya shrugged. 'Love! That is for Westerners and Hollywood. Our tradition is arranged marriages. It is much more successful, you know.'

'But more and more Indian women are choosing their own husbands,' Naarani piped up, from where she was watching some Bollywood movie that was all love and romance and dancing.

'It won't work,' Priya said airily, holding her embroidery up to the light. 'The truth is in the stars. A marriage of passion will not necessarily last. I know our mother has chosen well for me.'

Toni couldn't imagine putting her entire married fate into her mother's hands. It wasn't that she didn't respect her mother or think she had her best interests at heart, but really! This was archaic! What about women's lib? To prevent herself from saying anything rude, she decided to change the subject, and complimented Priya on the delicacy of her needlework. 'Are you making these to sell?'

'Oh no. This is for my married home.'

'May I?' Toni reached out and took the finely-stitched serviette. It was impressive. 'But you could sell these at the market and make good money!' she exclaimed.

'My husband will support me,' Priya said, taking the piece back after a moment to continue sewing.

'But... but then you'll be dependent on him!' Toni protested. 'Wouldn't you rather have your own income?'

'Of course I will be dependent on him,' Priya replied, looking at her evenly. 'He is promising to be my husband and support me my whole life.'

'But...'

'I will keep the house and raise our children. That will be my fulfillment.'

'I could find a buyer for this great stuff you're making,' Toni said, unable to let it go. 'I'm sure you could sell it for a really good price.'

Priya smiled. 'I am glad you like my work but it is not necessary.'

Toni tried again later with their mother but Srividya wasn't having a bar of it. In fact, she seemed shocked that a mere 'child' would have a business idea or want to discuss such things with the adults, Toni observed. Her own parents would have welcomed the suggestion and taken it seriously, but here... It seemed like such a waste! So much talent and potential would be wasted while Priya was busy meeting her household's needs.

'May I buy a few pieces to take home and show my family?' Toni asked, secretly intending to sell them at a fabulous price and totally surprise Priya and her stubborn mother by sending them the profit.

Perhaps Srividya guessed Toni's thoughts. 'It's all about money in these days,' she sniffed, after consenting. 'Everyone wants to make money! You used to be able to get a worker for fifty rupees a day, and now you spend one hundred and fifty!'

One hundred and fifty rupees... Toni did a quick calculation. That was about three dollars. This woman must be joking! No wonder India was in the poop. She watched as her hostess rapidly rolled curried patties between her hands and piled them on a plate. As ever, her gold bangles jangled prettily around her wrists with her movements.

'Indian women like gold – don't you?' Toni remarked, indicating the bangles.

'It is our insurance,' Srividya replied, pausing to raise one arm and admire her jewellery. 'Gold is good investment. Indian women hold eleven per cent of the world's gold,' she added meaningfully.

'Truly?'

Srividya bobbed her head in a kind of yes-no response.

'My mother has been collecting gold jewellery for me since I was born,' Priya said, entering the kitchen. 'I have gold rings and earrings and necklaces and hairpins – all in a beautiful jewellery box. Would you like to see?'

'I sure would!' Toni replied, standing immediately.

Mother and daughter smiled and nodded. Srividya washed her hands and they led Toni into the parental bedroom, with its sweet incense aroma and heavily brocaded scarlet bedspread and wall hangings. A jewellery box was carried to the bed and opened carefully, and Toni caught her breath at the glittering treasure inside. There was not only gold in here, but rubies and diamonds and emeralds too, studded into the gold pieces.

'Do you have a box for Naarani as well?' Toni asked, touching a necklace as if to check that it was real.

'Oh yes,' the girls' mother said proudly. 'No gold, no marriage. Even the poorest woman will have a gold nose ring at least.'

'My fiancé and parents-in-law will give me more gold also,' Priya said comfortably, letting a gold chain run between her fingers.

'But if a woman is widowed, she can be stripped of her gold,' Naarani said from the doorway. 'It goes back to the family. Some women still throw themselves on funeral pyres when their husband dies.'

'This old tradition is dying out,' their mother tutted, frowning. 'Most are lucky: their family looks after them.' She began to scoop the treasures back into the box while Toni stared at the three of them in barely-concealed horror.

'But this stores of gold is ruining our economy,' Naarani pointed out. 'It sits in vaults and on our persons and not used by exchanging to grow the economy.'

Her mother glanced at her irritably, and Naarani ducked out of the room.

Conscious that she was questioning many of their practices, and wary of causing a family quarrel, Toni steered the conversation in a safer direction. 'I know it's beautiful but why gold and not… silver, for instance?' she wondered aloud.

'Gold is a symbol of the Hindu goddess Lakshmi,' Priya replied. 'It is auspicious to possess gold. Also gold has healing properties. It is given to babies in their first food.'

'What – to eat?' Toni asked, startled.

'Yes, gold powder,' Srividya explained. She stopped for a moment, listening, then called out to her husband loudly, making Toni jump. He replied from the hallway, and Srividya nodded to herself in that sideways head-bobbing way Indians had.

'He is saying goodnight to the two sons of Parvati,' Srividya told Toni.

'You mean… to the statue in the hallway…?' Toni asked cautiously.

'Yes. We pay respect to our gods.'
What a different world this was.

Do you rely on your parents to provide for you, eg. food, shelter, material goods, services?

Do you help out around the house?

Are you paid pocket money?

Some parents believe it's their responsibility to provide it all, while others require contribution from their children.

What seems fair to you?

Which option develops more responsibility and more skills?

Is your family in a feud over money?

Is there anyone they won't speak to anymore?

Do the key players remember what the issue was about?

Do they want to make the family more important than the issue, or has the issue taken over?

What are the pros and cons of a life lived simply, close to the earth?

What are the pros and cons of a life lived immersed in technology?

What are the pros and cons of a rote-learning type of education?

What are the pros and cons of a creative, individualised type of education?

Should children be obedient to their parents?

How much of a role should traditions play?

The perpetuation of tradition is one of the factors that keep many stuck in poverty.

Would you consider an arranged marriage if you knew that the statistics for a long-term, fulfilling marriage were better this way?

Sometimes those statistics are better because women in arranged marriages can't afford to leave husbands who exploit them or are just not as suitable as expected, but often it's because the choices made are based on compatibility (and a whole host of factors) rather than simply attraction.

How do you plan to insure your lifestyle?

Will you invest in property or gold or other assets to build your wealth and guard against that rainy day?

CHAPTER 18

DAY 13: DIGESTING INDIA

Coming together again as a group after the homestay generated mixed feelings. For many, there was relief to be back with people who thought like they did, and to be somewhat 'cushioned' from the intensity of directly living such different lifestyles. But others were now so intrigued and fascinated by the different perspectives on this side of the world that they wanted more. A day had been set aside for relaxation and sharing their experiences, so they sprawled in the shade, exchanging stories and opinions.

'I was so nervous about staying with strangers!' one of the girls said, 'but they were really nice, really friendly.'

'And so generous,' someone else said. 'You can see they've hardly got anything and yet they would share everything.'

'But how are the contradictions!' one of the guys interrupted. 'Basic as anything lifestyles – you know, dirt floors, washing at a communal pump – but they've all got friggin' TV sets!'

'All countries must have these opposites but it seems so extreme here,' Jackson mused. 'Like corruption and spirituality: constant praying and gods and religious festivals, and also all the bribes and cheating. How's everyone wanting to be a traffic cop for the bribe money!'

'*Baksheesh!*' a voice called out, echoing the Indian cry for a tip – or bribe.

'Do they really mean it, all the constant praying and ceremonies?' Toni wondered. 'They're so quick sometimes, like it's just a meaningless ritual.'

'I reckon they do,' Chlöe said. 'They believe in it all so much, and the priests would take it all pretty seriously. But probably there are heaps of people who are just parroting the prayers.'

'Did anyone else go to school?' one student asked.

'I did!' Brooke said.

'Unreal, eh? All that rote learning. Seems so old-fashioned.'

'So you prefer our school, then?' Mr Plowright asked. His bald head was a bright shade of pink after three days lazing around and reading in the sun while he was 'off duty' during their homestays.

'Don't get too excited,' the student told him drily, suppressing a smile.

'Everyone here is cramming for the best scores since there's so much competition.' Brooke remembered being surrounded by dark heads bent over books – and Fathi diligently studying each evening.

'Survival,' Jackson stated. 'So many people! You've gotta be pushy to survive, to say nothing of get ahead.'

'So is our Western lifestyle too cushy?' Mr Plowright asked them. 'Not enough challenge?'

'Yeah...' a couple of voices conceded. 'We've got it easy. We're too soft.'

'Some things are definitely better here,' Brooke said. 'Like, I was staying with a single mum but she's not alone and struggling the way my mother is. She's a widow, so she doesn't even get alimony from the dad, but she's got this neighbor who just about lives at her place and they help each other out, and, yeah, I liked that. My mum would be much happier if she wasn't so alone but her best friends live ages away and she doesn't really know any of the people in our street.'

Life at home was not nearly as communal as in India, they reflected. In their world people got home after work or school and locked the front door – suburban streets were pretty empty; whereas here so much living happened in the streets and in shared spaces: cooking, talking, playing, business deals...

'Financial wealth, emotional wealth...' Mr Plowright scratched his peeling scalp and then put his cap back on. 'Which is better?'

'Neither,' Jackson said. 'Both. Pros and cons.'

Brooke immediately wanted to hear more about the royal lifestyle, and was taken aback by what he shared. Like Jackson, she'd always assumed that life was easier if you were rich – Toni, for instance: Toni had every latest gadget, her parents drove the latest cars, she had no trouble affording anything... no wonder she was so cheerful and confident! But here he was, popping the pretty idea Brooke had about rich, happy families...

Toni spoke up then, pointing out that inherited wealth was a very different thing to wealth you created yourself. Her own parents worked such long hours that they were hardly ever home. She'd been the typical latchkey kid, letting herself in after school for many years.

She shared this in a light-hearted tone, but Brooke wondered how honestly Toni was conveying her feelings. Also a latchkey kid, because her mother was the sole parent and sole breadwinner (aside from irregular contributions from Brooke's father), Brooke did not enjoy arriving home to a dark, empty house. Not since she'd been to Laura's, whose mother was a bright, warm presence always at home, baking and cooking and doing artwork with them.

'You don't necessarily need to work crazy hours to build wealth, though,' Mr Plowright said. 'I can give you an example from within our very ranks. Miss Harris –'

'Where *is* Miss Harris?' someone asked suddenly, looking around.

'She's with Dylan,' someone else replied. 'He's been puking.'

There were sympathetic expressions from the group since several, by now, had either had a stint of illness or witnessed someone who had.

'You're saying Miss Harris is rich?' Jackson asked sceptically. He'd had more to do with her than most of the other kids since she was the PE teacher and he was involved in a number of sports, and she didn't give the impression of wealth at all. She drove a Toyota Yaris, wore tracksuits and trainers to work every day, and brought her own lunch. Sure, she did a lot of overtime, like coaching team sports after hours and attending camps but that would all be part of her salary, wouldn't it, rather than extra income – so how could she be rich?

'It would be out of turn for me to divulge Miss Harris's financial circumstances to you without her permission,' Mr Plowright said, 'but what I can tell you is that she might live frugally, but she's probably one of the wealthiest members of staff.'

'Other than Mr Baxter, I guess,' a voice called out, referring to the principal.

'No, including.'

There was a little titter of surprise from the group.

'Inheritance?' someone asked.

He shook his head, a twinkle in his eye.

'Investments,' someone said knowledgeably.

He nodded. 'She's been saving diligently since she was about your age, and got into the property market very young. I think she bought her first property when she was nineteen or so, and since then she's amassed a portfolio of properties all over the country that are worth quite a lot of money. They're generating enough income that her work at school is extra – she only teaches because she loves you guys so much.' He said this with a grin, knowing the general student perception of Miss Harris, then added, 'And all those properties are increasing in value if she ever wants to sell them. Ask her about it. She'll tell you.'

Toni's respect for the sport teacher, whom she'd rarely given the time of day, had just soared. She made a mental note to quiz Miss Harris further. Jackson exchanged surprised expressions with some of his mates and Brooke raised her brows at Laura. As for Eric, he'd been very quiet since returning from his village experience. Now he remarked that the secretary of a friend of his family was wealthier than her CEO boss, who earned three or four times as much as she did.

'No shit! How?' someone called out.

'Lifestyle,' Eric said. 'The boss spends up big. He's got huge debts.'

Mr Plowright nodded. 'Living beyond your means is easily done. I'm guilty of that myself,' he added, with a comical expression. 'So, Eric, how was the village?'

Eric regarded him thoughtfully. 'To be honest, Mr Plowright, I didn't think I'd survive without my phone and the internet or TV, but... it was good.'

Their teacher smiled. 'I'm glad. India's is a very family and community-oriented culture, and the Bishnoi people are a great example of that. Our indigenous people are similar.'

'I think it's great to keep old traditions alive,' Toni said, 'but sometimes they just don't make sense. Or they're so old-fashioned it's ridiculous!'

'Arranged marriages?' Laura asked.

Toni gave an emphatic, wide-eyed nod.

'But the stats on arranged marriages run in their favour,' Mr Plowright said. 'It's all just different values.'

'The family I was with,' Chlöe interrupted, 'the mother put *turmeric* on her face!'

'Why?' Brooke demanded. 'Wouldn't that make your skin go yellow?'

'Uh-huh! They're trying to lighten their skin to look more Western.'

'That's weird.'

'But they're also kind of resentful of the British, which is understandable,' Toni said. 'So why try to look like Westerners?'

'People are complicated,' Mr Plowright said simply. 'We're all complicated.'

All cultures contain contradictions and polarities.

In fact, the more extreme wealth, the more extreme poverty.

Do you feel that the ideal society would be more balanced or do you think the extremes serve us?

Do you belong to a spiritual or religious family or community?

Do you engage in these practices with belief and attention or are you just going along with it?

Does your religious tradition believe that it is spiritual to be poor or that abundance is our spiritual birthright?

In the past, and in developing nations like India,

people dug their own wells and drew their own water, grew their own food, made their own clothes and tools, defended their property, and walked long distances since there was no car or public transport to jump into...

Do you feel that the modern western lifestyle is 'cushy'?

Have we become a dependent and unskilled people?

If there were a power breakdown and everything run by electricity simply stopped, how would you survive? (That would mean no water, limited food, no lighting, no heating or cooling, no computers, no devices of any kind...)

Does your family participate in the local community?

Do you know your neighbours or others in your street?

Do you recognise others in your shopping centre?

Do you feel alone or do you feel that you are surrounded by friends?

If there were a crisis, do you have people you can turn to?

Do you have prosperous emotional, family and community 'bank accounts'? (In other words, you feel abundant and resourceful in those areas of your life.)

Do you have the belief that rich families are happy families?

Do you believe that more money is the answer to your problems?

Have you heard the saying that a lack of money is never the problem; the problem is a lack of creativity?

Or that money follows when you do what you love?

Or that a happy person is always happy, no matter what they have or don't have, while an unhappy person is always unhappy, no matter what they have or don't have. What do you think?

Mothers who stay home to raise children put 'home duties' on forms as their 'occupation'. Most mothers do this work 'for free'.

Did you know that a mother's home duties have been valued at close to $120,000 per annum? That's what it would cost to pay someone to provide all the services a mother provides.

How many more women would stay at home if they were paid to do the housework and raise their children?

If the children are the wealth and future of a nation, do you think the roles of parent and teacher should be paid to reflect that importance?

Were you surprised to read that a secretary can be wealthier than her CEO boss?

It's all in the way money is managed.

If your lifestyle expenses exceed your income, be prepared for a shock...

CHAPTER 19

Days 14-16: From Village to Ashram to Seaside City via Overnight Train

The following day they bumped for ages along a road marred by potholes to visit a local village school. Donkeys and camels and goats shared the road with them, and a variety of vehicles rattled by on either side of them. They passed tiny roadside stalls whose owners were selling papaya or guava or pomegranate or passion fruit, or a whole array of items like biscuits and chocolate bars, shampoos in tiny sachets, and lollies in cellophane bags. You could even buy one single cigarette – because some Indians couldn't afford a whole packet at a time, their driver told them.

When they were still a kilometre or so away from the school they caught sight of many blue-shirted students looking out for them. The students grinned and waved and then turned and ran ahead of them to the school, while the bus followed slowly, dipping into potholes and bumping over rocks. When they pulled up in the dusty road beside the school and piled out, more people gathered around to stare at them, drivers even stopping their motorbikes in the middle of the road to look.

'I can't get over how famous we are!' Chlöe giggled, flapping at a fly. 'Wherever we go, we're celebrities!'

It felt even more like that a few moments later when, one by one, they were dabbed with red paint between the eyes as part of a welcome ceremony. Then each student was decorated with a garland of yellow flowers and guided past a whole row of students so that they could greet each other with a 'Namaste!' and a two-handed high-five that was so enthusiastic at times that **Eric**'s hands were burning by the time he'd reached the last student.

'They're so cute!' Brooke cooed in delight, as the lines of students dissolved into a chaotic crowd. She already had one small child on her hip and another two were hanging onto her spare hand.

Brightwood College was going to become a patron of this small, rural school and make regular contributions toward books and uniforms and equipment and new buildings. Today they were to be divided into two groups: one group would listen to children reading in English and interact with them, and the other group would assist with the building of an additional classroom. The following day they would swap, but first, a Puja Prayer Ceremony to bless the project with success and prosperity!

The ceremony was a blur of colour and incense, flowers and candles, and sing-song prayers in Hindi. Eric's own family was Christian but one day he intended to find out more about his ancestral family's beliefs and religion. He suspected that his forebears had participated in rituals such as these. When the ceremony was over, he and his group were directed toward the plot of land where the new classroom was to be built while the others headed into the shabby old classrooms with the children.

The 'builders' were each given a pick and a shovel, tools Eric had never handled before in his life, and spent the next few (tedious and painful) hours digging rocks out of the earth to make room for the foundations of the new building. Lunch came as a grand relief for his smarting hands. They sat on the ground with the Indian men who had been guiding their work, and tucked into a meal of rice flavoured with grated coconut and fried onion, and were then taught to make mud bricks. By the time they were driving back to their accommodation later that afternoon, Eric felt exhausted but satisfied; the following morning the satisfaction remained but he felt worse: muscles he'd never even known he had all ached at once.

He was glad to leave the construction work to the other group this time. Chattering, happy students welcomed him and his classmates into a bare room that boasted one blackboard, one piece of chalk, and one stick... for beating naughty kids? A picture of Saraswati, the goddess of education and music, was tacked to the grimy wall and some fifty more children sat on the floor and on a few hard wooden benches, gazing up at them.

The children were supposed to be copying English words from the blackboard into their books, and the Brightwood students' role was to listen to the children put those words into sensible sentences. Eric found himself sitting next to a small girl with big, serious eyes who was surely the only one not smiling in the place. He listened to her faltering English, but when he attempted to correct some errors that their teacher had made on the board, the little girl looked up at him with tear-stained eyes, and he felt terrible.

An older girl sitting next to them must have sensed his distress. She glanced across and, seeing the girl's wet cheeks, whispered to Eric, 'She is crying because she is beaten today. She want no school. She want to look after her baby brother but she must come school.'

'Oh,' he said. He couldn't imagine preferring childcare over school. And the kid was only some six years old herself! 'You speak very good English,' he complimented the older girl.

She smiled. 'I will be a doctor. I study hard.'

'Good luck,' he said. Her use of the future tense seemed to be more a measure of her certainty than of awkward English. She ducked her head back to her books, as if to demonstrate her dedication, and he turned back to the young child sitting beside him. The girl snaked her hand into his trustingly, and he no longer had the heart to correct anything.

On their way back to their accommodation later that afternoon, **Brooke** sat quietly in the bus remembering her walk along a narrow, steep and rocky path to collect water from the well with some of the Indian women. At first it had felt like a game, carrying the empty clay pot on her head and joking about how hard it was to balance even without water in it! The women had laughed good-naturedly at their visitors' awkwardness.

But then they'd arrived at the well and filled their pots, and she had nearly cried out at how heavy it was and how difficult to keep it centred on her head. Walking back slowly, with two hands gripping the pot to hold it steady, she'd kept a cheerful smile pasted on her face, but she had felt shocked and disturbed. At home, she flicked a tap on as often as she wanted every day, without giving it a second thought. All the water she needed for drinks, for cleaning, for cooking, for bathing was there in an instant. She took water for granted.

The Indian women who walked ahead of her and behind her said they made this trip up to fifteen times a day. It wasn't far – for them, sure-footed and experienced at balancing stuff on their heads, it only took a few minutes rather than the quarter of an hour it took Brooke and her classmates, but still… what if she had to make a walk like this every time she wanted a drink of water? She would certainly appreciate water much more. Her respect for the women had grown enormously with every step she took. One of the women said she had been living in that village for fifty years; she had married at the age of twelve and probably been carrying those jugs of water multiple times every day since then. Imagine that… A few times Brooke had stumbled and automatically looked down to check her footing, and then been doused as cold water sloshed over the rim of her pot. The whole experience had been a rude awakening. She felt humbled, tired, sad and grateful all at once.

'It's very different in China,' Eric said, his voice coming from behind her. 'China sends students to the West and pays for everything – fares, course fees and board – but the student is under contract to go back to China at the end of their course. And if they don't pass every subject, they have to pay the whole lot for themselves. So there's no brain drain out of China.'

'Ah,' Mr Plowright replied. 'That's quite an incentive. Whereas Indian students go West and then stay there?'

'Yes. And that rote-learning style of education isn't developing the skills they need to solve their problems. They're going to have to get very creative to figure out what to do about the over-population and the challenges that brings for meeting energy and infrastructure needs.'

'It always looks easier to fix from the outside,' Mr Plowright murmured.

'But they need to get outside their own perspective,' Eric said intently. 'You know what one of the older kids said to me today?'

'No, what?'

'That her teacher said that India was the most technologically advanced country in the world.'

Mr Plowright gave a little chuckle. His and Eric's voices continued in low tones behind Brooke. She was just beginning to doze off when someone called out, 'Look! There!'

Her eyes snapped open. Her classmates were standing up and cramming to the front and left side of the bus.

'What is it?' she asked, trying to see.

'Don't know,' someone called back. 'Crowds of people on the road singing and dancing.'

Brooke pressed close to the window, craning her neck. The bus had slowed down because the road ahead was swamped with people, and now the driver stopped altogether and announced, 'You are very fortunate, isn't it? This is an Indian wedding. We are nearly back to the hotel. You can visit here the wedding and then walk to the hotel from here. Go, go!' And he opened the creaky door and waved them out of the bus, beaming.

'What about our stuff?' someone asked.

'I will bring for you. Go, go!'

'But will they mind?' Miss Harris asked, stopping the outflow of students with her hand. 'We haven't been invited.'

'*Everyone* is invited to an Indian wedding!' their driver declared happily. 'Go, go!'

Grabbing her camera, Brooke descended from the bus with the others, and was immediately swallowed up in the crowd. There must have been hundreds of people in the street, all smiling and dancing around and throwing rice and flower petals. Somewhere drums were being played and bells were ringing and voices were chanting in Hindi, or perhaps it was their sacred language of prayers, Sanskrit. She was jostled along, laughing, caught up in this joyous, frenetic parade with no idea what was going on. At one point she caught a glimpse of a man dressed in white clothes and a turban on a horse – the groom? At another point she thought she saw Jackson talking to Ahmed – that guy turned up everywhere!

Without having any idea where she was going, she allowed herself to flow with the wave of partygoers until she found herself entering the bride's home. She hesitated on the threshold but it was impossible to turn back – she was being pressed forward! Deafened by the loud voices and traditional Indian music, bewitched by the smells of incense and spices, fascinated by the colours and people and ornate decorations on all sides, she allowed herself to be pushed this way and that… until there, seated on an abundance of plush cushions, she came upon the bride in a gorgeous hot pink sari, her bare arms and feet stretched out as women knelt around her applying henna in complex, swirling patterns, everyone happy, laughing, talking.

By the time Brooke had extricated herself from the strangers' home, dusk was falling. She had learnt that this was only one ceremony in a week's worth of wedding rituals and celebrations. The marriage ceremony was due to occur in a few days' time. Someone in the bride's family had warmly welcomed her back to join them. The marriage would be wonderful – she would love it! Brooke had promised to do her best to come back, and she truly hoped she could. Right now she was feeling a little sick after eating too many rich Indian sweets, but holy crap! That had been an experience to remember. These Indians sure did know how to celebrate!

The day after the wild pre-wedding they were driven to an ashram for a taste of spiritual India. Yoga and meditation, now so commonplace in the west, had once been completely unknown in their part of the world, and all of that had begun right here, in India.

They were greeted at the vine-covered gate to the ashram by a holy man who was naked to the waist. He wore only a white sheet that was wrapped around his midriff and between his legs, strings of brown, wooden beads around his neck, and a red dot on his forehead. His head was partly shaven. He waited for all the students to descend from the bus then held his hands together in the prayer position and bowed, saying, 'Namaste'.

'You know, we've been saying that all this time and I still don't know what it means,' **Jackson** murmured to Toni,

'I honour the divine in you,' she replied.

'What?' He was about to scoff at her for sending up the monk when he realised she was answering his question. 'Really?'

'Yep.'

'Oh...'

Their group was guided on a tour of the ashram, which was spread out across a large tract of land surrounded by vegetable gardens and fields, since they grew food for their many monks, students, and overseas visitors. The buildings included a meditation room, a large dining hall, dormitories, a library, and many more purpose-built spaces, most of them displaying pictures of gurus and spiritual teachers who wore beads or garlands around their necks. A curly symbol that apparently said 'Om' and meant a whole heap of things (including 'soul' and 'self' and ''Truth' and 'the entire cosmos') was on view everywhere too, along with images or statues of gods like Brooke's favourite, Ganesha the Elephant God, and the three Hindu gods: Brahma the Creator, Vishnu the Preserver, and Shiva the Destroyer or Transformer.

A god of destruction, Jackson pondered. It made sense that you would acknowledge the destructive force in life as an equal power, rather than just ignore it. After all, you couldn't start a new cycle if you didn't finish the old one.

He was taken aback to find the shape of the swastika in numerous places as well, and their guide explained that this ancient symbol had been 'hijacked' and stigmatised by the Nazis; to Indians it was a symbol of good fortune and the sun or the passage of time, and it had been used by Indians for some 5000 years before Adolf Hitler designed the Nazi flag.

In a courtyard, they paused to watch an Indian woman draw a mandala on the ground with white chalk that she sprinkled from her fingers, creating shapes that repeated themselves over and over within the circle. Their guide explained that the mandala was thought to bring good luck and to welcome the gods.

After the tour they were invited to join a yoga class on the lawn outside. Most of the students were white-skinned adult Westerners who were seeking peace or spiritual guidance at the ashram. Jackson and his mates repressed giggles as they tried to replicate the various postures and discovered where the limits to their flexibility lay. Some of the girls, who were dance students, stunned them with their ability to adopt any pose that was presented to them, and do it perfectly, and a few breakdancers in their school group impressed the crowd with their headstands. It was good to stretch, though, and a set of movements called 'Salute to the Sun' gave Jackson a quiet, centred feeling.

A vegetarian lunch followed the yoga class. They joined the crowds in the expansive dining room, which was remarkably quiet given how many people were present, and stood in the queue to receive a large tin plate with separate compartments for rice, dhal (the lentil mixture that was so commonly eaten here), vegetables, yoghurt, and the round Indian flat bread called chappati. Jackson found himself sitting at the long benches next to an Italian woman with a lovely smile. When he asked how long she had been staying at the ashram, she replied, 'This time, two weeks. But I've been coming here for eleven years now. I come every year. It's my sabbatical, my sanity.'

'Really? Eleven years!'

'It's difficult for Italians to explore their spirituality in Italy,' the woman, whose name was Gita, explained. 'With the Church so strong…'

She asked how he was finding India and he answered that it was good, although very confronting, and a dimple appeared in her cheek as she smiled at this. 'Not only confronting,' she said, leaning in towards him, 'but *magical*. Have you experienced India's magic yet?'

'You mean… that it's beautiful?' he asked, dipping his bread into the yoghurt.

'More than that,' she said. 'I really mean magic.'

He looked at her quizzically, chewing.

'For instance, you need something, and the next minute it's there. You turn a corner, and it's there.'

'Uh-huh,' he said, humouring her. 'Like what?'

'Like the time I wanted to buy a certain statue and the price was greater than I wanted to spend. A boy turned up at my elbow ten minutes later and asked if I wanted to buy the very same statue – and led me to a place where it was half the price.'

Ahmed flashed into Jackson's mind – but that had been different.

'Another time,' Gita said, warming up, 'I was walking through a village and a girl came to me and said, 'You have to see my grandfather. He is not well.' How did they know I do healing work? I don't know. I never saw them before. I went with her to her home and sat with her grandfather and he said, 'Guruji works through you.'' Gita shook her head in amazement; she was obviously still very moved by this experience.

'The magic is even more powerful here, in the ashram,' she said, looking around. 'Once I was at the end of my trip and I had to leave early for my flight home, so I took a seat at the back of the room to not disturb people when I left. The attendants wouldn't let me sit there – they insisted I get up and go right to the front to a spot exactly in front of where Guruji was sitting to give his talk. I tried to argue and explain, but they insisted. So I sat there. Guruji was chanting in their language and all of a sudden he stopped and looked right at me and said in English, 'You're not meant to have children in this lifetime.' How did he know that was my question? I cried and cried and cried.' She stopped speaking to dab at her eyes with the corner of her shawl. Jackson sat, food forgotten, spellbound by her stories.

'People think they come to India to bliss out but they come here to learn lessons,' Gita said. 'The love here brings anything unlike itself up to the surface. And the law of karma is very strong here. One time a bent old woman pushed me out of the way; minutes later a space opened up around her and someone pushed her and she staggered just as I had. Instant karma.'

'Karma,' he said. 'That's…?'

'The Law of Cause and Effect: what you put out comes back to you.'

'Oh. Yeah, I've heard of that.'

'There's even more magic,' she said, her meal forgotten. 'We have friends whose daughter was mixed up with a – let's say, not a very good man, and my friend's husband had a condition on his leg that was causing it to shrink. Guruji manifested a jar of ointment out of thin air for the man to put on his leg. After some months of rubbing on this ointment, his leg stopped shrinking. And the girl lost interest in that man, like Guruji said she would.'

'Out of thin air?' Jackson echoed. She was losing him now. That was too weird for words.

'Out of thin air,' Gita repeated. 'It happens all the time around here. Miracles all the time. All your beliefs about what is so and what is possible are confronted and contradicted in India, and especially in an ashram.' She picked up her fork to resume her forgotten meal, and then added, 'You know how crazy India is? Delays, power cuts, red tape… But if the Swami wants something to happen, it just happens. No delays. Like magic.'

'I'd like to meet him,' Jackson said. This was pretty weird shit. It was like wizard stuff for real – if it was. And if it was, that was wicked! It was seriously insane!

'He is speaking at two p.m. in the main hall,' she said. 'You should come.'

It turned out that they had no choice. His whole group was ushered into the hall that afternoon for a lecture on love and peace. Jackson sat cross-legged with the others, longing to see a miracle, but nothing out of the ordinary happened – that he was aware of. He saw the odd person in tears or smiling rapturously, but most were just listening quietly to their guru, very still on their mats, faces turned to the tall, grey-bearded man seated on the platform in front of them. He did have a very restful, deep, slow voice, and a calmness pervaded the room as he spoke.

Jackson was drifting sleepily when the session flowed from the talk into a meditation, and suddenly he was wide awake and restless as anything. Apparently they only sat in silence for half an hour but it felt like three or four hours to him. Everything that could itch, itched. Every irrelevant thought he could possibly have had passed through his mind. Every little sound around him distracted him from the task of breathing and focusing on the breath. If this was meditation, he wasn't sure that he was up for it, he thought grumpily, when they were finally free to stretch out their stiff legs and stand up.

As they walked through the courtyard on their way back to the bus, they passed a group of women sitting on the ground in saris and headscarves, singing and playing drums and bells and hand-clackers. The students paused for a while, watching and listening, and Jackson scoured the women for a sign of Gita, but she wasn't there. Her stories had left their mark on him though.

Their India trip was already drawing to a close. Tonight the group would be travelling to Mumbai via overnight train to spend their last few days in the seaside city before flying home. The state of Rajasthan had enchanted them with its wealth and grandeur, its warrior desert people and simple villagers, its animal sanctuaries and natural beauty. Packing her belongings, **Toni** promised herself that she would return one day to deepen and extend her exploration of this fascinating part of the country.

She and Brooke had managed to experience the actual wedding ceremony at the temple the previous evening, and they had watched, fascinated, as the groom led his bride in a circle several times and tied knots in a necklace signifying his promises to be good to her and make her a good home and share a good life together. Then his bride had led him in circles. She glittered and glowed in her red and gold sari, and was so decked out with jewellery and henna that she didn't have a single patch of bare skin.

One of the guests had described some of the other hilarious features of the wedding that they would miss out on – such as the rush to their seats at the wedding table to determine which one of the newly married couple would rule the roost; and the bride's relatives stealing the couple's shoes so that the groom would have to pay bribe money to reclaim them; and the symbolic foods they would feed each other; and the way their clothes would be tied together, also as a symbol of their union. And there would be Bollywood dancing and music until late, though the married couple would be stuck on a dais to receive congratulations and gifts for hours on end from the hundreds of guests. It sounded rich and marvelous, and they wished they could attend, but here they were, back in the bus on their way to the train station with all their luggage, ready for a new adventure of their own.

Arriving at the station, the Brightwood students stood together in a huddle while their teachers submitted their tickets – and returned in consternation because the stationmaster claimed that the tickets had not been confirmed. Their teachers returned to the office and the students hovered, laughing when one of the boys shot out of his seat in alarm at something, and then bumping together in shared anxiety when a big rat emerged from under his seat and sniffed around their pile of luggage. The girls squealed and darted away and the guys tried to look nonchalant, and the surrounding Indians laughed and pointed at them. All *they* did when the rat drew near was tap the toe of their shoe at it, and it ran away...

The train arrived and Toni's group hesitated, wanting to board but unsure if they were free to travel, and worried that any seats they might have had would be taken by the hordes of people cramming into the train. In the nick of time the official returned to acknowledge that yes, the seats *had* been confirmed after all. Hugely relieved, they climbed aboard and looked for their berths in the already-full carriage.

The sleeper train trip had been booked to give them a 'unique, cultural experience', and that was immediately apparent. 'You might not sleep very well tonight,' Miss Harris had warned, 'which is why we've scheduled a relaxed first day in Mumbai. So enjoy the journey!' There were so many people on board the train that it looked like it was going to be standing room only, but when the whistle blew, a number of people disembarked – probably family that had just boarded to farewell the traveller.

Toni had expected nice little carriages with cute little beds all made up. Instead, they found only seats, and stood around with their backpacks and suitcases at their feet, waiting for the carriage attendant to arrive and make up their berths. Why they weren't already made up, she had no idea, but she could see the fellow in the distance with an armful of pillows and sheets, adjusting seats from daytime to sleeping positions. And how all these people were going to fit, she also had no idea. There seemed to be twenty people for every eight seats. Her group was stretched out across one carriage and into the next, and she wondered if some of them were going to find themselves sitting up all through the night…

The train had barely rumbled into motion before the first person came through selling his wares. 'Chai, chai, chai!' the fellow called, squeezing among the passengers with his hot drinks. He was followed by another calling, 'Samosas!' and a woman with a baby slung on her back playing maracas and singing for money.

When this entertaining 'circus' had passed through, Toni took note of the passengers sitting nearby – the usual staring men, giggling adolescent boys, and mothers with children and what seemed to be all their worldly goods… and settled into an interesting conversation with a young

German woman who was spending a year travelling and volunteering at various places around the world. She was relaxed and confident as she rattled off the list of places she had already visited, inspiring Toni to add 'backpacking' to her bucket list. A family of smiling Indians joined their conversation and brought out a parcel of home-made pakoras that they insisted on sharing with Toni and Claudia. Toni bit into the cold but tasty deep-fried cauliflower, wishing that she had something to offer them.

At one stop, a pair of dolled-up transvestites came aboard, to her amazement. They approached the Indians for money and were either waved away or paid quickly, as if extended contact with them could bring bad luck, but they didn't trouble the Westerners, other than to cast them arrogant glances. More sellers pushed their way into the carriage with their wares: chai tea again, very sweet coffee, samosas, sandwiches wrapped in vine leaves, mutton biriyani, chicken biriyani, pastries, water… You surely wouldn't get hungry, but you also soon ran out of money. Toni showed her empty wallet to one insistent 'wallah', and shrugged that, much as she wanted to buy, she couldn't. He laughed, not believing her, but moved on.

She put off a visit to the loo for as long as she could, and then had to go. When she slid the door open she found Indian toilets only – squatting affairs. Not the easiest thing to do in a moving vehicle. On her way back to her berth she paused in the open doorway to look outside and get a breath of fresh air. Even this little space was packed: people standing and smoking, or sitting with their feet hanging out, all gazing at passing countryside where fertile farm fields were being worked by brightly clad folk. She stood watching for a while, until the scene faded into the gathering dusk.

It was close to midnight before all the berths had been made up. Their group mostly had upper berths, and Toni could understand why those positions weren't favoured by the Indians – it was a job to climb into them. But once up there, it was good to have a bit of private space.

There began a very long night. Someone seemed to be coughing or hawking or snoring all the way through those dark hours. Finally, unable to sleep, Toni stumbled from her berth, accidentally putting her hand on someone's face and mumbling an apology, and then grazing her shin on someone's massive tin trunk, which made her curse aloud… and squeezed her way back through the crowded corridor to the open carriage door where she found the usual small crowd enjoying the cool breeze that was flowing in, standing and rocking with the train's motion or sitting against walls, some fast asleep, others awake and chatting.

In the morning there was a constant queue for the toilet, which was not the most inviting place to visit by the time you succeeded. When they stopped at a station, people battled their way off the train with their luggage while even more people seemed to come aboard, including beggars and sellers, some of whom seemed to be boarding the train just to use the toilets… The carriage attendant eventually arrived to collect sheets and pillows and put their berths into the upright daytime position. Toni tried to straighten her clothes and hair. She felt like a horrible mess, with bad breath and bags under her eyes and dirty hands, but so did everyone else. Their expressions told her that her classmates had found the journey equally uncomfortable and entertaining.

Claudia pulled off her jumper since the day was already warm, revealing a grinning face on her t-shirt with the slogan, *'If you smile at me I will understand. Smiling is a universal language.'*

In developing nations, one's children are one's wealth

because they will care for the parents and provide for them in their old age, especially when the country doesn't have adequate social services, but keeping children at home means they remain uneducated and the nation becomes unable to break out of its vicious cycle of poverty.

Can you imagine being responsible for the care of younger children at the age of six?

Can you imagine marrying at twelve?

Can you imagine never or hardly ever going to school because you are working in the fields or caring for children?

Do you take water for granted?

Do you unconsciously waste it, since you haven't had to collect it?

With so many different cultures in the world, it becomes clear that all traditions are subjective; there is no one 'right way'.

This diversity creates a rich and interesting world.

Do you feel you would become more tolerant
the more differences you encountered, or more
threatened and protective of your own lifestyle?

Does your family engage in rich traditions?

Are they meaningful to you?

What do you make of the 'magic' in India?

Do you think it's just weird or possible?

The West holds a very materialistic, scientific view of the world; the East has a more spiritual and esoteric view of the world.

Together they provide a 'wholeness'.

Hinduism's three gods are testimony to this wholeness, a pattern we can observe everywhere in our lives:

our bodily cells are created, maintained for a
period, and then destroyed; our friendships
are created, maintained for a period, and then
give way to new friendships; our interests are
created, maintained for a period, and then give
way to new interests...

**Wealth is not just material.
Will you ensure that your life is mentally and emotionally rich and stimulating?**

Will you try new experiences like a sleeper train trip in India, or yoga and meditation?

Will you go backpacking or volunteering?

Will you give your money or time and energy to others? – there are benefits for them and you.

These are the experiences that build our character, our knowledge, our interests and our wisdom, all of which combine as our inner wealth.

How will you build yours?

CHAPTER 20

Days 16-19: Mumbai to Finish

It was raining when they arrived in Mumbai, a heavy, steady downpour. Being warm, this was not entirely unpleasant, but it was awkward being soaked while transporting themselves and their gear to their new accommodation. Many of the locals stood crammed together in shelters, but others just walked and talked regardless, as if it wasn't raining at all.

They spent the morning at leisure and then, when the rain had stopped, visited Dobhi Ghat, the world's largest laundry, where 730 laundry workers lived with their families in a slum district that extended for several city blocks. These 'dhobis' washed clothes by hand in individual stone wash pens, standing knee-deep in scummy water to do it, then beating the clothing against a 'flogging stone', boiling it and hanging it to dry, and then pressing and folding it, and personally delivering it to the surrounding apartments and hotels. Some million articles of clothing went through this process every day.

The group watched these human washing machines soberly, and when they caught glimpses of the shanty homes the workers lived in, some of the girls were moved to tears. In one tiny, cramped space six people would live, all sleeping together on a thin blanket the size of a single bed.

'It's no wonder Indians are so competitive,' **Toni** said, with crossed arms. 'You'd be doing whatever you could to get out of here.' If she'd been at home she'd have slammed a door, her usual response to feeling angry and helpless. They were standing crowded together in such a confined space right now that she had to hold her frustration in, but she could feel it buzzing restlessly inside her.

'The world will be screwed if everyone has the luxuries we've got in the West,' Jackson said, 'but you look at this and you get how you couldn't possibly stop these people from wanting what we have, or doing whatever they can to get it.'

Mr Plowright nodded. 'Some really creative thinking is needed on the planet right now: how to give everyone a decent standard of living without destroying Earth. Anyone got any ideas?'

Someone said, 'Leave it with me!' Someone else snorted.

They moved on through the city streets, gazing at the usual intense scenes – the smoggy skyline, vehicles of all types, people rushing and loitering and arguing and laughing, narrow dank lanes, goats tethered to posts, dogs scavenging, the crazy wiring, rubbish all over the ground, snake charmers, road work that they had to circumnavigate, beggars going through the garbage, street stalls where sellers were tossing chappatis in their hands and frying them in huge woks while a small queue of customers waited … Mumbai appeared to be a much more progressive city – girls could be seen walking with bare arms. In some areas there was a proliferation of bars and clubs and many of the high-rise buildings looked smart and modern. But there was also, as ever in India, the sense of having gone back in time to a previous era where life was hard and manual. And everywhere, contradictions: beggars talking on mobile phones; women in hijabs and jeans; smart, suited young Indians emerging from doorways in dirty cement-walled buildings…

'These roads really need to be widened,' Eric remarked, as they wove their way across one road between scores of jammed traffic. 'It's gridlock here.'

'Yeah, but how?' Toni asked. 'Everything's so on top of everything else. Where do you move the thousands of people living and working along the street edge to get the space to make it wider?'

'Even the city engineers don't know,' their teacher said. 'Or so Mr Baxter said, after speaking to some engineers during his last trip here.'

They wandered down to the beach and walked along the path beside the grey stretch of sea. Everything was grey today: skies, sea, and a light misty drizzle made the streets and buildings grey too.

Toni couldn't get the images of the slums and the hardworking washers out of her mind. They'd seen plenty of poverty since arriving in India, but something about that living laundry had hit hard. She thought about the new Toyota Landcruiser her parents had just bought, and about their large and comfortable home where each one of them had a bedroom that was big enough to house a whole Indian family – and more. She'd never stopped herself from buying anything she wanted, often making spontaneous purchases that she didn't really need and soon regretted. She'd spent hundreds of dollars to buy the most popular brand shoes. Her family all bought stuff when they wanted to feel better. They were typical materialist consumers who regularly engaged in retail therapy. It seemed very excessive when compared with the laundry workers' lifestyle.

The intense productivity at the laundry had struck home too. She left the housecleaning to her mother and their weekly cleaner, just doing the barest minimum herself and claiming that she was too busy with homework for much more. These Indians *had to* work hard, and so they did; she didn't have to, and so she didn't. Was that what it boiled down to? Could she rouse herself out of her self-centredness to contribute more, or would these impressions and resolutions fade as soon as she arrived home and settled back into her old habits? She withdrew inside herself, pulling away from the group, feeling bad and determined at the same time.

That night they were led up onto the roof of their accommodation to watch a film. The rooftop had been strung with fairy lights and looked utterly magical. They stood near the edge, gazing down at the ever-busy streets, into lighted windows in the buildings opposite where families cooked evening meals and argued, and at the distant blur of sea. The rain had stopped but the ground was damp so they spread heavy rugs and scattered cushions and lay there in the warm evening, relaxing and enjoying the film... until the power cut out halfway through.

'India!' someone chortled.

The film, called *Dhobi Ghat*, was about a young man who worked in the laundry and dreamed of being an actor, an emotionally-locked-up artist who discovered personal video tapes of a previous tenant, and a young woman on sabbatical who fell in love with the artist. It was poignant and well-made. Not the fast-paced Western drama they were used to watching, but they had now settled into India's rhythms and were charmed and interested in the story. Their host fussed and apologised for the power cut and promised to show the rest the following evening.

In the morning they visited Gandhi's Museum, watching film clips and gazing at miniature displays about the inspiring leader who had launched the idea of non-violence on the world. **Eric** felt a great deal of admiration for the skinny, bespectacled man. Gandhi had protested against racial segregation when working in South Africa, and had urged his own people to throw off British control and oppression, leading the famous 250-mile Salt March to collect his own salt from the sea rather than pay taxes to the British for this basic foodstuff. He had raised the status of both women and the untouchables (the lowest caste in India who were looked down upon and relegated to the dirtiest tasks in society), promoting peaceful civic disobedience, spending periods in prison, and undertaking numerous fasts to make a point. Six attempts had been made on his life, until he was finally assassinated in 1948, an event that had actually triggered celebrations in the streets by his enemies, although now the date of his death was a national holiday.

'Holy crap!' Brooke exclaimed, leaning close to read a plaque. 'Gandhi and his wife got married when they were *thirteen*. Can you imagine that! And they friggin' *stayed* married till she died when she was sixty-two! Far out...'

He and Brooke looked at each other. If it were them, they'd already have been married for two years. They moved on hurriedly in opposite directions.

Eric also admired Gandhi because he was so well educated. He had studied in India and in Britain, and, despite being a mediocre student at first and struggling to find work at times, he had achieved great political influence. Eric had no desire for political influence – he couldn't think of anything worse than being in the limelight or having to lead a whole country or being the target of assassinations, but he admired anyone with a clear mind and the ability to argue a point soundly.

As a child, when Eric had learnt that his mate Chris was being paid to wash the dishes, he had informed his mother of this situation, hoping that she would take the hint. She had stopped spooning leftovers into plastic containers and had turned to look at him thoughtfully, saying, 'You'd like to be paid for doing the dishes too? Okay. We'll pay you fifty cents each time you do a load.' And then, as his heart leapt with delight, she'd added, 'And you can pay us two dollars fifty for each meal you eat.' And he'd crashed. But he couldn't help admiring the justice in this, and how it encouraged responsibility and accountability. He had passed on the wage and extra expenses…

Gandhi the activist would have liked the concept of microloans, Eric mused, now a vast industry where individuals could borrow as little as one hundred dollars to start their own business and lift themselves out of poverty. The 'Great Soul', as he was called, was all about empowerment.

After lunch and a stroll, they were booked into an Indian Cooking School, where they were going to prepare their own dinner in traditional style. The man who greeted them was possibly the happiest fellow Eric had ever encountered. His short and curly black hair was shot through with white hairs, and his face was a riot of laughter lines. He welcomed them into his kitchen with large gestures, and handed out aprons, asking them about their trip and joking and jostling, so that by the time he was ready to begin the class they all felt as if they'd been friends for years.

Eric, who rarely entered the kitchen at home, other than to pour himself a bowl of cereal or raid the fridge for snacks, found himself standing in front of a chopping board with knives and spices and a range of vegetables laid out in front of him.

'This is a team-building cooking class!' Ajay winked. 'If you are making a delicious meal in good timing with no errors, you are eating your dinner. If not...' He showed them a downcast face for all of two seconds and then burst into a broad smile and elbowed the student nearest to him.

For the next few hours they diced vegetables, kneaded and rolled dough, ground spices, and wept over onions while Ajay shared snippets about his life and family, and educated them about the dishes they were preparing and how they fit into India's culinary history. They were all surprised to learn that Indian food was originally spiced with black pepper, and that chilli came to India with the Portuguese.

The resulting meal tasted superb, even if some of their dishes didn't look as elegant as Ajay's. Butter chicken, golden puffed poori bread, and a vegetable that was new to most of them: 'ladies' fingers', or okra, an edible green seedpod that was cooked with tomato and spices and coriander – kind of slimy but tasty all the same.

After the feast Ajay gave them gifts of spice packets that were stapled to cards containing some of his recipes, and urged them to visit again. Eric felt very full and deeply relaxed as they broke out into the cool evening, chattering and laughing. He couldn't see himself becoming a chef or a teacher but there was something to be said for a vocation that made you and your clients as happy as you were productive.

It had rained incessantly all night, and in the morning their clothes were damp to the touch. They had no choice but to wear them because the humidity would allow nothing to dry, and there was no (working) dryer in their accommodation.

Jackson emerged from his room to hear Brooke complaining about the state of her clothes – and her hair now that she'd run out of shampoo, and how many mosquito bites she had acquired during the night – there must be a hole in her net. Toni ignored all of this and asked if they were going near shops today.

'Yeah,' Jackson said, 'I think that's where we're going now. Hope so, anyway. I need an internet café.'

Their first stop was the Gateway of India, one of the biggest landmarks in India and the arrival point via ship of English King George V and Queen Mary in 1911. They gazed up at the huge stone archway monument that had been built at the water's edge in recognition of the royal couple's arrival (although it had been constructed two years *after* their arrival), then joined other tourists in ambling around the vast, brick-paved square, past sellers whose wares of souvenirs, jewellery, shoes and sunglasses were spread out on sheets on the ground. On the other side of a stone wall, all manner of boats bobbed about in the water.

Originally there were seven islands of Mumbai (formerly called Bombay), Jackson read in the tourist guide; however, an English governor, William Hornby, decided to link them together into one single island with a harbour. The project was started in 1782 and took some fifty years to complete. When the sea wall collapsed multiple times, the chief engineer dreamed that the Hindu goddess Laxmi was in the sea; they searched, and a statue of the goddess was actually found. A temple was built on that site with Laxmi as the idol and as an offering for successful completion of the project.

It was interesting that *nothing* was built or done in this culture without a prayer or offering or sacrifice of some kind, Jackson reflected, stuffing the guide into his back pocket, and *everything* at home was built or done without the slightest attention to 'otherworldly influences'. He grinned at the idea of himself praying to a statue before going to school.

Their wandering took them past Victorian architecture and an abundance of shops selling carpets, tailor-made suits, handicrafts, leather goods, clothing and music. This was their last chance to go shopping before flying home, and there was some serious buying going on. A number of students had had to email their parents and ask for more funds to be deposited in their accounts, and there were lots of frowns as students stood deep in thought, determining the urgency of the purchase and the state of their finances. Jackson had kept a tight hand on his supply of cash to absolutely avoid calling on his parents for more money, and he still had a reasonable amount in his wallet... as well as products to sell when he arrived home. Tucked away in his backpack was a little bundle of kohl, the black eyeliner pencil Brooke reckoned would sell. And right now he needed an internet café to get in touch with Ahmed about the first test supply of hair...

'There's one over there,' Toni said in his ear, pointing.

'Oh. Thanks!' He looked at her more closely. 'You look pretty happy with yourself.'

She grinned. 'You know that embroidery I bought from my homestay family? I just sold it for, I dunno, double, I think. They're going to be so excited when I send them the money! With a little cut for me, of course.'

'That's great,' he enthused, but he didn't say anything about his own entrepreneurial efforts. Toni was a natural at this while it felt uncomfortable and risky to him. He'd tell her when, and if, he pulled it off.

'But,' she said glumly, 'I've lost my friggin' charger again, so if you see...'

He laughed. 'Will do. The internet café should have some, you know.'

'Good thinking.' She followed him in and ended up staying with him during the ordeal that followed, where he had to enter his name, full address, age and passport number in a ledger before being permitted to use one of their old computers. The manager even took a copy of his passport, which made Jackson nervous – stolen identity issues! Apparently it was just that security was tight following recent terrorist activity.

The café didn't have chargers but the manager relayed some instructions to Toni as to where to find some, so she ducked out (thankfully, Jackson thought; he hadn't wanted her watching as he composed his message to Ahmed), and he pulled out the scrap of paper with Ahmed's email address and began to type. He'd left this kind of late, having spent so long wondering and agonising, so the hair would have to be sent to his home. He hoped that wouldn't be too expensive. The cost for the use of the slow, old computer, however, was only a few rupees.

He was just hitting 'send' when Toni returned. 'So funny,' she chortled. 'I'm in the queue and this American guy is asking for a gigabyte on the one-month plan and the sweet young Indian lady goes, 'I am being very sorry, sir. I am being afraid that we do not have a one-month plan, sir. But we do have a 28-day plan, sir.'

Jackson grinned, standing up and hoisting his daypack. 'I'm done. Let's go.'

They wandered back through a market, eating fruit bought from the heavily laden baskets at one stall as they walked, and debated the wisdom of trying the local street food one last time – the *sev puri*, a kind of potato-and-chutney pizza, was supposed to be excellent; *bhel puri* a mixture of puffed rice, onions, spices and hot chutney was another favourite among the locals. Finally they agreed to risk it together, and tentatively tasted both *puris*, soon forgetting their concern since the food was delicious. They passed Brooke, who was buying an imitation Louis Vuitton bag from a hawker. She blushed a little when she saw them, then stared and came closer, peering at Toni's nose.

'What?' Jackson asked, following her gaze.

'You've got a diamond nose stud!' Brooke squealed.

Toni smiled. 'Like it?' she asked, turning that side of her face toward Brooke.

'It's gorgeous! I want one! Where did you get it?'

Toni thought for a moment, turned in circles, got her bearings and pointed, giving Brooke a series of landmarks.

'I'm so doing that too!' Brooke exclaimed. 'Thanks!'

'No probs,' Toni replied, and she and Jackson strolled on.

Vegetable markets on one side, high-rise buildings on the other, trendy restaurants and galleries, tree-lined streets, Victorian architecture with an Indian flavor, children playing in the streets and people sleeping in the streets, an old Muslim man in white clothes and white prayer cap driving a horse and carriage, poverty rubbing up against wealth and elegance... they were going to miss all of this colourful chaos.

On their final day in India they were booked in for a Bollywood experience. **Brooke** could barely contain her excitement. Would they see an Indian movie star? Their guide laughed and said that he couldn't promise anything but if he saw anyone of note, he would point them out. (Not that they or anyone they knew would recognise the stars, so they wouldn't get much joy boasting about the experience!)

None of the school group had visited a film set before so they had no idea what to expect, and while none of them would have voluntarily played the music or watched a film at home, actually hearing real Bollywood music and seeing a troupe of dancers gyrating in front of a camera was thrilling. The liveliness was infectious – toes were tapping as they watched from their corner, and in a completely unexpected development, they were invited to mingle in a street scene that was being filmed next.

'We're going to be in a real Indian film,' Brooke marveled to Toni, who peered at her nose.

'You did it.'

'Yeah. So pretty! Mum will kill me, but.'

Toni shrugged. 'It's your money and your nose.'

Brooke said nothing. It *was* her nose, but...

After lunch they were invited to have a Bollywood dancing lesson themselves. The girls delightedly attempted to don the gorgeous saris and veils, and were soon tied up in knots. The attendants laughed and made them stand still while they wound the fabric around them and pinned it, Brooke and the others obediently lifting and lowering their arms as required, having no idea how this outfit worked despite some of them having tried in their rooms with saris they had purchased at their first shopping expedition in India.

Many of the boys declined the dance lesson, pulling horrified expressions, and Brooke was surprised to see Eric joining in, his face suffused with colour as he valiantly wobbled his hips and waved scarves around. The girls cheered as he and Mr Plowright got into it. Stern Miss Harris blew them away with her unexpectedly seductive dance moves.

The ending of that *Dhobi Ghat* film had been kind of sad, kind of unfinished, kind of lovely, and very moving. Leaving India would be like that.

India's population is 1 billion.

> How many Indian families would fit in your bedroom?

Many of the people living subsistence lifestyles don't know what other lifestyles are possible while others are very aware of the disparities.

> If everyone in the world wants to be as rich as the West, should that be encouraged? Digital cameras and iphones and ipads for everyone?

> What if it means more pollution and mining and deforestation for the planet as a whole? What if it puts everyone in danger?

> Do you think we're capable of coming up with win/win ways of meeting everyone's needs and wants?

Are you an impulse shopper?

> Do you often make purchases that you later regret?

> Do you engage in retail therapy?

Do you do the bare minimum at home or more than your share?

> Are your parents' rules and requirements fair?

> Are they mollycoddling you or encouraging you to develop skills and responsibility?

> Do they pay you to help?

Do you pray?

Do you feel that your life would be richer if you took more time for the intangibles?

There are 7 areas in which we can be wealthy:

Physically, mentally, spiritually, socially, familially, vocationally and financially.

Do you deliberately seek new experiences to build your 'experience wealth'?

Wealth doesn't just arise from money, possessions and assets; it's our life experiences that make us feel rich or poor.

Would you rather be a Scrooge sitting alone with buckets of hard cash or someone whose life is rich with new experiences and relationships?

Do you see opportunities for making money wherever you go or do you never notice stuff like that?

Would you like to be so financially successful that you are independent and free to do what you want while you're still young?

Do you believe it's a question of luck or education and good management?

Keep reading for some practical tips – and some warnings...

PART III: Mastering Money

CHAPTER 21

Strife At Home

It was good to sleep in his own comfortable bed again, but if **Jackson**'s family had been in financial stress before he left, things were way worse now. Jackson had arrived home to find his bed squeezed against the wall to make room for his brother's bed since his brother's bedroom now housed a boarder.

Not only that, but his mother was working out of the house in a full-time job after only working two days a week from home throughout his whole childhood. Apparently it had been a case of 'make these changes or put their house on the market'. All this because Jackson's dad had kindly given a personal guarantee for a friend's new business and the new biz had gone sour, dragging Jackson's family with it.

It seemed that his family lurched from one financial crisis to another, Jackson thought, irritably stepping over his brother's schoolbag and clothes and cricket bat that were lying on the floor in his room. Having come from India, he knew that he had no right to complain about these new, cramped living conditions but it wasn't fun to be so quickly reacquainted with that knot in his stomach.

Their boarder was a quiet Malaysian student who joined them for meals and then locked herself away in her room. She seemed pleasant enough, although so shy that she barely held eye contact for more than a few seconds, so while that meant she was not very intrusive, it also meant that they were constantly aware of having a stranger in their midst. Jackson took to doing his homework in the school library and then cycling home the long way to limit his experience of the oddness and tension at home.

On the bright side, his mother seemed to be quite happy about her extra work. She moved about the house much more quickly than usual, as if there wasn't a moment to waste in her busy schedule, and she was particularly cheerful and very definite whenever she spoke; the old vagueness seemed to be gone.

Jackson would have liked to sit his father down and lecture him for being so inappropriately generous with that loan but he knew the guy his father had helped out – it was a long-time friend they called 'Uncle Mo', someone the whole family loved who kept them entertained for hours whenever he came by for a meal. So there was no point criticising; he, Jackson, would probably have offered the guarantee too. Apparently the numbers had looked solid at the time Jackson's father had checked it out but Uncle Mo's accountant had misrepresented the new business's liabilities. Meanwhile Jackson's real uncle, Dave the ex-accountant, was on Skype every day with Jackson's father, helping him brainstorm ways of cutting expenses and making his business more efficient.

Lying on his bed and staring up at the movie posters on his wall, Jackson reflected that fortunately this was neither the time nor place where boys of fifteen were asked to leave school in order to go to work and help pay the family's bills – unlike in India, of course. All the same, he began to think much more seriously about how he could contribute, or at least earn more money of his own so he didn't have to ask his parents for anything beyond food and a bed.

Brooke's mother had noticed her nose piercing from the very moment she clapped eyes on her daughter at the airport. Being a nurse, she was immediately concerned that it might not have been done properly and Brooke would end up with an infection. Brooke had insisted that it was fine; she was determined to say nothing about the slight itchiness she felt there at times.

Instead she had talked excitedly all the way home, pouring out a stream of news and impressions of India to distract her mother's attention from the gem in her nose, and hardly giving her mother a chance to say a word. Finally, when they were around the corner from home, her mother pulled up against the kerb and switched off the engine.

'Why are we stopping here?' Brooke asked, looking around. (Had they moved house while she was away? If so, she hoped she had a bigger room!)

'There's something I have to tell you,' her mother said, turning awkwardly to face her. 'Kelly's back home.'

Brooke stared. Kelly? Who had sworn she would never, *ever* return home after storming out that miserable night last year when she and their mother had just about screamed the house down?

'Leo overdosed and nearly died and is *still* refusing rehab,' Brooke's mother said. 'So she's finally getting to see who he really is. Thank God.'

'Holy crap...'

Her mother nodded grimly. 'But of course he spent most of her money while she was with him so she's got nothing to her name now but debts. Their landlord's kicked them out – turns out they owe him three months' rent. I don't know how Leo is going to pay his share of it. I hope, for his sake, that he gets his act together but...' she broke off then finished with a hard note in her voice. 'He had better not ever come anywhere near my daughter *ever again*.'

Listening to this, Brooke remembered Kelly's starry-eyed declarations of love for Leo. She and her sister had been quite close until the night of her stormy departure, and after that it had seemed as if Brooke had been lumped into the same category as her mother: Not To Be Communicated With. How would this new Kelly be? This licking-her-wounds-Kelly?

'There are a few serious conditions governing this arrangement,' Brooke's mother said, 'and I need your co-operation. Remember that

Monopoly game we played? I played it with Kel the other night and we are tracking every single cent she earns. So there are no sisterly shopping sprees on the agenda, okay?'

'Okay,' Brooke said.

'I mean it.' Her mother touched Brooke's knee lightly. 'I don't want to spoil your homecoming, but this is serious. And, while we're on the subject, it won't hurt you to keep the wallet zipped up either. I notice you used that emergency credit card a few times.'

Brooke flushed. 'Only when it was important and I'd run out of money,' she said. 'I'll pay it all back – I promise!' In fact, she had hardly noticed herself using the credit card. In the excitement of the moment it had always seemed like a reasonable thing to do… Thinking back now, she couldn't one hundred per cent guarantee that she'd only used it for important things. Would souvenirs and gifts for her family count?

'Is Dad coming to see me?' she asked, partly to change the subject.

Her mother snorted and switched on the ignition. 'Who?' she asked in a sour tone as the engine fired. 'Oh him! He's Missing In Action again.'

Toni had become so used to her nose piercing that she hardly noticed it anymore, but she was a tad disappointed that her parents didn't notice it either. They picked her up in the new Toyota Landcruiser, eager to hear her news and full of their own news, which they conveyed via barely disguised hints so that when they finally arrived home after the long drive from the airport, she was not surprised to find architectural plans spread out across the dining room table for the extension they were planning.

Did they really need a bigger deck and a brand new kitchen and family room? She didn't ask, but with images of India still so fresh in her mind, she was certainly wondering. The spaciousness of the home they already occupied seemed almost criminal by comparison – and yet deliciously so. She found herself walking around and appreciating every long white wall and every big window and each of the three bathrooms. (That sounded a lot but it wasn't *so* extravagant – just the main bathroom, her parents' ensuite, and the toilet downstairs.)

Toni had been greatly inspired by the grand architecture in India – and she didn't want to live a cramped life herself – but could she live with herself if she resided in a mansion while others were crowded together in slums? Maybe she could somehow become rich enough or clever enough to make such a difference in the world that *everyone* could enjoy a good standard of living! Then again, Mr Plowright had explained to them that there was already enough wealth in the world for everyone to be a millionaire; it just wasn't distributed fairly. Maybe her generation would turn that situation around. They were a creative and fair-minded generation that didn't automatically persist with old traditions. Maybe they would find solutions to the various crises. Once she had money she would personally invest in energy-renewing technologies!

That was an exciting possibility, but she had also heard of brilliant inventions that were stalled for years by powerful organisations that had an interest in keeping things as they were. Surely by now electric cars should be widely available? What or who was stopping that from happening – oil companies? And why was coal still being burnt? And wasn't there something that could be used instead of uranium to create safe cheap power? Or the energy of the oceans… some doco she had seen had claimed that only one-tenth of the energy generated by waves crashing against the shore could provide three-quarters of her country's electricity.

Toni wandered out the back door, past her parents who were standing on the grass and pacing out where the new deck would go. She walked to the pool and around the ledge on its raised, tile perimeter, then sat in a deck chair and gazed up at the sky, wishing for answers in the clouds.

Eric had been aware of his parents' imminent divorce, of course. The main issue concerning him was where *he* was to live, and it seemed that they were intending to share him fairly equally. (He didn't much like this sense of himself as an item of property, but that was sometimes how it came across.)

The divorce arrangements had progressed while he'd been away. The value of their family home and investment properties had been tallied and divided, but according to his mother, it hadn't been done fairly. Or so he discovered on the night he returned from India when he came downstairs for a glass of water (still jet-lagged and unable to sleep), and overheard them talking in the dining room.

'You got the bank to value this house at under market value and then you valued the Bennett Street house at over market value and you're giving that one to me,' his mother said in a low voice. Low and angry. Eric hesitated in the kitchen, frozen to the spot. 'And now you're telling me that you want to keep this house for yourself *because of the cellar.*'

'That's my wine collection down there,' Eric's father interrupted.

'The wine that you're telling me is only worth ten dollars a bottle! Your exclusive French wines that you've been collecting for the last twenty years to fund your retirement, and now you're trying to make me believe that those bottles are only worth ten dollars each! You must be joking.' There was a sound of paper rustling and a small thud as she laid something on the table. 'This is rubbish. I'm not stupid, Paul. As if you'd have bought cheap wine! I want a proper valuation done by a wine expert.'

'See what a problem you're causing wanting this divorce!' Eric's father exploded.

Eric shrank back toward the kitchen door. He wouldn't bother with the water. He would rather not be listening to this conversation.

'Don't pin the divorce on me,' his mother said coldly. 'You had twenty years to make our marriage work – you put more time into your wine collection than into us! I won't be screwed just because you don't want to lose face.'

'What are you talking about! You're always at the hospital. We haven't had a marriage for years,' Eric's father retaliated bitterly.

Eric turned and walked away. He thought he heard his mother call after him but he didn't stop moving until he was back in his room with the door closed.

Lending money to friends can be very dangerous...

If you want to help out a friend, respect yourself and your friend by making a clear, written agreement about the total amount of the loan, the repayment amounts, the dates of repayment, and what you're both going to do if you have a falling out or if your friend doesn't honour the agreement.

It's unpleasant but important to think this stuff through. Many a generous person has been caught out because he or she didn't...

The beauty of working is not just earning your own income; it's also the self-esteem, confidence, and independence that income gives you.

Those good feelings flow on into the rest of your life.

If you've got an emergency account, how do you define 'urgent'?

Make sure you're clear so that impulses don't suddenly count as urgent.

The pain of regret can be much worse than the pain of self-discipline.

Needs vs Wants

How do you determine what's a need and what's a want?

If you can't have it, will your survival be affected?

If not, it's a want.

What is your parents' 'money DNA'?

It's worth knowing because the chances are good that you have adopted their beliefs about money, and their spending and saving habits.

A big part of our behaviour is the result of 'programming' from our environment.

There really is enough wealth on the planet for everyone to be a millionaire but

(a) the 'haves' don't have the desire to share it evenly, and

(b) the 'have nots' generally don't have the desire or ability to manage large amounts of money well... or they'd keep it when they acquire it.

(c) there are too many vested interests for a scenario like this to be organised from the 'top down', and would that even be wise or sustainable?

(d) Besides, if everyone were a millionaire that status would lose its value since only rare things are considered valuable...

On the other hand, creating a world that works for everyone is an exciting challenge for your generation.

How would you achieve that?

Buckminster Fuller talks about Spaceship Earth and the very real possibility of making the world work for everyone by sharing energy.

Jacque Fresco has created something called The Venus Project that enables all people to share resources without involving money.

What would you do?

Learning to manage your money well will do wonders for your relationships.

It can be very painful to have financial strain and resentment destroy what was a loving relationship.

CHAPTER 22

STRUGGLING

Jackson and Toni were not officially a couple but they seemed to be gravitating together more and more often. He was toying with the idea of asking her out to the movies or something. He was pretty sure he wouldn't have to pay for her – most girls were okay with paying their own way, which was a relief since he was still trying to repay his parents for the trip and still only had occasional lawn mowing jobs.

'You glad to be home?' she asked as they sat on the grass of the school oval, legs stretched out to catch the sun.

'Not really,' Jackson said. 'We've got a boarder now and Mum's working full time and Dad's up to his ears in all sorts of shit at work.'

'What kind of shit?' she asked with interest.

'Just the usual,' he said vaguely. 'Problems with suppliers, and orders being held up, and people not paying accounts on time.' He was wishing he hadn't mentioned it now because he wasn't all that clear on what the problems were, just aware that there always seemed to be something wrong and his father always looked strained. Plus the Uncle Mo thing had put another big pressure on the family business to generate more income, though he didn't want to mention that. Instead he added, 'Mum used to do the bookkeeping for Dad but she's got a full-time job now and Dad is still training up the new person, so nothing's going very smoothly at the moment.'

'Hm,' she said, opening a packet of something with her teeth.

'What's that?' Jackson asked, cocking his head to read the name on the bag. Toni always had interesting food.

'Fruit leathers,' she said, proffering the bag. 'Dried fruit straps. Pretty good but they get stuck in your teeth.'

He took a purplish piece of 'leather' and bit into it. It took a lot of chewing to soften but there was quite a nice flavour. Blackcurrent, he thought. 'I reckon I'm gonna do a trade,' he said through his mouthful. 'Pays well, and, basically, anything to get out of dad's clutches for working in the family biz.'

'What sort of trade?' Toni asked, rolling a green fruit leather around her finger.

'Dunno. Building, maybe, but def not air conditioning. That's Dad's thing.'

'Yeah? We know someone who could maybe give you a job. He's got this huge property development company, and Dad reckons he's always taking kids in for work experience. Maybe he can get you a few hours on weekends.'

'Awesome,' Jackson said. He could see what she meant now about these fruit leathers getting stuck in your teeth. He poked at his molars with his tongue.

'But meanwhile what's happening with Ahmed? Have you heard from him? Has he sent the hair yet?'

'Nah.' That was a sore point; Jackson felt stupid about all of that now. The kohl pencils were still wrapped up and shoved in the corner of a drawer where his mother was unlikely to look.

'Have you sold the eyeliners you bought?' Toni persisted, as if reading his mind.

Typical Toni, Jackson thought. Dog with a bone. 'Not yet.'

She gave him a look and dragged the rolled-up green leather off her finger before popping it into her mouth. 'Why not?'

He shrugged. 'Like, just go up to girls and ask them if they want to buy make-up from me?' He made a face.

Toni laughed. 'You sound like they'll think you're a creepy old man trying to get them into his car.'

That was exactly how Jackson was feeling. He grinned, hoping she wouldn't pick that up.

'Honestly, Jackson. I'll buy one – there you go: that's your first sale. And I'll ask around. You should mention it to Brooke too, she's good at spreading the word about things like that.'

Brooke! That was an idea.

'How much are you going to charge?' Toni persisted.

Jackson looked blank.

'Ask Brooke,' Toni said again. 'She's on top of all that sort of thing. I'll pay whatever it is.' She pulled out a red fruit leather, tore a piece off with her teeth, and chewed, her eyes closed, face toward the sun.

Jackson thought about working on a construction site during the weekends. That would be good. He'd like that.

Eric and Chris were playing chess in the school canteen while they ate lunch. It was a slow, distracted game because they were both simultaneously playing online games with other partners. Managing multiple games at once was an excellent challenge for the brain – Eric's idol was a Romanian who could play as many as eight games at the same time. Insane!

'So have you heard from your dad, Brooky?' a female voice behind him said.

'Not a word,' he heard Brooke reply. 'It's like he's left the country.'

'Geez.'

'Yeah.'

'Wanna go sit in the sun?' The girl asked after a moment. 'It's freezing in here.'

'Yeah, okay,' Brooke replied. 'In a minute; I'll just finish this.'

'I'm going to get a juice,' Chris said, pulling Eric's attention back to his own table. 'Want anything?'

'No thanks.' As soon as Chris had headed toward the fridges, Eric swiveled in his chair to face Brooke. She was sitting on her own, writing an assignment, tongue poking out of the corner of her mouth.

'Hey, Brooke,' Eric began, and at that exact moment someone dropped a whole tray of food with a tremendous crash. Brooke didn't hear him but she looked up in the direction of the sound, and then caught him watching her. She looked back at him with narrowed eyes.

'I couldn't help overhearing,' Eric said, flushing, 'about your dad.'

She continued to look at him.

'Is he... has he abandoned you?'

Frowning a little, Brooke glanced down at her page and then back at Eric. 'I wouldn't say that exactly. He's just out of communication for some reason. Which is nothing new. He doesn't live with us anymore and he's often away on business. But it would be nice if he'd stay in touch with his own flesh-and-blood daughters.' Her eyes flashed.

Eric wanted to ask more. Having spent his whole life in the relatively comfortable cocoon of a typical nuclear family, the new uncomfortable scenario of divorce-plus-mother-moving-out had unsettled his world. Everything felt uncertain and rocky. He was embarrassed about asking Brooke questions, but learning more from other kids' whose parents were divorced could perhaps provide some landmarks for this new territory he found himself inhabiting.

'Did they... divorce a long time ago?' he asked, spying Chris in the queue with his drink. He'd be back soon and Eric had barely even discussed this divorce with his oldest friend.

'Years ago. I was in primary school. Why?'

'My parents...'

She nodded sympathetically. 'While we were in India?'

'No, it was already happening. But now they're dividing the property and that's really...'

'The pits,' she agreed. 'Not that *we* had any property, but the money fights. Holy crap. That's why my folks split up in the first place.'

'Oh,' he said, watching Chris out of the corner of his eye. He'd stopped to talk to someone.

'I hope your parents manage it better than mine,' Brooke said, leaning back in her chair and capping her pen. 'My folks have never stopped arguing about money, even after separating. And I'm always the meat in the sandwich because Dad's half of the school fees or parenting payment or whatever is usually late. In fact,' she said, leaning forward again, 'Mum is still mad about the money he put into the trip – she calls him a 'Disneyland Dad'. You know, swoops in with presents so I'll love him and then disappears again and isn't around to help with the hard stuff. I defend him like crazy but it does look like that. Which makes me feel like crap.'

Eric hadn't quite expected this download. Chris was on his way back and he still hadn't figured out his next chess move. He made a sympathetic murmuring sort of a sound, not sure what to say or do next.

'It's okay,' she said airily, gathering up her stuff. 'You don't have to feel sorry for me. I'm used to it. Good luck with yours.'

'Thanks,' he said, turning back to his table and the chess game. Would one of his parents disappear? Would he become used to it? The certainty of his previous existence was dissolving. It felt as if he'd grown up with a clear history and a clear destination (of sorts: do well at school, make married parents proud, do well at uni, make married parents proud, get a great job, make married parents proud…), and now the path ahead of him was breaking into pieces before his eyes.

CHAPTER 23

Stepping Up

'Hair arrived?' **Eric** asked Jackson. They were standing at the crossing outside the school, Eric to catch a bus and Jackson to pedal home on his bike.

'Nope. Reckon he saw a sucker coming in me,' Jackson said sourly. 'Lucky little git.'

'I don't imagine your fifty dollars, or whatever it was, put him on easy street,' Eric contradicted. 'Hang in there. I reckon he'll come through. He had an honest look about him.'

'You reckon?'

'Yeah... Have you sold those make-up pencils?'

'Brooke did – most of them, anyway.'

'Cool. So I suppose you've had to pay her a commission.'

'She said not to bother.'

'But you will, won't you?' Eric said.

Jackson looked at him a little strangely. The lights changed to green and they began to cross together, Jackson pushing his bike alongside.

'If you're running a business, I mean,' Eric said.

'Am I?'

'Well, you've bought some products at wholesale, imported them into the country, had a salesperson sell them for you, and now you're waiting to hear from your supplier about another product line. Sounds like you're in business to me.'

Jackson whistled. 'When you put it like that...' They were due to part ways but stepped out of the path of passers-by to finish their conversation against the fence of a neighbour's house. 'That's a bit of a different take than Toni's 'go for it' advice!'

Eric smiled. 'Toni is full of good intentions but not necessarily good plans. You've got a chance to do something here, Jackson. I'd be making a business plan if I were you.'

'Really? I wouldn't have a clue how. Running a business is not something I've ever seen myself doing.'

'Is your dad in business? Or your mum?' Eric added, being politically correct.

'Dad is but I'm not asking him!'

Eric gave a little nod. 'Fair enough. I can help if you like.'

'Yeah? Sweet.'

'You got a savings account?'

'Nah. Well, Mum and Dad have one for me but I keep most of my cash in my room in a jar under my bed so I can get at it when I want to.'

Eric shook his head. 'Open one *immediately*. Or start using the one you've got. In fact, you need two.'

'Why two?'

'A savings account for the usual purpose and a prosperity account where you put ten per cent of everything you earn and you never, *ever* touch it.'

'What's the point of that?'

'Makes you feel rich,' Eric smiled. 'I've got just over $500 in my prosperity account now. Goes back to when I first started getting pocket money when I was seven. I'd put fifty cents a week in that account and it's just steadily increased since then. My dad's got tens of thousands in his.'

'What about your usual savings account?' Jackson asked, with a distasteful expression, as if he didn't really want to know the answer. 'How much in that?'

'Nearly two thousand,' Eric said.

They were silent for a moment. Eric checked his watch. His bus had never been so late.

'So… a savings account and a prosperity account…' Jackson echoed. And Eric had thousands in his regular savings account even after paying for India! How did he do it?

'And a business account,' Eric said. 'Where most of the income will go and where you pay bills from.'

'Gawd… And pay Brooke a commission.'

'It's only fair.'

'How much, do you think?'

'Twenty-five per cent?'

'Geez, there'll be nothing left. It wasn't much money to begin with, you know.'

'Not for that first supply because you were testing the waters, but once you get bigger orders… Have you sussed out other places you can sell the things?'

'Nah. Brooke reckons her sister's a hairdresser and she might know what to do with the hair, if it ever gets here.'

'Cool.' Eric hoisted his schoolbag onto his shoulder. 'My bus is coming. I'll help you if you like. You're usually in the library after school these days. We can talk then.'

'Great. Thanks, bro.' Jackson held up a fist and Eric awkwardly met his in a bump that nearly missed.

'No probs.' Eric headed toward his bus, thinking about money. It was a real trap for the unwary. His mother had apparently asked her lawyer to initiate the division of property conversation but his father had objected to so much of their wealth lining the lawyer's pockets; instead, they could figure it out themselves with their accountant, he had argued. And argued had become the key word. Eric's loyalties were divided very equally between his parents and he wanted them to get their act together asap. Meanwhile he would help Jackson avoid some of the pitfalls he was headed for.

There was definitely a case for people understanding money and being in charge of their own.

Brooke had arrived home from India to find her sister Kelly reasonably friendly though quite subdued. No longer the bright and bubbly party girl, she was silent on the subject of Leo and the drugs, and totally focused on working as many hours as she could to get her debts paid and move the hell out of there again – or so she had confided in Brooke.

They were a delightful household, Brooke reflected as she peeled potatoes for dinner. Kelly left for work at eight a.m. and arrived back home at eight p.m., tired and cranky. Meanwhile her mother was typically tired and cranky since she was doing extra shifts at the moment, including night shift, and that always screwed with her mood. And Brooke, who was supposed to be studying, was cooking dinner seven freaking nights a week.

Kelly would be back soon, ravenous. Brooke had a mere twenty minutes to cook a whole meal (because she'd been distracted in her room watching a movie and snacking on dried fruit, so she hadn't felt any hunger pangs to remind her of what she should have been doing). Right now her mother was sleeping so Brooke couldn't even turn the music up to take the edge off the boredom of making dinner.

She was just wondering if she was brave enough to use the pressure cooker to speed things up when she heard Kelly's key in the lock. Shit. She peeled faster, listening as the front door closed quietly and something thudded to the ground in the entrance. Her sister stifled a curse and moments later came into the kitchen, bringing a delicious aroma with her.

'You got pizza?' Brooke asked, swinging around.

Kelly grinned. 'I was starving. Couldn't wait. I've saved you some.'

'Thanks!' Brooke wiped her hands on her bum and lifted the lid of the box her sister was holding out to her. 'Capriccioso?'

'Of course.'

'Yum.' Her lack of hunger aside, Brooke lifted out a sagging slice with both hands and took a big bite.

'Wotcha making?' Kelly asked, kicking her shoes off and sinking into a seat.

'Mashed spuds and chops.'

'Height of gastronomy!'

'You can start criticising me when you start doing the cooking,' Brooke retorted through her mouthful. 'Until then, zip it.'

'Okay, fair enough.' Kelly sighed and stretched back in her seat. 'Sit down, wench. You'll get indigestion if you bolt it like that.'

Brooke sat. She swallowed the first divine mouthful and took another. 'Shaving any for Mum?' she asked through the food.

'What? Oh. If you think she'd want some. The ogre sleepeth?'

'Yeah.'

'Thank God.' Kelly folded her arms on the table and rested her head there. 'I am so tired.'

Not knowing what to say to that, Brooke just ate. It was quiet in the kitchen, aside from the fridge humming. Outside, a dog gave a sudden shrill bark.

'I'm so depressed,' Kelly said, her voice muffled by her arms. 'I totally get how people can neck themselves and do shit like that.'

Brooke slowed down her chewing. She put a tentative hand on her sister's back.

Kelly stiffened a little, and then relaxed. 'I feel like such an idiot,' she muttered. 'It was totally obvious to everyone how he was using me and I didn't get it until it was way too late. You know what?' She sat up, turning her pale face with its dark ringed eyes toward Brooke. 'I reckon Leo frittered away about *five grand* of my money. That's everything I had saved plus my wages for however long we were living together. You'd think I could have read the writing on the wall, wouldn't you?'

'I'm not very good with money either,' Brooke confessed. 'I keep overspending and buying things I shouldn't and stuff like that.'

Kelly sighed. 'We're a pathetic family when it comes to money, aren't we? You know what I think? I think I was buying him.'

'Leo?'

'Yeah. Buying his love. Crap way of having a relationship, isn't it?'

'It sounds familiar,' Brooke said.

'Dad?'

'Uh-huh. Do you want more pizza?'

'No. It's yours.'

'Disneyland Dad and his Disneyland Daughters,' Brooke giggled. 'Not that it's funny.'

'No. And we've got the Wicked Real-Mum cracking the whip. Although she's right, which makes it all the more painful.'

'I heard she played Monopoly with you.'

Kelly made a face. 'You too?'

'Yeah. I like the idea of saving lots of money, truly. I just find it so hard to *do*. So hard to resist all the stuff in the shops – especially the sales. I can't stand watching my friends buy stuff I want to get too, except I haven't got the money and they have. It sucks.'

'We've just got to work our arses off and turn things around,' Kelly said. She yawned and stood up. 'Sorry I dumped on you. It's been going round and round in my head all day – all week…'

'I'm glad you did,' Brooke said. 'We haven't had a D&M in ages.'

'Yeah. Well, thanks for listening. Want a hand with those?' Kelly indicated the spuds, which were going grey on the chopping board.

'It's okay. You treated me with the pizza. I'll do them.'

'All right…' Brooke's sister was heading out of the kitchen when she stopped at the door. 'Heard from Dad?'

'Nothing.'

'Bastard.' She walked out.

The toilet in their mother's ensuite flushed and Brooke leapt to her feet to finish the evening meal, a meal she had even less appetite for now. She had no idea what had triggered her sister's sudden confidence in her, but she was glad. A first step on the road to their old closeness, she hoped.

Jackson followed Toni up the long, wide driveway, feeling awed. 'How rich is he?' he asked, yet again.

She stopped walking and grinned at him. 'I dunno. Squillions.' Then, digging him in the ribs, 'Multi-millionaire, I think. But he's human.'

'And you're sure he doesn't mind?'

'His son is pissed with him and they hardly talk to each other, so he has a soft spot for any kid who's willing to work hard and learn from him. He's going to love you.'

They had climbed the steps and were standing in front of the large front door. Toni reached out to press the bell; Jackson grabbed her wrist and stopped her. 'What's his name? I've forgotten.'

'Arnold, I think. Dad set this up for you. The last time I saw him was months and months ago, before India. He had us over for dinner.'

'Okay.' The peal of the doorbell had died away. Jackson listened for the sound of approaching feet from inside the house. There was nothing. 'Do you think he's forgotten?'

Toni pressed her face to the narrow glass panel next to the door, but it was a smoky stained glass, impossible to see through. 'I wouldn't think so…'

'Hello there!' a voice called from behind them. They turned to see Toni's tall, wealthy family friend walking rapidly up the drive toward them. 'Sorry, kids, I was held up.' He leapt lightly up the steps and held out a hand to Jackson. 'Hello mate, I'm Arnold.'

'Jackson,' Jackson said, shaking the hand. It was a strong hand, and the eyes looking at him were used to assessing people quickly, he could tell that much.

'How's Toni?' Arnold asked, planting a kiss on her cheek.

'Pretty good,' she said.

'So this is your friend who wants some labouring work?'

'Yes, if you've got some,' Jackson said.

'You prepared to work hard?' Arnold asked, looking sideways at him as he unlocked the front door.'

'Definitely.'

'He wants to find out if he'd like to get into building. For a trade,' Toni explained as they stepped inside.

'He can talk for himself,' Arnold said. He looked questioningly at Jackson.

'That's right,' Jackson said at once. 'I'm not an academic sort of person. I think a trade would suit me and I like the idea of building, but...'

'It's a good idea to check it out.' Arnold beckoned them to follow him. 'Juice? Soft drink?'

'I'm fine, thanks,' Jackson declined, looking on either side into large rooms with polished floors and big windows and plush furniture and artwork.

'I'd love a juice, thanks,' Toni said.

They walked after him through a swinging door into the kitchen and he opened the paneled wooden wall, revealing a fridge. Turning to Jackson, he said, 'You saying no to be polite or because you really don't want anything?'

Jackson hesitated.

'Juice all round,' Arnold said, bringing out a jug of tropical juice and closing the fridge door. 'I've got a job on at the moment just near to here that will suit you. I'll text you the address. Turn up any time from eight a.m. on Saturday morning and we'll give you a crack at it. It'll just be labouring – nothing very exciting. Digging, clearing rubbish, moving bricks... If we like each other, we'll find you enough to do to keep you busy for a while.'

'That's great. Thanks!' Jackson said, trying to hold the excitement back to not sound like a little kid, and totally failing.

Arnold opened a cupboard and brought out three tall glasses. He poured the juice and they toasted each other then swallowed the golden liquid.

'If you work hard, you'll do well. But if you work hard *and* smart, you'll do even better. Any young person who shows even a skerrick of interest gets my attention and support.'

You see? Toni said to Jackson with her eyes.

'Thanks. I really appreciate it.' Jackson was entertaining a stream of images of himself with sleeves rolled up and a spade in his hands, tossing dirt aside... his father smiling and patting him on the back and saying, 'Well done, Jackson. We're proud of you...'

'Show me your thanks by what you do with the opportunity,' Arnold said. 'Now, Toni, I've got something for you to give your parents.'

'Sure,' she said.

'Wait here and I'll go get it.' He strode out of the kitchen and the doors swung behind him.

Jackson took a deep breath. 'He doesn't stop for long, does he?'

Toni walked through the empty house with her dirty plate and cutlery. She pulled the dishwasher open and slotted the things inside and closed the door again with a frustrated little bang. Now what? Another evening all alone stretched ahead. Her parents had rushed in from work, eaten or changed or grabbed stuff, and then rushed out again to meetings. Separate meetings. Her father was on some board and her mother belonged to a philanthropic organisation, and they barely ever had time to themselves, it seemed.

She scowled, noticing that the dishwasher door had bounced open again, and gave it a hard push so that it would close properly. It clicked shut and she stood there, arms folded across her chest, brooding. Last night she'd turned her favourite music up loud and danced around and enjoyed being on her own; tonight she felt depressed by the large, silent house. She wanted to go somewhere herself – *do* something – have some new experience instead of the 'same old' of homework and bed.

Still brooding, Toni wandered back to her bedroom and slid onto the chair in front of her desk. Jackson's meeting with Arnold had made her restless for her own new source of income. She had no desire to 'get onto the tools' with him, so what could she do? She picked up her phone and scrolled down her Instagram feed idly, but there was nothing interesting there. Some of the India-trip people were still talking about it and posting pictures, which made her remember that she had enjoyed organising the Fundraising Crew; or at least, she'd enjoyed it until there were too many cooks spoiling the broth. Toni preferred to be solely in charge of her projects. So what could she do that *she* could be in control of?

Stupid phone just died again, Laura posted. *Was fully charged this morning then died when I was at Athletics. Driving me nuts!*

You need one of those solar chargers like they had in India, someone commented a moment later.

What solar chargers? Toni wondered. And then an image came back to her of a market stall somewhere in India with piles of solar chargers for mobile phones. She hadn't seen them much over here but it made sense that they'd be in high demand in India where there were still lots of people not connected to the grid.

She popped up the lid of her laptop and typed in the URL for ebay then began to search. There were stacks of them! She paused in her scrolling to read a few of the ads: 'Waterproof, Made for iPhones, Range of Colours, Free Postage…' One seller had a deal going where you could buy a batch of ten for eight bucks each. Eight dollars! Surely she could sell those to kids at school for fifteen! It was a no-brainer. That would be seventy bucks straight into her pocket *and* she'd be doing something good for the earth at the same time.

Toni clicked the 'Buy Now' button.

Do you have a Savings Account?

What about a Prosperity Account, where you <u>never</u> withdraw the money?

One of the principles of good financial management is Fair Exchange,

which means that you receive appropriate payment for your goods and services and you give appropriate payment for the goods and services you acquire; the two elements should be of equal value.

Is there someone in your life who tends to buy your affection?

Or someone whose affection you are buying?

Are you prepared to work hard <u>and</u> smart?

What does 'working smart' mean to you?

Do you prefer to be in charge/a leader or are you more comfortable as a follower?

Do you check things out before you buy or do you tend to act on impulse?

CHAPTER 24

Creating a Gap

'He's *bankrupt*?' **Brooke** echoed, stunned.

Her mother nodded.

'Shit.' Kelly drew her feet up onto the couch and wrapped her arms around her knees.

'What does that mean?' Brooke asked. 'Like, for his life. Will he go to gaol?'

'No,' her mother said. 'It just means he's let a lot of people down.'

'Tell us about it!' Kelly said with feeling.

'No wonder he didn't want to see us. He must be feeling terrible.'

'I hope so,' Brooke's mother said, and then added quickly, 'I don't mean that in a nasty way; I mean I hope he's getting the lesson.'

Brooke surveyed her mother and sister thoughtfully. Their mother was actually being quite good about it, she'd noticed; no mean comments, no 'I told you so's'. And Kelly, who had surely been nursing a private hope that their father would turn up with one of his windfall gifts and help her out, looked shocked but not devastated.

'Do you think that trait is in our DNA?' Kelly asked suddenly.

'What, gambling?' Brooke looked at her mother, the biology expert.

'I don't know if it's in your DNA, girls, but you certainly do have his habit of living beyond your means,' their mother said. She was sitting in her favourite armchair for this 'girls' talk', her slippered feet on a footrest.

'You're not destined to gamble any more than he was; it's all choices. It's up to you to learn from your father's mistakes and make some changes.'

'Dad should have cut his credit card up, the way you made me,' Kelly said. 'That would have sorted him out!'

'He'd just have got another one,' Brooke said. Then, as the question occurred to her, 'Where's yours, Mum? Do you have one?'

'In the freezer,' their mother replied. 'Sitting in a block of ice.'

Both girls stared.

'I can't melt it fast or I'll ruin it, so waiting for it to thaw makes me think twice about using it,' she said with a smile. 'Believe me, living with your dad and watching my hard-earned cash pour out the window was no party.'

'I get it,' Kelly muttered.

'Best to just have a debit card. That way you're only spending money that you actually have,' their mother said.

'Yeah. I don't get how people can have this magical thinking about credit cards,' Brooke agreed, 'as if you're getting money as some sort of present and not thinking about paying it back. Like the kids who think their parents are getting money for free out of the hole in the wall.'

Brooke's mother looked as if she were going to hold her tongue... then didn't. 'But living beyond your means is exactly the same thing. Buying more than you can afford is as bad as using a credit card.'

'Yeah but at least you're not paying all that interest,' Kelly intervened. 'You're just not saving much.'

'True, but either way you're losing out. On the other hand, if you were saving instead of spending, you would be *accruing* interest on the money you have in your account. The bank would be paying you.'

'At piss-weak rates.'

'Only until you've built up a reasonable amount – then the interest grows. And grows. Have you heard about compound interest?'

The girls exchanged glances and shook their heads.

'What are they teaching you in school these days!' their mother said in despair. She lifted her feet off the footrest, heaved herself off the armchair, and knelt down by the coffee table, scrabbling around amongst the clutter in search of a pencil and scrap of paper. Finding them, she wrote *$1000 @ 5%* and said, 'Suppose you put $1000 in the bank at 5% interest and you commit to adding another $10 each week. At the end of the year you'll have more than $1,500 in your account, of which $63.00 would be interest.'

'Woopy-doo,' Brooke said.

Their mother raised her hand in a stop sign. 'Hold on. If you deposit another $10 each week for ten years, you'll have nearly $8000, of which some $2000 is interest. Does that sound better?'

'Just putting $10 in each week? That's pretty cool.'

'Very cool. It's called the magic of compound interest because the interest is calculated on the *total* amount in your account, including all previous interest, rather than just the money you've deposited. Over time the bank rewards you for continually putting money into your savings. The more you deposit and the bigger your deposit amount, the more you'll be rewarded. If you put more of your income from The Burger Place into that savings account you'll be surprised how quickly it will start to grow.' Their mother looked around the room. 'Is there a calculator in here?'

Brooke produced her phone.

'All right, watch this. Say you keep depositing that $10 every week...' She tapped at the phone keypad and then jotted more numbers on the page. 'In five years' time you'll have $4,000 in your account. But in five years you'll be working full-time and able to save quite a bit more, let's say $50 a week. At that rate, in another five years your savings will be more than $18,000!'

'Very cool,' said Brooke.

'So you're kind of getting money for free,' Kelly said.

'Not exactly for free but it does mean your money is working for you. And if the interest is calculated daily instead of monthly, the amount grows even faster.'

'But that all takes years and years and basically in the meantime you just want us to live on no-name brands and put all of our money into savings,' Brooke said glumly.

Their mother gave a little sigh. She put the pencil down and sat on the floor, stretching her broad legs straight out in front of her. 'Brooke, honey, it's not about what *I* want for you. Sure I want you to save, but what I really want is for you to understand how important this is and want it for yourself! You'll never get your act together financially if you're doing it for me; you've got to do it for yourself –because *you* get how much sense it makes.'

'One bag instead of four,' Kelly said to Brooke. 'Four pairs of heels instead of eight –'

Their mother looked alarmed. 'Why on earth would you need four bags!'

'Colour co-ordinating, of course,' Brooke said. 'Black for black outfits, red for red outfits –'

'*One* – maybe two bags,' their mother said firmly. 'Until you've earned the right to have a range of colours. It's not that you can never have them, it's just that until you have enough spare money for luxuries like that, you simply shouldn't be buying them. You can't spend money on luxuries because you might need that money for important bills. If you live beyond your means, it will eventually catch up with you.'

'Like it did with Dad,' Kelly said.

'Exactly. And why designer brands? You're only fifteen, for God's sake, Brooke. You don't *need* Gucci and Louis Veeton or whatever his name is.'

'But you can get fake good brands!' Brooke pointed out, remembering her India purchase of a Louis Vuitton copy that was still hiding in her cupboard…

'Yes, but often the workmanship is dodgy. Just buy something decent and affordable.'

'Decent and affordable is boring.'

'So is spending time in prison,' their mother said.

'You said Dad wasn't going to gaol!'

'I know, I'm teasing. I'm just trying to say that if you tighten your belt now you can afford lovely stuff down the track, whereas if you lash out now, you'll be in trouble later.'

'It's like Matt says about fitness,' Kelly put in. 'Work hard now and look good later, or be lazy and eat everything you want now and regret it later.'

'Exactly,' their mother agreed. 'Matt. Have I met him? Is he that nice boy –?'

'Very hot but off the topic, Mum. And anyway, he's taken.'

'But if you just buy cheap brands you look like everyone else,' Brooke mourned.

'You can buy expensive brands and look like everyone else too!' their mother said. 'Whereas with a bit of creativity you can put a fabulous wardrobe together out of the opp shop. Honestly! Get a tattoo to 'express your individuality' and you end up looking like every other tattooed person on the street! It's ridiculous.'

'That's different.'

'Not really.' Their mother glanced at her watch. 'I'm going to have to go soon. My point is this: make a budget and stick to it. Buy according to what you *need* instead of everything you *want* – just until you can afford everything you want.'

'But that might take forever,' Brooke wailed.

'Then work smarter. Look for opportunities – ethical, legal ones, of course! You have to earn the right to a higher standard of living. Otherwise, if you're going to live the high life one week, you'll have to tighten your belt the next week. It stands to reason.'

'Reason is so boring.'

Their mother looked at Kelly. 'Are *you* getting this?'

'Of course.' Kelly poked Brooke in the side. 'If you do some research you can usually find good deals pretty cheap.'

'Ouch.' Brooke pulled away with a sulky expression. 'It's not fair.'

'It is what it is,' their mother said philosophically. 'That's a good point, Kel. I've been having a lip wax up the street here and it's been costing me eighteen dollars for a two-minute procedure. I thought that was way expensive but I didn't have time to shop around. Then the other day –'

'You found a place where you can get it done for eight bucks,' Kelly interrupted. 'You could have asked me. Hairdresser, right?' she said, indicating herself with a comical expression. 'We work right alongside waxing girls.'

Their mother made a face. 'Silly me. I didn't even think of asking you. But you're right – that's exactly what I found. Eight dollars. Unbelievable. To think I've been throwing all that money away for years.'

'If you're so sensible, why did you marry Dad?' Brooke demanded.

'Come on, you know, Brooks,' Kelly said. 'Opposites attract. Right, Mum?'

'Must be,' their mother said, shaking her head and slowly getting to her feet. 'Yes, he was fun and exciting at first. But I also wasn't very sensible when I met your dad – I became more practical as a result of the pain of all our frittered-away money!' She brushed grit off her backside. 'Who's supposed to be vacuuming? This carpet is gross!'

'I guess your impulsive thing was marrying Dad then,' Brooke grinned. (A change of subject was urgently required.)

'Maybe it was,' their mother mused. 'Look, he's not a bad man; he just doesn't think. So get the lesson: think before acting. Walk away before you buy so you can check that you really need it.' She held up her thumb and forefinger. 'Create a little gap between seeing it and getting it, just so you can check if you *really* need it.'

'What I need is a buying conscience,' Brooke said. 'A Jiminy Cricket sitting on my shoulder.'

'I'll be your conscience,' their mother said. 'Just think of me sitting there.'

'You're too heavy.'

'Cheek!' Her mother tossed a cushion at her and headed out.

'No but really,' Brooke said to Kelly in a low voice after she'd gone. '*She* needs to create a little gap between seeing cake and eating it.'

Kelly giggled. 'You're right. Everyone's got their blind spot!'

'I wonder if *she* sees that it's the same thing?' Brooke mused aloud. 'I mean, food is her pleasure and buying stuff is ours. I suppose we've all got to find other ways of feeling good and rewarding ourselves. Any ideas?'

Kelly shrugged. 'Nope. But let's think on it. I don't want to end up like Dad.'

Toni was on her way out of the shopping centre when she caught sight of Eric emerging from the iMac store. He was wearing one of the shop assistant t-shirts! She increased her pace and flagged him down. 'Hey! Eric!'

He turned and waited while she caught up.

'You work there?' jerking her head in the direction of the store.

'Just started. A couple of weeks ago.'

'Is it good?'

'I enjoy it,' he said. 'They know a lot, those guys. I'm learning heaps.'

'I bet,' she said. 'Do they have good deals for staff?'

'A bit of a discount. I've been thinking about upgrading the old Dell I've had for years to a Mac so it's good to get all the insider information on it.'

'Sweet,' she said. She was going to mention the solar chargers she had just ordered but hesitated.

'Then again,' he continued seriously, 'I might not. I hate taking money out of my bank account.'

'Really?' she asked. 'You can always make more.'

'True, but I prefer to see it grow. Taking that money out for the India trip was physically painful.'

He was joking, sort of. She wasn't sure…

The double glass doors of the shopping centre slid open for them and they walked out into the cool evening.

'Going out tonight?' she asked after an awkward silence.

'No,' he said. They walked a moment and then he said, 'You?'

'Birthday party.'

He nodded without comment.

'What will you do tonight?' she asked curiously. What did Eric do when he wasn't at school or studying?

'Probably a bit more research. Although I've pretty much decided already. Most technical development lately has been focused on reducing power consumption so that batteries last longer, so there haven't been any great advances in performance for a while. Which is a good reason not to upgrade yet.'

'Uh-huh,' she said slowly. Seeing her mother's car ahead she gave a wave. 'Want a lift?'

'I'm right, thanks. I don't live far from here.'

'Okay... Well... see you Monday.'

'Yep,' he said, and walked on with barely a backward glance.

Toni jogged to the car and pulled the door open.

Her mother was texting. 'Get what you needed?' she asked, without looking up.

'Mm,' Toni said, strapping in. Gift card for the birthday girl. They all gave each other those cards, with an agreed limit. Not very creative but then you didn't have the stress of thinking about what to buy or outdoing each other on gift amounts, etc. She thought about Eric as they drove home, with his very considered approach to his possible purchase. She never analysed the pros and cons of something so thoroughly – just leapt in and did it and trusted that she'd bounce back if it didn't work out. Well, there were probably pros and cons to both approaches.

Jackson was enjoying the labouring work. For one, he loved hanging out with the boys. They didn't treat him like a kid and he was gaining all sorts of fascinating insights into the world of men. He liked working hard alongside them and feeling the burn in his muscles. He liked the tiredness at the end of the day and the sense of achievement when he could look at the site and see the result of his efforts. And he liked the cash in his hand – a whole $80 every Saturday morning, and as much as $160 when he worked a full day. If he had his choice, he'd turn up here on weekdays too, but he couldn't see that happening. He still had three years of school to go – unless he left school and started an apprenticeship, which was more and more appealing…

Arnold wasn't often on site and when he did turn up he never said much or stayed long but he seemed to command respect from all the guys. And he always stopped for a word with Jackson. Once he came with his father, a stocky man who smoked continuously and kept pointing to various spots on the site and making comments. Everyone listened; it turned out that he had started the company years ago.

Jackson wondered how his own father's employees viewed him. Did they work hard for the company or only when he turned up to check on them? What was the feeling in the factory? Was his father a good boss, a good leader?

For himself, he would rather follow than lead. He didn't like the spotlight or being solely responsible for something, and leaders had to be good at that. He would rather put in a good day's work and take a wage and clock off, and then come back fresh the next day without any of the headache his father carried home. Definitely. And yet, here he was, as Eric had said, running his own business. It was nuts!

He had asked Brooke if she'd help with the hair when it finally arrived (*if* it ever arrived), and she'd said yes. Meanwhile he'd paid her a commission for the eye pencil sales. She'd been thrilled about that. She was such a social butterfly it was effortless for her to spread the word and it made the whole exercise far less painful for him. It was a very good deal. She was happy, he was happy… He would email Ahmed to send more of those kohl eyeliner pencils – and ask again about the hair. He'd received one very formal email from Ahmed explaining that there had been an unavoidable delay but he had posted the hair and it should arrive soon. So now to see if the guy was for real or not…

And he'd opened all those accounts, with Eric breathing down his neck to make sure he did it. It felt good. Even just twenty bucks in an account with your name on it felt good. Eric was insisting that he track all his income and keep records, and while he grumbled about the fiddliness of the work, he felt good – proud of himself. He realised, with a flash of surprise, that he hadn't had a bellyache in quite a while.

The Magic of Compound Interest

> 'Compound interest is the eighth wonder of the world. He who understands it, earns it… he who doesn't, pays it.' – Albert Einstein

Learn more about it and put this principle to use in your life if you want to see your money grow significantly.

Do you see the value in creating a 'gap' between your desire, your impulse to buy, and actually making the purchase so you can check if you really need it?

To feel better about disciplining yourself, don't say 'I can't afford it', say, 'This isn't a priority right now.'

Do you figure out the pros and cons of the things you want before committing to them?

Do you do your research before buying a phone package, for instance?

Never assume all providers are equal. When hiring someone to do a job for you, always get three quotes to compare rather than accepting the first one.

Gifts for friends can be tricky.

Do you have a 'ceiling' agreement re what you spend or is there pressure to outdo each other?

This gets especially tricky with boyfriends and girlfriends…

Working hard (at something you don't love)

might seem boring but there is truth in the old proverb that 'slow and steady wins the race'.

However if you work smart <u>and</u> hard, you can compound your advantage.

The best is working smart and hard at something you love.

How do you reward yourself?

Does the reward always cost money or do you have non-monetary ways of feeling good?

Some of the wealthiest people in the world have created teams so that they do what they are best at and they pay others to do the things they are not so good at.

This system of delegation is a key factor in building a successful business.

CHAPTER 25

A Balance of Risk and Caution

Jackson frowned at his Facebook messages and scrolled through, looking for Ahmed's name. Nothing. He clicked across to emails and searched for something from Ahmed. Nothing. His fingers drummed on the table as he calculated. He had paid for another set of kohl pencils some four weeks ago, and was *still* waiting for the delivery of hair. What could have gone wrong, or was this just confirmation of the sneaking suspicion he'd had since the beginning that Ahmed was a con man?

Tapping at the keyboard, he launched online banking and took a quick look at his account balances to boost his morale. Fifty-seven dollars in his savings account, thirty-two in his prosperity account, and two hundred and forty in his business account (which included his income from the building site work). He'd given his parents the savings in his jar as a contribution towards India, refusing to crumble in the face of his mother's objections. Holding strong had felt good. As for Ahmed, that con man wouldn't be seeing one more cent of his money; the rest of it was going to accrue in his bank accounts until he had enough to buy a car and move out of home. Forget about being in business; he would just work hard in an ordinary kind of job.

Logging out of online banking, he wandered out of the bedroom and into the kitchen, wondering when dinner would be ready. His mother was nowhere to be seen but Adelia, their Malaysian boarder, was cooking noodles at the stove. She ducked her head at him in acknowledgement of his presence.

'Chicken noodles?' he asked, those being her favourite.

She nodded and blushed, and poked at the contents of the pot.

'I'm hungry too.' Glancing at the clock, he saw that it was already close to six p.m., which was when his mother would usually be found preparing the evening meal. Just as he thought this, the front door slammed and hurrying feet approached. His mother came in with a full shopping bag in each hand.

'Oh good,' she said, seeing Jackson. 'Would you bring the rest out of the car?'

By the time he had emptied the boot, his mother was well underway frying patties that had been waiting in the fridge. The aroma was appealing, so he hung around. Adelia was sitting at the kitchen table, quietly slurping her noodles and reading a school text. Probably the reading was just a pretext so she wouldn't have to converse, although surely that was the point of boarding in a foreign country: to master the language! It made him remember his homestay experience in India – he understood her conflicting desires to be part of the family and yet keep her privacy.

Thinking of India made him think again about Ahmed, and he took the risk of mentioning the situation to his mother. Cautiously. One little detail at a time... casting it all in the most positive light he could.

'You're what?' she asked, turning to face him, spatula frozen in the air above the sizzling frypan.

'I'm doing this kind of... business deal with a guy I met in India,' he repeated, beginning to wish he'd said nothing. 'I bought some make-up pencils really cheap and sold them over here and made a bit of a profit, so I'm going to do it again. And I bought some hair – to be made into wigs.'

'Hair?'

'Yes. For wigs and... extensions.'

'I heard. Why?'

'It's cheap in India and worth a lot over here.'

'But you haven't received it yet.'

'Not yet. It's on the way.'

'You hope.'

'Yeah,' he said, and then, to demonstrate more faith in his supposed business partner, 'Yeah definitely. It should be here any day.'

'It all sounds very risky to me,' his mother frowned, turning back to the frypan and beginning to flip the patties.

'Well, yeah, but not so much. It wasn't, like, thousands.'

'Thank God for that,' she said with feeling. 'We've taken enough risks around here lately.' She sighed. 'At least you've got that nice job now. But Jackson, don't send that Indian boy any more money, will you?'

'I won't,' he said. He wished he hadn't said anything. Now she'd worry and he had wanted to present his parents with a success, not uncertainty.

Adelia took her mug to the sink to wash it. 'I think this is good business,' she said. 'You make good international relations.'

'That's what you're studying, isn't it?' Jackson asked after a moment. 'International Relations?'

'Yes. This Indian boy, he will respect. He will see good opportunity.'

'I hope so,' Jackson's mother said fervently, lifting the first patty onto a plate.

'Oh well, move on,' Toni said, when he broached the subject with her the following day. 'Next! You've got the building thing going so it doesn't really matter. Besides,' she added, eyes sparkling, 'I've got this new business venture of my own. It might give you some other ideas!'

Eric was philosophical about it. 'You know India,' he said. 'Communication issues, red tape, delays, corruption. Obviously the internet was down the first time you were trying to reach him and it could be anything else now. Hang in there.'

Brooke looked disappointed. 'What a pity,' she said. 'I've got, like, four more people who want kohl pencils. And my sister reckons she's interested in the hair. She's got a client with really black, straight hair who wants a hair extension.'

'Little import business, eh?' Arnold said, surprised and smiling. 'Good for you! Very entrepreneurial. Well, don't stress about it. It's not the end of the world if it falls through. If you're going to be wealthy, you've got to expect both successes and failures. You know the average entrepreneur fails three or four times before succeeding?'

'Really?' said Jackson. He wasn't sure he was up for that, but then again, he still didn't see himself as an entrepreneur.

'My word,' Arnold confirmed. 'A balance of risk-taking and caution, that's the path. You've got to do what you can to guard your money from loss but also keep increasing your ability to earn, which you're doing. Good job.' He gave Jackson's shoulder a short, strong squeeze and walked on.

If you knew that your first three or four businesses were going to fail, would you keep at it?

They say that success is as simple as getting up one time more than the number of times you've fallen down.

A baby falls down approximately 6000 times in the process of learning to walk. Imagine if you decided it was all too hard after falling down the first three times...

One of the important principles of wealth creation is to Guard Your Money From Loss.

We can lose money by

• spending on things that are over-priced (because we didn't shop around first),

• buying things we don't really need or want (because that's what our friends are doing),

• buying on impulse (eg. clothes we buy for 'later when we intend to fit into them'),

• lending money to friends who don't repay us,

• not keeping money in a safe place (if you don't value it, you might find that you lose it; whereas if you value your money, you'll manage it well, know where it is and know how much you have.)

- We can also lose money by not investing wisely, by not keeping appropriate track of our investments, or by not insuring our valuable purchases.

Another important principle of wealth creation is: Keep Increasing Your Ability To Earn, ideally from passive income.

Earning follows Learning:

(i) Educate yourself about money.

This information is rarely taught in school so hunt it down.

Warren Buffet, one of the wealthiest men in the world, was said to have read every book on wealth creation in his local library by the age of sixteen.

Even if that's not strictly true, there is no doubt that he is very well studied in the area of investment.

(ii) Get a real life education on the job.

Work your way up the ranks of whatever industry interests you. Many people who are today leaders in their fields began at the bottom.

Their love of the product or service stimulated a level of creativity that eventually attracted the attention of their managers and employers; with that attention comes opportunity.

If you are the best person in your field, you'll always have people wanting your product or service.

CHAPTER 26

Correcting...

'Hey, Brooke!' **Toni** called, pressing her way through the crowd toward the lockers. Brooke turned, her arms full of books.

Toni caught up, delving into her backpack as she spoke. 'Check these out! You know how annoying it is when you're out for the day and your phone runs out of battery? Well, dah-dah!' She produced a black device with a hot pink edge to it. 'Solar chargers! My new little biz. Only fifteen bucks. Whaddaya say? They come in a range of colours!'

Brooke took the thing and looked at it admiringly, then handed it back, shaking her head sadly. 'Sorry, Tone. I'd love to buy one but my mother would seriously kill me. I've promised to cut back on spending because I owe her heaps, but my boss gave away some of my hours while we were in India and I've got so few shifts that I'm hardly making any money at all.'

'No worries, you can pay back later or in installments,' Toni breezed.

'Geez, I'd love to get one,' Brooke said earnestly. 'But I've got literally no spare money and Mum won't lend me a cent, that's for sure, and Dad's... in the shit financially. And, to top it off, I dropped my phone last week and the screen cracked and Mum won't replace it because it's my second one this year.' Brooke gave a 'terrible me' grimace. 'She totally freaked and I've had to pay the cost of the insurance premium as well. I am *so* up shit creek. Honestly. I would if I could.'

'Sure. No probs.' Toni stowed the charger away in her backpack again. There would be other people who could afford it – there was a whole school here! She found her own locker and pulled out the items she needed for her next class, and was heading there when she saw Jackson coming back from an inter-school soccer match.

'Hey! Jackson!'

'Hi,' he said. There were streaks of mud on his face, clumps of it in his hair, more on the front of his jersey, and caked mud on his knees and shins.

'Good game?' she asked. 'Didya win?'

'Yeah.'

'Winning shot!' someone said affectionately, batting Jackson across the head on their way past.

He grinned and ducked, looking after them.

'Remember what I was saying about a new business?' Toni persisted (despite the little voice at the back of her mind saying, 'This might not be the best time').

'Yeah,' he said, glancing around and past her, as if he were looking for someone.

'Well, I've got them! Solar chargers. Remember how we saw them all over the place in India?' She pulled one out of her backpack, adopting a TV commercial voice: 'Never run out of battery again!' (Oops – hot pink. She pushed that one back into the bag and pulled out one with a green edge to it.)

Jackson looked but he was clearly distracted. 'I really want to help you out with this, Toni. You've helped me heaps. But you know, my money's all tied up in the kohl and hair. Once I shift that stuff, it should be okay. Keep me in mind!'

'Okay…' she said, opening her mouth to offer her 'pay later, installments' options, but he was already moving on.

'Gotta get cleaned up. I'm running late for Maths.'

Toni stood, thinking. She'd expected this to be a no-brainer but her first two customers, whom she'd assumed would be sure things, had both declined. Well, there was a whole school! She headed to class, and in the doorway ran into Eric.

'Eric,' she beamed. 'How'd you like to buy a solar charger? Never have those pesky dead battery problems again!'

Eric looked at her quizzically, and then at the packet she was producing from her backpack. 'How much?'

'Fifteen.'

He reflected on this as they entered and took their seats. 'I'll have a proper look later.'

'Later' Eric decided he would buy one, after examining it carefully during lunch, but despite her best efforts (including a colourful hand-written poster tacked to the wall in the locker room with lots of exclamation marks and a big bright picture of the sun), she had only sold four chargers, two of which were on promise of payment the next day.

At home that evening, Toni decided to create her own store on ebay. She'd sell them there for sure! But, as she was entering the information, she was stopped in her tracks by the question, 'Postage?' When she'd purchased from China the postage had been free but if she was going to have to post them to people… She opened a new tab and pulled up a postage calculator. Shit. Ten bucks. That was going to eat up most of her profit.

Toni pushed away from her desk and scowled at the screen. Damn. She had screwed this up. She stood up so suddenly that the chair fell over with a crash, and then when she tried to pick it up her hand slipped and it dropped to the floor again. She was feeling very pissed off by the time she got to the kitchen.

Her mother was stirring something on the stove and sipping from a glass of wine. Toni's father stood at the bench, frowning at their plans for the extension. A neighbour had objected to the height of the structure on their side because of windows overlooking their place, so they were back to the drawing board.

'Dinner will be ready in ten,' her mother said, seeing Toni enter. 'Set the table, would you, darl?'

'Okay. You know those solar chargers I bought?' Toni said, opening the cupboard door to get the plates. 'I've screwed up *again*. I've only managed to find four takers at school, and if I sell them on ebay I've got to add ten bucks postage, which I hadn't factored in, and that's going to pretty much wipe out my profit.'

'Don't think about it like that,' her mother said. '"Screwed up again." That's not a good attitude to take. You're learning from experience. It's okay.'

'Sell at cost to get rid of them if you have to,' her father said in a distracted voice. 'Next! You can't agonise about these things.' And then, to Toni's mother, 'Honey, we'll have to see how they feel about the window if it's got a smoky glass. Bottom line we're going to need some light coming in there.'

It struck Toni later that night that she was a chip off the old block: her parents were risk-taking entrepreneurial types who always had a new idea to pursue but didn't always think it through properly (eg. the extension…?), and she was exactly the same. She'd leapt in and paid for those punjabis in India up front rather than with a deposit, so when she discovered that the quality wasn't good enough, there wasn't much she could do about it. The products had been made and delivered and fully paid for, and she and the other girls had had to suck it up. At the time they'd all thought it wasn't such a big deal since they were pretty cheap, but now she'd done it again. She'd leapt in without thinking things through, and she was definitely going to lose money on this one because why would people buy a solar charger from her with postage when they could buy their own direct without, and for half the price?

She twirled her seat around in circles, jaw set, stewing on it. Those punjabis were probably going to fall apart soon. Why had she and the other girls valued their money so little? Why were they so comfortable just tossing money around, as if there was an endless supply of it? She supposed it was because, for her, at least, there virtually *was* an endless supply. Her parents were pretty well off and that was how they lived – spending easily, buying what they wanted when they wanted it and not thinking too much about it.

But maybe – and this was such a new and unsettling thought that she braked suddenly with her feet – maybe they weren't as well off as she thought. Maybe her parents' finances were *not* stable and she was just assuming things were okay based on their behavior. After all, buying new cars, extending your house... surely you needed enough funds to be able to do that sort of stuff? But maybe they were over-extended and hadn't thought things through properly themselves? If, like Toni, they acted first and thought later, and then had to make expensive corrections, then perhaps their rich-looking behavior wasn't a very reliable indication of the actual state of affairs.

Brooke was a big spender too. Toni had been surprised by her restraint in not buying a charger – she was usually up for anything that was going, but clearly she had over-extended herself one time too many. Eric, by comparison, was very anal. You could imagine him getting stuck in paralysis by analysis, checking out every single little detail, but he was probably much less likely to be burnt with a bad purchase. And, from what she had gathered he had a fair bit of money tucked away, so that must be working for him. She wondered why he'd bought one of her chargers since he could probably have figured out in two minutes that he'd get them cheaper himself online, and could only conclude that he wanted to help her out in her business venture. That was a humbling thought.

She sighed. Clearly she had to temper her impulsive nature. She liked her ability to see opportunities and act on them! Surely making quick decisions was a good trait? But, on the other hand, it did look like she needed to discipline herself to do more research as well or she was going to come a serious cropper one of these days. Maybe, instead of assuming that her money supply was unlimited (since she always had her parents' wealth at the back of her mind as a safety net), she should act as if it was in short supply, and so everything needed to be very carefully assessed. Maybe, instead of rushing to the prize, she needed to spend more conscious time on the journey. Especially when she was investing in stuff she knew nothing about – maybe that was her fatal flaw. If she focused on investing in things that she was actually interested in, she might be more successful. Maybe knowing more about something made you more savvy when it came to turning it into a business… So what *did* she know about? What was her area of 'expertise'?

'Mastering The Gap'

means pausing before you purchase to do your research and/or check if you really need it.

Do you do this?

Everyone has strengths and weaknesses.

Being a risk-taker is a great trait – and a risky one.

Being good at analysis is a very useful trait – and it can immobilise you.

Playing it safe is often wise – but it can keep you from expanding.

Joining in on what others are doing makes you warm and appealing – but can distract you from some of the hard realities; it's wiser to make sound decisions rather than just doing what the 'in' crowd is doing...

The wisest path is to draw upon the best of those four approaches:

You save steadily rather than frittering money away and you research a purchase before leaping in, but you also take some risks and you allocate some money to pure enjoyment.

And you aim for a balance of financial abundance and 'life-experience wealth'.

CHAPTER 27

Food For Thought

'So,' Arnold said, coming to sit on the low brick wall next to **Jackson**. 'How's it going?'

'Yeah, good,' Jackson replied, hoping there was no tomato sauce on his face. The sausage roll had exploded when he bit into it.

'I thought I'd join you for lunch and have a chat.' Arnold put a small esky on the ground at his feet and popped the lid open. Glancing sideways, Jackson caught a glimpse of fruit, an abundance of fruit.

'That's pretty healthy,' he remarked, cracking open his coke.

'I feel good when I eat like this,' Arnold said simply. He lifted out a red apple and took a big bite. 'Lots of energy. But when I was your age I ate like everyone else – burgers, pies, coke… and it showed. I had a face covered in pimples, I was tired all the time – I'd fall asleep in class. And I was headed for obesity. I was a good twenty kilos overweight.'

'No way,' Jackson said, staring disbelievingly at the trim, strong-looking man beside him. Arnold's sleeves were rolled back to the elbows on arms that were muscled and brown. There wasn't a spare roll of fat anywhere on this man. Jackson's own body was pretty trim but he did sometimes wonder where his diet was taking him… After all, he ate a lot of pastry and soft drinks and crap like that. And his father was pretty solid, if that was any indication of what lay ahead for him. 'How'd you turn it around?' he asked.

'The question is 'why', Arnold grinned. 'A girl, of course. I fell in love and I knew she wouldn't give me a second glance looking the way I looked so I started to clean up my act.'

Jackson nodded. The coke in his hand felt good and cold and the taste was as delicious as usual, but was it taking him down a path he would regret?

'So how's the deal with India?' Arnold asked, taking another huge bite out of his apple, a bite that included half of the core. Surprised, Jackson looked away, self-conscious about staring.

'Still nothing,' he said. 'I spoke to Ahmed on Skype for a few minutes but there was too much interference. He reckons it's all on its way, but.'

'Okay. Well, it's still a great learning for you. The wealthiest people in the world have lost whole fortunes on business deals – you know that? They just pick themselves up and carry on. The ideas in here,' Arnold tapped the side of Jackson's head, 'are more important than the money in your wallet. With ideas and courage you can always start again.'

Jackson thought about this. He didn't want to show himself in a bad light to his mentor but the idea for this business hadn't been his, it had been Ahmed's, and he had resisted it pretty strenuously. And it was Eric and Brooke who were helping him get it together… He really hadn't done anything much himself at all, other than cough up a bit of cash.

'Just a thought for you,' Arnold said, taking a raw corn out of his esky. 'You might want to check out the government regulations for importing hair. It's possible that you'll need permission, since hair is a biological product.'

'Shit!' said Jackson. 'Didn't think of that.'

Arnold shrugged, peeling the corn and tossing the protective leaves and silk back into the box at his feet as he spoke. 'I don't imagine you'll have the cops after you in a hurry. But worth looking into, especially if it does take off. These are all the hidden details of running your own business.' He took a large bite of the golden niblets.

'You're eating that *raw*?' Jackson couldn't help the tone of distaste in his voice.

Arnold laughed. 'It's delicious. Very juicy and sweet. Here, have a bite.'

How did you turn down a taste of your boss's lunch? It felt uncomfortable but he risked a nibble from the untouched end of the cob. And it was juicy. And sweet. Not bad…

'What do you think?'

'I prefer them hot, with loads of butter,' Jackson confessed.

Arnold laughed again. 'I was the same at your age but tastes change, especially as you get better informed. People think of the wealthy as always living the high life – grog, rich food… and some do. But a surprising number prefer salads and wouldn't touch junk food. They make their own lunches, exercise regularly, are fitter than people half their age.'

'I'd like to learn more about being wealthy,' Jackson said in a burst, surprising himself. 'My family does it really hard financially and I don't want to be like that.'

Arnold nodded. 'Good for you. You might think I'm joking when I say this, but start with your diet. A big part of becoming wealthy is self-discipline. See if you can get the junk food calories down and the wholefood calories up.' He turned the corn around in his hands, looking for any areas he hadn't yet demolished. 'What would you like to know?'

'Basically… how do you do it? What are your tips for getting rich?'

'Okay…' For a few minutes they chewed together in silence. Then Arnold said, 'First thing, of course, is to have some sort of income, which you're doing, and then to be religious about saving a percentage of it. It's a principle called 'Pay Yourself First'. Do you save at all?'

'I've got a savings account and another one, a prosperity account that I'm not supposed to touch – ever,' Jackson said with a flush of pride.

Arnold whistled. 'I'm impressed. Who told you to do that?'

'A mate at school.'

'He's worth listening to.'

'I put about ten per cent in each one.'

'Good job.' The shaved corncob fell into the esky and Arnold lifted out a packet of almonds, which he offered to Jackson. 'The next tip is to live below your means. No lashing out. You buy stuff you can afford or you don't buy it. It's that simple. Mate of mine made his family live in a tiny two-bedroom apartment until he could buy their dream house *for cash*. They hated the long wait, and him, I suspect, but everyone's pretty happy now. It's either the pain of discipline or the pain of regret – you make your choice.'

'For cash'. Jackson remembered his jar, stuffed full of notes. He'd always enjoyed the feel of the money and he missed it now that it was in the bank. Still, he got the value of having it somewhere safe while it grew, and he liked the idea of fronting up to buy whatever he wanted in cash. He could just see himself with wads of notes, counting them out… He wondered how much a ute would cost. Could he set the goal of saving several thousand by the time he finished school so he could buy his own for cash? That would be very cool. A goal like that would turn him on.

'Lots of wealthy people are extremely frugal,' Arnold was saying. 'Zuckerberg drives a 30K car and he's a multi-billionaire.'

'Geez,' Jackson said. The founder and CEO of Facebook driving your average mum-and-dad car and not a Merc?

'Tips…' Arnold said thoughtfully. 'You want a balanced approach, Jackson: live within your means and guard your money from loss on one side, and do what you can to expand your earnings on the other. You're having a crack at that – working here weekends and starting up your little import business on the side. That's all good. And you're planning on an apprenticeship after school, which is a great way to earn while you learn.' He gestured around the building site. 'There's always work for a good tradie.'

Jackson felt warmed, not only by the sun beating down on them, but also by the sense that he was on track, that he was beginning to take charge of his destiny.

'It's important to work at things you love to do because that's what you'll be best at and where you'll be most self-disciplined. If you value it, you'll value it. Stands to reason. Money in itself is worthless. You can't eat it; it won't give you any pleasure in and of itself. Its value is as a medium of exchange, right? That you can use to acquire and do the things you *do* value. It's important to keep that in mind. You're not building wealth to have a stockpile of cash; you're building wealth so you can create the experiences you want to have, and so that you're able to follow through on your ideas and interests.'

One of the builders came over with a question and Jackson watched and listened as the two men conferred. When he'd gone, Arnold picked up his trail of thought.

'People get very judgemental about the idea of making money – they think wealthy people are obsessed with money and putting it up on a pedestal and making some idol out of it. That's rubbish. It's actually the other way around. Wealthy people have money working *for them*, while poor people spend their whole lives working for money. They're the real slaves to money.'

'Makes sense,' Jackson said. His family were slaves, there was no doubt about that.

'Something else to understand,' Arnold said, putting the last of the nuts back in his esky and locking the lid in place, 'is that wealth is not just about the cash; your true wealth is what you're left with if you lose all your money and possessions: it's your knowledge, your skills, your attitude, your work ethic, how flexible and adaptable you are, your creativity and courage and persistence… You get that stuff right and the money will flow; you'll be ahead of the game.' He glanced at his watch. 'There's lots of practical stuff to know, of course, like the difference between assets and liabilities. We'll save that for next time. I've got to jump. Got a meeting in town at two.'

'I reckon Toni would be interested in learning this stuff too,' Jackson said.

'She's welcome. I'll give any kid who's keen a leg up.'

Toni looked at Jackson curiously. He was clearly on the verge of saying something to her – he was blushing, which was kind of cute. 'Spit it out,' she said. Which made the blush deepen.

'Just wanted to say thanks,' he said at last, 'for introducing me to Arnold. He's great value, and I'm really enjoying it.'

'Oh, that's fine,' she said, a little disappointed. 'I'm glad.'

'He's been giving me some tips for getting rich. You want to join in on that?'

'Sure. Like what?'

'You know, just saving and stuff, but it's best hearing it straight from him.'

'Okay.' She nodded her head in the direction of the exam timetable that was tacked to the wall of their homeroom. 'You feel ready?'

'Nope,' he said automatically, and then, 'And I was wondering if you want to go to the movies this Friday night.'

So that was the reason for the blush! Toni felt a smile on her insides. 'Sure,' she said again. 'What to see?'

Eric was studying. The exam timetable was tacked to the wall next to his computer, and next to it he had tacked a colour-coded study timetable. He'd leapt at the job at the Apple store when it came available but the timing wasn't ideal with exams starting soon. Perhaps he had been too impulsive taking that job just now…? He would have to be very disciplined to make sure he achieved all of his goals.

Brooke had been avoiding the mall because she knew what she was like when it came to window-shopping: if she saw something she liked she would soon talk herself into buying it, especially if it was on special. But she had to do an errand here for her mother, so she had roped Kelly in for moral support. 'I'm going to walk all the way down there,' she said, pointing straight ahead, 'without even *looking* at those clothes shops,' waving a hand on either side of them.

'Go, Brooks,' Kelly said. 'But isn't the point being able to look and *not* buy?'

'Impossible,' Brooke said.

'Crap.' Kelly set off. 'Tell me if you see something you want. I'm an expert at this now.'

'But I don't want to look,' Brooke objected, holding her hands on either side of her eyes as blinkers.

'Get over yourself,' Kelly replied. 'You look like an idiot.'

Brooke quickly dropped her hands to her sides. Shit. Her favourite store had *'Sale Now – Everything 25% Off!'* signs emblazoned all over the windows. She turned away, biting her lip.

'You like their stuff, don't you?' Kelly asked, veering toward the store.

'What are you doing?' Brooke wailed, following her like Mary's Little Lamb. 'We promised!'

'You're not going to buy anything,' Kelly said. 'You're going to look and think about it and create a little gap.'

'I can jump over little gaps in a single bound,' Brooke said miserably. Her hand trailed along the outfits on the rack in the open doorway.

'Have you thought of asking for a job in here?' Kelly asked.

'Oh no, that would be too dangerous. I'd spend my whole pay here.'

'Okay… Just an idea. Because there is layby, you know.'

'I know. I already have something on layby in here,' Brooke confessed.

'So what would you like to buy?' Kelly asked, almost like Santa Claus.

'We're not, are we!' Brooke exclaimed, with a little thrill.

'No, just asking.'

'Oh. Well, just about everything. That jacket. This top. That dress hanging up there. The pants and scarf on that model…'

Kelly shook her head. 'So… about three hundred bucks' worth.'

'Is it?' Brooke winced. 'But I wouldn't. It's just what I would *like* to buy.'

'I know. So that's your incentive. You've got to get some kind of job that will let you earn that kind of money if you want to buy that much stuff. So look at it, feel how good it will be to wear all that stuff, imagine yourself in it… and get focused on a job.' She turned Brooke by the shoulders and steered her away. 'Meanwhile, how else can you reward yourself? Other than chocolate, of course.'

Walking away from that shop without taking advantage of the sales gave Brooke, like, an actual physical pain. She walked in silence for a while, brow furrowed. 'What?' she said after a while, remembering that Kelly had asked her something.

Her sister caught her by the elbow. 'Come in here. My shout.'

Sitting on a comfy, padded bench seat with drinks, they watched the shopping mall crowds flock past. People of all ages and sizes and genders hurried and dawdled, plastic bags in hand, some with fixed expressions on their faces, many speaking into phones or sending text messages, a few laughing with friends…

'Still no joy at The Burger Place?' Kelly asked.

'One shift a week. Two if I'm lucky.'

'So what else can you do?'

Brooke thought back to the conversation she'd had with her mother before India. Dress-making, her mother had suggested. Or photography. She picked up a pen that someone had left on the table and began to doodle on the paper placemat. 'I dunno.'

Kelly watched the caricature come to life on the page. 'You've always been good at that,' she said admiringly. 'Bitch. Wish I could draw.'

'You can cut hair,' Brooke said, absorbed. 'We could go into business together. I'll draw your customers while you cut their hair.'

'Sounds like a no-brainer,' Kelly said, stirring her drink with the straw. 'But seriously, you could go to kids' parties and draw funny pictures of the kids. You're very quick and you're good. Why don't you?'

'Mum said that,' Brooke remembered, still sketching. 'Do you really think so?'

'Sure. A few ads in a primary school… I can ask if we can put some ads in the salon. Plenty of mums come in there.'

Brooke thought about it. To make money drawing, which she enjoyed, would actually be pretty cool. 'Okay,' she said. 'What would I charge?'

'I'll ask around this week – what they're paying for face painters and all that stuff.

'I think Toni used to work for a lady who had a kids' parties business,' Brooke said. 'I'll ask her too.'

'Good plan. So now,' Kelly turned her face sideways to look into Brooke's eyes. 'Tell me how you feel about those clothes. Do you still want them?'

'Of course.'

'But is it urgent?'

Brooke reflected. To be honest, she would have to say no. The pain had receded by walking away and not thinking about those clothes for a few minutes. She'd successfully Created A Gap.

Kelly gave her a thumbs-up gesture. 'See? Mum's right. If you just walk away and think about something else for a bit the urgency dies down. And if you stay away for long enough, you can even forget all about it.'

'Yes… it was all just a lovely dream,' Brooke murmured, as she put the last strokes to her drawing.

'Sign that,' Kelly instructed as they stood up to leave. 'Someone is going to acquire a future-famous Brooke Hamley picture.'

CHAPTER 28

Looking For The Way Forward

'**Jackson**! There's a big package just arrived for you,' his mother called.

Jackson bounded through the house to the hallway where his mother stood leafing through envelopes. She handed him the parcel, which was taped and stamped multiple times.

'At last!' He ripped into it and a number of sealed plastic bags, each containing a bunch of straight, black hair, fell out. A tightly wrapped bundle that was probably more make-up pencils began to slip out of the package too – he grabbed it before it hit the floor.

His mother shook her head. 'Slow down, Jack.'

Jackson beamed, scooping the bags of hair up. 'See! It's all good!' He made a beeline for his room, turfed the products onto his bed, and grabbed his phone to text Brooke.

The whine was growing closer and louder, until it was almost deafeningly loud, and then it cut off. **Toni** hopped to her bedroom window, one leg stuck in her twisted jeans, and peered outside. It was her brother – on a brand new motorbike! He was parking it in the drive and then sitting there, relaxed, undoing a helmet. She tore the jeans off, shook them out, and tried again. She could hear voices outside now: her father admiring the bike and her brother replying.

They were coming inside as she ran toward them, and then past them, calling, 'Is it yours?'

Her brother grinned. 'Yep. Lock, stock and handlebars.'

Toni circled the bike, admiring the shining metal, the padded seat, the black helmet... When she joined them inside, her brother was slinging his brand new leather jacket across the back of a chair.

'Very cool,' she enthused. 'Is it fun to ride?'

'The best! Zipping past cars stuck in traffic... Love it.'

'Just wait till the weather cools down, though,' their father said. 'Might change your mind when it's raining and cold.'

'It's not like you to rain on someone's parade,' Toni's brother countered, in mock disappointment.

'Been there, done that,' their father replied. 'I remember it well. So! Tell us about the new business.'

'You've got a new business as well?' Toni demanded. 'How come I never hear about these things?'

'You're hearing now. It's all just happening.' He hoisted himself onto a bar stool at the kitchen bench. 'It's the hottest company in the direct sales industry at the moment. Supplements, protein shakes, stuff like that. They get awesome results for people – huge weight loss, that kind of thing. The guy who signed me up is going gangbusters with it already. Anyone care to sign up?'

'You'll have to give us a better spiel than that,' their father said. 'Coffee?'

Toni's brother unzipped his backpack and pulled out a couple of plastic containers. 'The drinks are on me. I want you to taste this stuff. It's wicked!'

As Toni and her father reached for the containers her brother added, 'But I'm serious – especially for you, Tone. It's a business you can run. It's direct sales so there's hardly any start-up investment – just your joining fees. They reckon network marketing is the way of the future. For a few hundred bucks I'm in business doing something I believe in, and you could be too. The income potential is unbelievable.'

Toni's phone buzzed and she glanced at the screen. Mrs S. She hadn't heard from her in ages!

Parties ramping up – I need you! she read. *Have a great deal to offer: work for me in exchange for horse riding lessons. My new partner offers lessons, trekking – you name it!*

Hm. Toni laid the phone on the bench, thinking. She'd always wanted horse-riding lessons, ever since she was a kid. Her mother had probably shared that detail with Mrs S, since they were friends. But did she really want to be *paid* in lessons? That meant no cash of her own to do with as she wanted. Plus there'd be the challenge of getting out there, since her parents were never around to drive her… And it meant she was committed to those lessons even if she changed her mind and would rather have, say, singing lessons, or just save the money, or go into business with her brother.

Nope. She would rather have the cash and the control over it herself. Picking up her phone, she texted back: *Thanks Mrs S. I really appreciate that but horse-riding lessons are not a high priority at the moment. Happy to work for cash!*

'Are you studying hard?' **Eric**'s mother asked. She had dropped in from the hospital for a brief visit between appointments since the house was so close. 'Do you need any help?'

'He always does well,' Eric's father said.

'That's exactly the wrong attitude,' she snapped. 'What are you trying to teach him?'

'I'm going fine,' Eric interrupted. 'Exams have already started. I had Biol today and Maths is tomorrow.'

'It's not just about study,' Eric's father continued. 'Better be the uneducated guy who owns the business than the person with all the degrees who's just an employee.'

'There are many more uneducated people in dead-end jobs than running businesses,' Eric's mother said tightly. 'And it's also possible to be a well-paid employee and build security rather than a high-risk entrepreneur.' She turned away from her ex-husband to her son. 'Have you been thinking more about your career path?'

Eric knew they didn't mean to fight over him all the time like this; it was just that they were both so stressed at the moment about the divorce and everything that entailed. Still, it was horrible being the meat in the middle.

'Not much,' he said. 'Something with science or maths… Maybe engineering, like Dad. Or IT… The guys at the Apple Store are making me interested in designing apps. I've got lots of interests.'

'Mm-huh,' she said, looking pointedly at Eric's father, who was not supposed to hover like this when she dropped in. He registered the message, picked up his glass of wine, and left the kitchen.

Eric's mother waited a moment for his echoing footsteps to die out. 'I'm sorry about that,' she said. 'I'm always on edge around your dad lately.'

'It's all right,' he said, because what else could you say?

She touched his cheek gently. 'I know you study hard. I… actually, I've been feeling a bit left out. You used to ask me for help and you haven't done that in ages.'

Eric stood still, uncertain what to say.

His mother glanced away and then back at him with a bright smile. 'It's all right. You're growing up. It's fine. So… good luck tomorrow then.' She woke up her phone to check the time. 'My place this weekend, right?'

He nodded, and she leaned in to kiss his cheek. 'Don't rule out medicine, Eric. You used to want to be a doctor, remember?'

'Yes… okay…' he said. He had let go of that plan a long time ago but this wasn't the right time to tell her. It was funny how his parents had swapped positions; his father used to be fixated on university and his mother would be encouraging him to have more life experiences, and now they were reversed.

He watched her walk down the path toward her BMW, and felt a pang in his chest. She looked lonely. She saw him watching from the door as she climbed into her car, and smiled and waved. But when she'd closed the car door he saw her brush at her cheek, and the pang in his chest deepened.

'Kel reckons that a full head of hair from Russia or Europe sells for a grand,' **Brooke** informed Jackson, as she peeked into the package. 'Can you believe that? But India and China, it's more like a hundred bucks, three hundred bucks...'

'Still,' Jackson said, 'even half of that is decent money, so don't lose it, will you?'

She looked at him scornfully. 'Are you kidding? I'm earning almost zero and I owe stacks. You're saving my life right now with the extra bit of cash I'm making helping you.'

He followed her to her locker, saying, 'I don't know if you're interested but the guy I'm working for wants to help kids understand money. He's mega-rich –'

'What was that?' someone asked.

They both looked around. Track-suited Miss Harris was standing at Jackson's elbow, a clipboard under her arm.

'What was what?' he asked back.

'What you just said: "Some mega-rich person..."?'

'Oh. Yeah. My boss. He wants to help kids get their heads around money.'

'Do you think he'd come and speak to the Year 9s?'

'Sure,' Jackson said. 'I dunno. I can ask him.'

'Please do,' Miss Harris said. 'We've got an opening after the exams finish for a guest speaker, and I think that would be an excellent topic.'

Remembering Mr Plowright's comments in India about Miss Harris's personal wealth, Brooke plunged in. 'Or maybe you could be the guest speaker, Miss H. I don't mean to pry, but we heard you're pretty rich too.'

Miss Harris scrutinised them. They were both taller than her but she was still a formidable presence. 'I think an expert from outside of the school, from the world of business, would have far more impact on the students than me,' she said at last. 'However, I would be quite willing to contribute. There's far too much ignorance about money among youth, and too many atrocious habits.'

When she had gone, and Jackson had loped off for his next exam, Brooke took her study notes to sit in the sun and cram before her own next exam. She noticed that she had accidentally taken her Gratitude Diary out of her locker with the textbooks. Her mother had given one to her and one to Kelly. They were pretty – colourful designs and quotes about the power of gratitude – and the girls were supposed to be noting at least three things a day that they felt grateful for. She and Kel checked out each other's entries each night and she hadn't written anything for today yet. Thinking of things you were grateful for while you were in the middle of exams was not the easiest!

She scanned the list she'd jotted so far. One of the challenges they had set each other was to list new things rather than repeating the same old things over and over. So far she had:

1. *Mum.*
2. *Dad.*
3. *Kel.*
4. *A home to live in.*
5. *Plenty of food.*
6. *Clothes.*
7. *I'm healthy.*
8. *I have friends.*
9. *Pizza.*
10. *Jackson paying me for selling eyeliners.*
11. *First exam over! Yay!*
12. *Kel and I are close again.*
13. *Dad finally called.*
14. *It was hot today – summer coming!*

15. Don't have to worry about survival. Have a home and food.
16. India trip – the best.
17. My nose stud!
18. Laura's b'day party the night exams finish.
19.

A shadow fell across her page. She looked up. Toni was standing over her, blocking the sun.

'I spoke to Mrs S about you drawing pictures at the parties,' Toni said. 'She reckons she'll give it a go. I'll send you her number.'

'Hey thanks!'

'No probs.' Toni wandered away, and Brooke added:

19. Possible job at kids' parties drawing caricatures.
20.

She doodled in the margin, wondering what else she could be grateful for – although she shouldn't spend too much time on this because she was supposed to be cramming. Ah!

20. School term nearly over. Holidays coming!

Brooke wasn't sure if things in the future counted in a gratitude list as much as things now but she was definitely feeling grateful that the holidays were near. But then she remembered that several of her friends were going away for the whole summer, so she'd be alone for most of it. That wasn't something to look forward to… Maybe, Brooke reflected, maybe instead of hanging out at the beach and poolside all summer, she would surprise everyone (and herself) and work through the entire school holidays and make piles of money!

Brooke liked the idea of piles of money much more than the idea of working all the way through the summer holidays… She thought about The Burger Place. It was easy work – she just had to smile at people and take their orders and use the cash register and do a bit of cleaning… But it wasn't the most inspiring place to work. Most of the employees saw it as a path to something else, so they did the bare minimum and got out of there. And most of the customers ate there because they couldn't afford anything better. Well, she supposed that was why. I mean, why would you eat fries and preservative-laden, processed burgers, she wondered, if you could afford a classy restaurant with dishes like slow roasted meat, herbed potato wedges, wild mushrooms, caramelized onions, wilted spinach, rustic bread, salads with cherry tomatoes, goat's cheese, grilled eggplant, spicy peppers – and chocolate mud cake with berries…? Her mouth watered as she recalled the special birthday dinner they'd had the previous weekend for her mother.

Yes, The Burger Place was definitely a stopgap. She would prefer to do something creative; her mother was right about that…

Drawing at parties would be fun but would she make much money? Somehow she doubted it, and Brooke wanted a way to have fun *and* make money. Her parents were not the best role models. Her mother loved helping people but she always looked exhausted; Brooke didn't want that. Her father loved finding the next exciting deal but he was always right on the edge, taking risks, and lately, crashing and burning; Brooke didn't want that either. Somehow she had to find a path that was a balance of security and enjoyment. Brooke felt sure that she was cut out for the high life. She could just imagine herself, the life of the party, in stunning outfits… The question was: how could she get into that world of wealth safely?

What's top of your gratitude list?

Could you find three unique things every day?

Have a go...

1.

2.

3.

4.

5.

6.

7.

8.

9.

10.

11.

12.

13.

14.

15.

16.

17.

... now keep going!

Is a job just about the money you earn or more than that?

If you're like many young people today you don't just apply for a job because of the pay packet but also because of the satisfaction you'll get doing the work. That's wise: if you're going to invest your life energy into it, make sure you're doing work you enjoy that aligns with your values and makes you feel alive and fulfilled.

Network Marketing or Multi-Level Marketing is considered by some financial pundits...

(eg. Robert Kiyosaki, author of Rich Dad, Poor Dad), to be the way of the future – an ethical way to make limitless income by being of service to others. (Beware of its 'lookalike' – pyramid selling.)

Traditional schooling is not, in and of itself, a guarantee of jobs or success in life.

A university degree is linked to higher incomes during one's working life but 'soft skills', like your ability to talk to and relate to people, can be even more useful.

You'll find people on unemployment benefits who are highly qualified yet out of work.

You'll find people who dropped out of school running multi-million dollar international businesses.

Likewise, you'll find people who dropped out of school on the dole, and people who scored straight A's in top level positions.

There are no guarantees.

So... what will guarantee your future job fulfillment and financial success?

How can you live the life of your dreams AND be secure?

CHAPTER 29

Money Talks

The assembly hall was buzzing. Not only were the students high on nervous energy with the relief of exams being over and the long summer holidays ahead, but today they had a speaker from 'the real world', as adults liked to call it, who was going to talk to them about making money. They watched the guy chatting to their principal while the last stragglers took their seats, and hoped this would be interesting.

Mr Baxter gave his inevitable long-winded introduction, but when he listed off Arnold's achievements, both Jackson and Toni (who were feeling chuffed that they'd organised this), were as impressed as the rest of the crowd. Millionaire by age thirty. Owned property all over the world. Friends with Richard Branson and Elon Musk. Philanthropist. On the board of several non-government organisations, especially working in the social enterprise arena.

'Did you know all that?' Jackson asked Toni with his eyes. She shook her head, joining in with the applause as Arnold took to the stage.

'So you've finished your exams, eh?' was the first thing he said. The students exploded into cheers.

'Well done.' He raked them with his gaze. 'I'm possibly going to say a few things your teachers won't like.' A titter rippled through the auditorium. 'Because an education is all very well, but are the facts you're learning here going to help you pay your bills or realise your dreams?' He paused, and they waited.

'Schooling is correlated with financial success in life but it's not the cause of it. A high IQ doesn't guarantee that you will rise above everyone else. Research shows that 85 per cent of your financial success comes down to your personality and ability to communicate, negotiate, and lead – your EQ, Emotional Intelligence, and only 15 per cent to factual knowledge. People would actually rather do business with a person they like and trust than with someone they don't like, even if the likeable person is offering a lower quality product or service at a higher price.'

He picked up a marker pen from the flip chart stand behind him and said, 'Here's a question for you: if you had a million, how would you spend it? Come on!'

Someone called out that they'd travel. He asked where and a few voices shouted destinations, which he wrote on the page. He turned back to the students and another voice called, 'Buy a yacht!' so he added that to the list.

'Buy the house of my dreams!' someone said.

'Shoes!' a girl added, 'and a new wardrobe!'

'Uni fees so I don't have to work,' another voice called out.

'Go snowboarding and skiing all over the world,' one of the school athletes added.

'Buy a footy club,' the class clown shouted, and Arnold turned around, capping the pen.

'You're joking,' he said. 'You think a mill would do it? But...' he turned back to the list, jotted the comment then faced them again. 'What else?'

'Pay my parents' mortgage,' one student said, and Jackson swivelled around to see who that was.

'Set up an animal rescue centre,' someone else called out.

'Okay.' Arnold added the last few suggestions and then surveyed the list. He circled the 'Buy a footy club' idea and turned to face them. 'Of all of them, this is a rich person's thinking; the rest is poor person thinking.' He waited for the chatter to die down, then continued.

'Poor people consume: they buy stuff to have, to use. Rich people invest: they buy stuff that will make them more money.' He paused, looking around the room.' But that's all years away, right? When you're adults!' A pause, and it was as if he had put his finger on the thought everyone was thinking – *Give us a break, mister. We're just kids…*

'Wrong,' Arnold said, a steely glint in his eye. 'Wealth and poverty are *habits*, and you're building your habits right now, as teenagers.' He walked to the front of the stage and perched on the stool. 'How many of you save?'

A smattering of hands rose, and he rolled out some sobering statistics about how little most people saved, and how many were dependent on social security or their families in retirement. They watched as he scrawled the numbers on the next page of the flip chart.

<u>7 BILLION PEOPLE IN THE WORLD</u>

1% HAVE EXTREME WEALTH

1.2 BILLION LIVE IN RELATIVE WEALTH

4.3 BILLION ARE SOMEWHERE ALONG THE SCALE FROM POVERTY TO SUBSISTENCE

1.5 BILLION LIVE IN ABJECT POVERTY.

'It's a sad thing,' he said, 'but most people your age assume that you'll do okay in the future and don't actively prepare for it. Most of those people,' walking back to the flip chart and banging the scribbled statistics, 'assumed they'd be okay. They were *sure* they'd be okay. And they didn't take responsibility for putting money aside. Most people spend more time reading the instructions on their iPhone than designing their own lives.' He gave them a comical stare and they broke out laughing; who spent any time reading iPhone instructions?

'So listen,' he said in a more relaxed tone. 'Millionaire at thirty – that's out of date. Kids of *twenty* are making their first million. It's doable, folks, if you want it enough. And, sure, you need a cracker of a business idea to make that much money that fast. But if you want to be ahead of the curve, if you want to retire young and spend most of your life doing what you want, you're going to have to discipline yourselves to make money and *save*.'

He returned to the stool. 'You people are starting to get casual jobs, part-time jobs, holiday jobs. In a few years you're going to leave school and look for some kind of work, either full-time or on the side while you're studying. But whatever work you do, you're going to start at the bottom. That's appropriate. You know nothing about how the world works! You've been here, learning this stuff. But once you get out *there*, make sure you pay attention. Do your job well – give it your best. The worker who goes above and beyond what is expected of them is noticed and rewarded. Opportunities will come your way because the boss feels he or she can trust you.'

He stood up and went to the front of the stage. 'But the most important pathway to wealth is to manage your money well, and the best way to do that is to save. Make saving your new religion. Have a savings account for your everyday stuff but also put 10% of everything you earn into a Prosperity Savings Account that you never touch, because 10% of everything you earn should be yours to keep.'

He looked at them seriously. '*You never spend that money – never.* It sits there, growing and making you feel wealthy. Got that?' There was a low rumble of voices in response, and he walked a few paces to address the students on the other side of the auditorium. 'There's a funny law in this universe called the law of 'The More, The More; The Less, The Less': 'The more you save, the more you'll receive; the less you save, the less you'll receive'. So do yourself a favour and start the saving habit *now*. Even if you only save one per cent to begin with, *start saving now*.'

He paced back the other way, then stopped and asked, '10% in your WHAT?'

'Prosperity account!' someone yelled back.

'Bingo. The goal of your prosperity account is that it grows to such a degree that it earns you more in interest than you can make by working. Another 10% goes into a regular savings account, where you save for things like cars and holidays and houses. And 10%, I would suggest, goes into a charity or some kind of community goodwill. And another 10% is for investing. Let's talk about that. What's investing?'

'Putting money into stuff that makes you money!' someone called, and he asked for examples, and they listed off property and stocks and owning your own business and collectables like stamps and cars and artwork.

'Do you have to understand all this now?' he asked, and the response was a muddle of 'Yes!' and 'No!'

'No,' he said, grinning, 'but you do have to *start* learning! How many of your families talk about money at the dinner table?'

Toni nodded. In another row, Eric nodded. Jackson rolled his eyes – please, no; money conversations always caused stress. Brooke shook her head; her mother never permitted conversations about money during mealtimes, although they were constantly happening at other times, it seemed.

'I won't ask how many of you actually *have* dinner with your family around a table,' Arnold said, with a meaningful glance toward Mr Baxter and the other teachers. 'Although family meals are actually linked to greater achievement later on... But listen, folks, ask your parents about money. Ask them how your family stands financially. You're old enough to start understanding this stuff. *You* pay the household bills one month – I don't necessarily mean out of your pocket, but do the job so you get a reality check on how much it's costing your family when you have a twenty-minute shower or forget the heater on or break things. Do the weekly grocery shopping. Find out what the stuff you stick in your mouths so unconsciously is costing your parents.'

Toni remembered the time her mother had given her and her brother two hundred dollars cash and the shopping list, and then sat in the car outside the supermarket with a book while they trailed up and down the aisles doing the weekly shop. She had loved it. She'd felt so grown up, at all of nine years old, clutching all that money and doing a whole trolley's worth of shopping.

'So get educated,' Arnold said powerfully. 'Wealth know-how doesn't just magically drop into your lap at a certain age; it's something you can begin developing *now*. Start a spending diary – track everything you buy, keep all the receipts. Find out how much you're spending on sweets at the corner shop, or whatever it is you guys indulge in these days. That few dollars here and there adds up, sometimes significantly. Reuse, recycle, upgrade instead of buying everything brand new. Don't try to keep up with the Joneses, they're going down the financial gurgler.'

Brooke wondered if he was speaking to her specifically. He sure seemed to be looking at her right now. Her gaze faltered and fell to her lap, and when she looked up again he had moved a few paces across the stage and was looking at someone else.

'Prioritise your purchases, guys. If there's something you want, figure out how much you need it on a scale of one to ten. Did you hear that? I said 'need it' – not want it. Your needs are things like food, shelter, clothes – basic, not the latest styles – dental care...'

Someone groaned. Brooke wondered if he'd been speaking to her mother...

'Your wants – well, you get to earn the money and pay for those yourselves. Don't expect your parents to provide them. "I need a new phone," he said, mimicking a teen speaking to a parent. 'No, you don't. You *want* the new phone. There's a big difference. Does it sound like I'm lecturing you?'

For a moment the auditorium was silent. 'Here's the thing,' Arnold said, perching on the stool again. 'Would you go to a butcher for brain surgery?' He waited, scanning the room, but no one spoke. 'I promise you guys, if you want to be financially free, listen and act on at least something you hear today. When I turned thirty I didn't have to work a day for the rest of my life because I worked hard and smart when I was your age. I *do* work, because I love it, but I don't have to. I have choice.'

He bent down to the briefcase leaning against the stool and pulled out a packet of marshmallows. 'Anyone want a marshmallow?'

A few voices called 'yes'; others hesitated, waiting for the catch.

'Have you guys heard of the Marshmallow Study?' He was ripping the packet open. 'Got a little video clip to show you. See if you can hang onto these without eating them until it's over.' He began tossing marshmallows randomly into the crowd. Students leapt up to catch them, and there was the odd crash and laughter and swearing...

When the pack was empty, he gave a nod to someone at the back of the auditorium and the room went dark. The screen lit up with a black-and-white movie taken in the seventies of five-year-old kids being given marshmallows – one now, but if they could wait fifteen minutes before eating it, they'd get a second one.

The students watched as the children sat on their own in a room and stared at the marshmallow on the table in front of them. Some looked around, to check if anyone was observing them, then licked it or took a nibble. Some ate the thing outright. Others waited the agonisingly long time until the adult returned.

When the short clip was over, Arnold asked who still had their marshmallow, and a number of hands waved the little white squares in the air. He asked what they would have done, age five, and waited while they chattered and commented. 'That study was about the ability to 'delay gratification'. It means: can you wait or do you have to have everything *now*?'

'Now', thought Brooke, wincing. She really needed to grow out of that. She wasn't five anymore...

'The people who can delay gratification are the people who typically end up earning more,' Arnold told them. 'If you need it, fair enough, but if you just want it, see if you can wait. Delay. Check if you *really* need it. The less you spend now, the more you have later. It's called 'Mastering the Gap'. If you can pause before you spend, just that moment of extra thought and there's a decent chance you'll be able to put off the purchase – and put that money into your savings instead! You want to get so that you love the idea of your savings growing. You want it to feel so good that it's painful to take any money out.'

Eric knew that to be true.

'A good rule of thumb is that you only get to spend more on your lifestyle, on the stuff you want, when you can increase your savings by the same amount, so build the habit of regularly bumping up the amount you save. Say you only start with five per cent, so the next month it's six per cent or seven per cent. If you keep pushing yourself to raise your savings, you'll find that you earn more too, because you're valuing your money, and money likes to go where it's valued.'

Oh, Brooke thought, surprised. That was a different way of seeing it – as if money was alive, a 'person'. That would help...

Arnold turned to a new sheet and wrote two words on the page. 'Who knows the difference between an asset and a liability?' he asked.

A few people mumbled answers. While they spoke he wrote:

<u>ASSET</u>

PUTS MONEY IN YOUR POCKET

<u>LIABILITY</u>

TAKES MONEY OUT OF YOUR POCKET

'You guys want to buy a car soon, right? Asset or liability?'

'Liability!'

'What about your family home?'

'Asset!'

'Only if it's significantly increasing in value and then you sell it. Or if you're renting rooms. But your own house where you live,' he shook his head. 'That's costing you. What about your own business?'

'Depends,' a savvy student said.

Arnold nodded. 'Exactly. Your business is an asset if it's making a profit and a liability if it's costing you or putting you deeper into debt.'

Toni thought about her brother's new business. Health and fitness products. Would anyone buy those from her, a kid?

'Do you people own any assets?' There was silence. He looked around the room. 'Come on, *think*. What do you own that you could sell if you needed to?'

'My doll collection,' a girl called out.

'Good. What else?'

Computers, phones, skis, game consoles, old Pokémon collections and autographed celebrity photos were listed. Arnold nodded. 'But remember, that stuff only counts as an asset if you actually sell it and turn it into money in your pocket. The money in your bank accounts is another asset. Next question for you.'

He walked back to the flip chart stand. 'How many ways are there to make money?'

'Get a job!'

Earned income, Arnold wrote on the page.

'Inherit.'

'True, but you don't want to be waiting around for that. What else?' He surveyed the room.

Passive income, Eric thought.

'You people heard of passive income?' Arnold asked. 'You write a book and make royalties from it. Or a song. Or you earn rental income. That's all passive – it comes in without any ongoing effort, after the initial effort or purchase. This is a big key to wealth creation: rich people are good at making money work for them, whether they're working or not. What else?'

Portfolio income, Eric thought.

'Stocks and bonds,' a voice called.

'Precisely. Same principle as passive income: it generates income while you sleep. It's called 'leverage' – when other people or products are earning money for you.'

A light bulb went off in Jackson's mind. There he was, feeling guilty that Brooke and Eric and Ahmed were all helping him make an income from the Indian products when actually he was just applying leverage. He was being a good businessperson. He smiled.

Arnold checked the time. 'Okay. I have two last things to cover. First, is debt good or bad?' He stood at the edge of the stage, rocking backwards and forward.

'Bad!' they yelled.

'Good!' someone called out.

He grinned. 'Both answers are right. There's good debt and bad debt. Good debt is money spent to increase your income, like when you borrow to buy an investment property. Bad debt is money borrowed to buy a car, or something that's going to depreciate in value. What about credit cards?'

'A trap,' one of the teachers said from the back of the room.

Arnold laughed. 'Very often! Actually, used well a credit card can help you to establish a good credit rating if you pay it out fully every month. But if you just pay the minimum payment option you're heading for disaster. The amount can snowball and before you know it, you're in deep doo-doo because the interest rates are nasty. Do you know how long it can take you to pay off a credit card debt of, say, $2000.00 at 20% interest when your minimum monthly repayment is $34?'

Silence. Then someone called out, 'Five years?'

Arnold shook his head. '*Twenty* years.'

The silence deepened.

'Shit,' someone said.

'Exactly. They are killer rates. You'll find that your credit card debt will be increasing even though you haven't bought anything new. It's like burning money.'

He pulled out his phone and waved it at them. 'This is really important for your generation. You're growing up in a cashless society – people are using plastic and transferring invisible money all over the place in the blink of an eye. Putting aside the whole issue about money losing its value since it's not backed by gold anymore, and the fact that we're moving into being a cashless society, I'd recommend that, wherever possible, you keep it concrete and pay with real hard cash, or debit cards if you have to use a card, so that you're only spending money you actually have. You don't need to do that forever, but I recommend it as a set of "training wheels" while you're establishing good money habits.'

He put the phone away. 'The fact is, guys, you don't need millions to be financially free. There are plenty of millionaires who are up to their eyeballs in debt. Or they might be asset-rich and cash-poor, whereas other people on fairly ordinary incomes are financially free because they've mastered saving and investing and they have no debt.'

Toni wondered about her parents. Were they in debt? Would they reveal the actual truth about their finances if she asked?

'The last thing I want to cover is *you*,' Arnold said, resting on the edge of the stool. 'Play to your strengths. Find work you love to do. Some of you are good with your heads, some with your hands, some with numbers, some with ideas, some with people, some with animals, some with plants, some with movement... No one of those is better than the others; everything has its place. Do what turns *you* on and you'll stand the best chance of doing well at it and making money from it.'

What would he do, Eric wondered, thinking back to his conversation with his parents. Everyone knew that today's youth weren't going to stay in one job for forty years like their parents had; they would jump around every few years, from job to job and even from career to career, switching dramatically at times. He was determined not to stress about it. He would just do the thing he was most interested in at the time and then change when he needed to...

'So don't blame the world for not being the way you want it to be,' Arnold was saying. 'Don't blame your parents, your teachers, the system, 'bad luck'. Just get off your arse and do whatever you need to do to turn the situation around. Act as if you're responsible even if you think you're not, simply because it's more empowering. You'll feel more confident and stronger than if you go around handing your power over to someone else by complaining that it's their fault. And don't waste time being envious of others' good luck. Go create your own.'

Yeah, Jackson thought. He had a tendency to feel envious and resentful. *Cut that out*, he told himself.

Arnold was standing again. 'Same deal when you're looking for work. Employers like people who show initiative, who have a good attitude, who are there to learn and contribute. They don't care so much if you don't have many skills in their industry yet; you can teach 'people skills' but you can't easily teach a good attitude. You might be Gen Z – or whatever we're up to – but a good work ethic still counts. It's important that you *give* to the job; don't be a bludger, just doing the minimum, grabbing your pay packet and running out the door; give your all. The return on your investment will flow to you in all sorts of ways, like extra opportunities and introductions to people who can advance you along your path.'

Arnold paused and looked around the auditorium. Jackson and Toni exchanged glances, ready to jump out of their seats and head up the front to formally thank him for the presentation.

'Becoming wealthy is simple,' he said.

- SPEND LESS THAN YOU EARN.

- SAVE.

- INVEST AT LEAST 10% OF YOUR EARNINGS AND LET COMPOUND INTEREST DO THE REST.

'We don't have time to talk about that, but Einstein considered it to be one of the most powerful forces in the universe, so check it out.' He kept writing:

- GUARD YOUR MONEY FROM LOSS.

- BUILD YOUR ASSET BASE AND MINIMISE LIABILITIES.

- THE GREATER YOUR NET WORTH, THE GREATER YOUR SELF-WORTH.

- FIND YOURSELF A FINANCIAL MENTOR. BUILD ON YOUR STRENGTHS.

- EXPAND YOUR ABILITY TO EARN.

'After school, your banker won't ask for your report card – she'll ask for your financial statement, so if you have dreams you want to realise, this all matters. Well, that's it from me. Any questions?'

'Do you have any more marshmallows?' some joker yelled.

The Principles of Wealth Creation

1. Pay Yourself First

Set aside a percentage of every dollar of income toward the goal of financial independence. Have a savings account where you save for important items and experiences, but make sure you also have a 'Prosperity Account' where you save for investment and financial growth. This account will give you emotional stability and peace of mind.

2. Control Spending

Don't spend unnecessarily. Live with less / within your means.

'Master the gap'.

Don't assume that a bigger income will solve your cashflow problems; chances are you will just spend more – unless you have sound budgeting skills.

Avoid liabilities.

3. Make Your Money Grow

Take advantage of the power of compound interest and look for ways of earning more money (especially passive income), and acquiring assets.

Investment is usually about being in there for the long haul.

4. Guard Your Money From Loss

Don't lend money unless you're sure the borrower will be able to repay.

Don't invest unless you understand the deal exactly.

Seek financial advice from someone someone who is qualified (= wealthy).

Avoid and quickly pay down high-interest debt.

Protect against disaster by insuring pricy items like cars.

Avoid 'get rich quick' schemes. If it looks too good to be true, it probably is.

'First rule: Never lose money. Second rule: Never forget the first rule.' – Warren Buffet.

5. Increase Your Ability To Earn

Focus on what you love – aim to make a career out of your interests and skills.

Keep educating yourself.

Become an expert at something by mastering it. (Experts earn more.)

Find a mentor who can support and challenge you in earning more.

True wealth is not money and possessions,

it's your knowledge, your skills, your attitude, your work ethic, how flexible and adaptable you are. It's your creativity and courage and persistence – and your life experiences.

And being wealthy is not about luck, it's about strategy.

The key one is saving.

Start today.

CHAPTER 30

THE NEXT GOAL

Toni, Eric, Jackson and Brooke gravitated together after Arnold's talk, wandering out of school and across the road to a favourite café. Brooke had news to share with Jackson about the hair and potential income from Kelly, and Eric was about to help Jackson set up an invoice book. Toni listened, struck by the professionalism and degree of detail in Eric's thinking and approach.

She had discovered that she was too young to start a network marketing business – you had to be eighteen – but the idea of it was growing on her. Meanwhile she had heard back from Mrs S, who was offering just a few hours a week of paid work so she really needed to find something else, ideally something where she could 'play to her strengths', which were…?

Bossing people around, she thought, suppressing a smile. Well, maybe not that exactly, but organising people. She was a good organiser, a leader… What sort of work could a fifteen-year-old do where she was in charge and paid for it? Could she perhaps inspire Mrs S to give her more control of the kids' parties biz…?

Toni was all fired up by Arnold's talk – she wanted to set some definite goals and work towards them now rather than waiting till she left school. And while she wasn't too bad at saving, she was also prone to dipping into the account when she felt like it – she now wanted to resist dipping in and see that amount grow.

'That's easy,' Eric said. 'You just put your money into one of those no-touch accounts.'

'Scary,' Toni said. 'What if I need it?'

He gave her a look. 'Inspiring level of commitment there. You have parents and you're underage. They'll bail you out if you really need the help. *Need*, not want,' he added teasingly.

Eric was thinking about everything Arnold had said, too. He was enjoying helping Jackson – that really was playing to his strengths, and he was feeling pleased with himself that he had completed his exams successfully without losing his job at the Apple store. Not that he knew what his results were yet, but he was usually pretty good at judging how he'd gone based on how he felt during the exam. He liked hanging out with the computer nerds at the store and felt that his brain was going at full capacity learning new things and solving problems. He loved that. Whatever lay ahead for him in the future, it would involve learning, systems, numbers, code, patterns… And in that sort of industry, intelligence really did count.

Jackson felt more relaxed than he had in a while. The exams were over, thank God, and he and Toni had been on a first date, which had been nice… And his boss had just wowed everyone at school and inspired Jackson himself even more about getting his financial act together.

At home, things were okay. Adelia was still there, a quiet noodle-eating presence. He'd had the odd interesting conversation with her about international relations and was feeling, again, the desire to travel more. His father had found a way, with Uncle Dave's help, to cut costs significantly in his business, and their humbled uncle Mo was doing his damnedest to help reduce his friend's burden, so Dad was a little less stressed now. And his mum still seemed really happy about being back at full-time work, so things were cruising along okay, although he couldn't wait to get his brother out of his bedroom. Geez, *that* was a royal pain.

His real source of pride, though, was that his two savings accounts were steadily growing, if only very slowly. It was reassuring to know that Arnold would be there to advise him how to invest 10% when he was ready for that. Working hard at the building site felt good to him, and taking that risk with Ahmed now felt worthwhile. All in all, things were pretty good.

Brooke received her cappuccino and admired the smiley face that decorated the top. She watched the waitress walk away, twitching her black mini skirt down, and suddenly thought, *I could work here!* Across the road from school – that would be easy for shifts. And weekends she would have those kids' parties. The first trial had been very successful. Brooke was so good at chatting to both the kids and their mums, and quick at sketching and capturing an entertaining likeness, that Mrs S had said she would trial a new party theme that would almost exclusively feature Brooke!

Brooke's mother was delighted that she was using her skills to make money, and especially that she actually hadn't done any more shopping!!! largely thanks to Kelly's support and discipline. It was a relief to not always be feeling guilty…

Today's gratitudes would include Arnold's talk and that lesson about the marshmallows. Maybe she'd buy a packet and hang it up on her bedroom mirror as a reminder… She was grateful for her friendships, too. Looking around the table at the other three, she was struck by their similarity to the four characters in the Wizard of Oz, which had been the theme of the party she'd attended when she was drawing caricatures of kids.

She would be the Scarecrow who needed a brain because she really needed to think things through before she opened her wallet. Eric, who had the brain, was like the Tinman who needed a heart. He was a little stiff and could do with more fun in his life, she reckoned, watching him draw sample invoices on the napkin. Jackson, who'd been so timid about starting the new business with Ahmed, was like the Lion who needed courage, but he was on top of it now, she could see that. And Toni, Toni was a little like Dorothy herself, who headed out on grand adventures though part of her just wanted to feel loved and needed.

As for the Wizard, who was that? Arnold? Or all of them, as they each figured out how to create real magic in their lives? Yeah. At any rate, it was clear to her that if they wanted to be rich (which meant having the money to buy what you wanted, including more experiences like that trip to India), they would have to get their acts together (which meant becoming savvy, switched-on people who saved and researched and mastered the gap and took reasonable risks). It would be an adventure all right. Plenty of traps for the unwary, as her mother said, but if you just plugged away with regular saving and didn't take any stupid risks, you would surely end up with money in the bank and the potential to create the life of your dreams.

The End

Glossary

Arse	=	Australian slang for buttocks.
Blockchain	=	a digital ledger in which transactions made in Bitcoin or some other cryptocurrency are recorded chronologically and publicly.
Brain drain	=	the emigration of highly trained or qualified people from a particular country.
Cryptocurrency	=	a digital currency in which encryption techniques are used to regulate generation of the currency and transfer of it – all independent of banks.
Elon Musk	=	an American business magnate, philanthropist, investor and engineer with an interest in space exploration, artificial intelligence, and a sustainable future for humans.
Freebies	=	things received or jobs done where no payment is expected.
Hijab	=	a head covering worn in public by some Muslim women.
Khamma Ghani	=	a Rajasthani greeting in the Marwari language that might mean 'many blessings' or 'much forgiveness' or just 'welcome'.
Richard Branson	=	a wealthy and influential businessman, investor and philanthropist who founded the Virgin Group.
Robert Kiyosaki	=	a financial educator and author of *Rich Dad, Poor Dad* and the Cashflow Game.
Warren Buffet	=	one of the wealthiest men in the world.
Windfall	=	a large amount of money that is won or received unexpectedly.
Wotcha	=	Australian slang for 'what (are) you?' eg. Whatcha doing? = What are you doing?

The Four Money Personalities

1. 'Northies'
- Strong, action-oriented, results-driven, competitive, loves to win
- Popular, charismatic, inspiring
- Quick at making decisions, a risk-taker, impulsive, loves a challenge
- Doesn't stop to plan and keeps changing the plan and the rules
- Tends to be over-confident, direct, dominant and bossy
- Can be self-centred, impatient, insensitive, and annoy others
- Fears loss of control
- Entrepreneurial; makes and loses money easily

2. 'Westies'
- Systems-oriented; loves instruction books and planning
- Values accuracy, information and logic rather than intuition
- Great ability to see the big picture and challenge assumptions
- Research, research, research – rarely impulsive
- High standards and ideals; critical of slipshod methods
- Fears criticism and being wrong
- Reserved, quiet, a loner
- Good at saving and planning but can over-analyse

3. 'Southies'
- Caring, loving, salt of the earth
- Patient, calm, a good listener, humble
- Solid, hard working, diligent, responsible
- Co-operative and helpful, generous
- Overly accommodating; can feel like a doormat
- Dislikes change, values security, fearful, risk-averse
- Needs to do lots of research and get lots of opinions before deciding

✧ Saves money in jars and under the bed, but can also fall for get-rich-quick schemes

4. 'Easties'
✧ Friendly, fun-loving, sociable, charming and optimistic
✧ Chatty and happy – loves bringing people together
✧ Wants to belong and look good; craves approval and acceptance
✧ Confident but also easily affected by life's ups and downs
✧ Overly values others' opinions and puts them on pedestals
✧ Disorganised, lacks follow-through, impulsive
✧ Fears being left out and fears missing out
✧ Needs to plan more, be more responsible with money and less attached to what others think/what others are doing

About the Author

QUEST FOR RICHES is Liliane Grace's third 'personal development novel' for youth, following *THE MASTERY CLUB® – See the Invisible, Hear the Silent, Do the Impossible* (2007 Independent Book Publisher's Award for Youth Fiction), and sequel *THE HIDDEN ORDER*. The *Mastery Club®* has been translated into Mandarin and German, and gave rise to a 10-session goal-achievement program for youth that has been taught in England, Scotland, South Africa, America and Bali, and a program for transforming the bullying dynamic – 'Let's Bully On Purpose In Schools' (by making Communication Skills a compulsory subject).

Liliane created two children's picture books in collaboration with her artist sister, Yvette Bentata-Moore: *THE BOY WHO BARKED* (about human behaviour specialist Dr John Demartini) and *THE BOY WHO FOUND HIS PULSE* (about health revolutionary Don Tolman). She has also written a book for women entitled *WANTED: GREENER GRASS – a novel about love, envy, and a crazy kind of courage.*

Liliane is a public speaker and workshop leader on a range of topics to do with personal empowerment and creative expression. She lives in rural Victoria, Australia, and has three young adult children who are all actively pursuing their life interests and saving money.

https://lilianegrace.com for more information and your free gifts.

www.ingramcontent.com/pod-product-compliance
Lightning Source LLC
Chambersburg PA
CBHW032028290426
44110CB00012B/721